LINGUISTICS AT LARGE

CONTRIBUTORS

Professor Basil B. Bernstein
Professor Colin Cherry
Professor Eugénie J. A. Henderson
Dr Edmund Leach
Professor M. M. Lewis
Professor John Lyons
Professor Frank Palmer
Professor Randolph Quirk
Professor R. H. Robins
Claire Russell and Dr W. M. S. Russell
Dr George Steiner
Professor P. F. Strawson
Professor Stephen Ullmann
Professor Oliver L. Zangwill

LINGUISTICS AT LARGE

The fourteen linguistic lectures presented by
the Institute of Contemporary Arts
London 1969–70

Edited by

NOEL MINNIS

LONDON
VICTOR GOLLANCZ LTD
1971

ISBN 0 575 00506 8

Printed in Great Britain by
Ebenezer Baylis & Son Limited
The Trinity Press, Worcester, and London

CONTENTS

Foreword

NOEL MINNIS

Principal Lecturer in English,
Wall Hall College of Education

The lectures at the Institute of Contemporary Arts in London during the winter of 1969–70 proved, if nothing else, that linguistics has caught on. Tickets were sold out, extra seats were placed on the rostrum, and lecturers accustomed to facing their audiences found themselves obliged to lecture on three fronts, and answer questions from all sides.

Many were puzzled by this spate of interest in a hitherto recondite subject. As a writer in *The Times* remarked, "linguistics is a semantic jungle", which few people dare to enter. Yet so many applications of linguistics are now in the news that curiosity is overcoming fear, and more want to explore the territory.

The series set out to answer the questions: "What is the nature of language?" and "What is linguistics?", with an introductory lecture followed by three outlining the linguist's approach to phonology, grammar and meaning. These, therefore, examine the main structures of the language, and go on to explain briefly the transformational generative approach to each. The concluding lecture brings home the value of these theoretical studies by answering the question: "What bearing has linguistics on our language, and on us as users of English?"

The rest of the lectures range over some of the topics in which current developments have a distinct bearing on linguistics, or derive from it. The span is wide, stretching from philosophical argument to the study of animal behaviour. On the one hand, the nature of linguistic meaning is explored in a close examination of the conflict between the "communication theorists" and "the theorists of formal semantics"; while on the other hand, a survey of current investigations into various kinds of animal communication reveals how some creatures can convey complex and detailed information to each other. While this invites the comparison between forms of animal communication and human language, and may even suggest at what point in the evolution of man language emerged, it cannot account for the curious fact that there is no such thing as a primitive language. All known languages, past and

1*

present, various as they are, seem equally complex, and equally able to express all the needs of their speakers. Furthermore, all normal infants master their mother tongue in the first four years of their lives. How they manage this is of absorbing interest, not only to their parents, but also to psychologists and teachers, the more so now that the "rules" of language are seen to be so complex that a page of diagrams is sometimes needed to show how a simple utterance is generated and understood.

Whether this ability is innate or whether it derives solely from the child's imitation of others is a controversial point, yet certainly both sociological and neurological factors are involved. For injuries to that fragile yet powerful nervous communications system of perception, understanding, and muscular control, by which we hear and respond to language, produce linguistic defects, or forms of aphasia, which have for some time come under the scrutiny of neurologists. Sociologists, on the other hand, are currently investigating the effect of social background on children's use and understanding of language—and therefore on their ability to learn from their teachers at school. They suggest that teacher and child may use different language codes; but how these codes are constituted, where they differ, and why some children cannot easily adapt to the teacher's code, raise very complex questions.

The study of language as part of, or even as the controlling factor in, the culture of a society belongs to anthropology, which for this reason has given great impetus to the study of linguistics. But since language can be regarded as a type of conventional behaviour, comparable with other behavioural patterns which regulate the attitudes, customs, and actions of societies, anthropologists are now looking afresh at language as a possible structural model for non-linguistic forms of behaviour.

Sociologists, however, join forces with teachers of English in their common concern about the ability of children to use the language adequately. Here the linguists have a special responsibility, for by discrediting traditional grammar teaching, they have caused confusion without suggesting, at least until recently, any more positive means of improving children's command of language. The urgency of this problem is brought home by a glance at the extent of illiteracy at one end of the educational scale, and linguistic incompetence at the other. At least the linguist's explorations into the enormous variety of ways in which people speak and write in different situations provides a promising starting point from which a lively awareness of the range and subtlety of language may grow. Such awareness is still largely confined to the study of literature, but there is immense scope outside it.

Nor can the literary scholar claim to be the sole arbiter of literary studies, for the linguist must be concerned with the language of literature, not only as one among many varieties of English, but also because it is unique in that its form and substance are in a way as important as the message it conveys. To some of the literary minded this may seem the trespassing of heartless Philistines on hallowed ground, while to some linguists the intuitive perceptions of literary men may be mere vapourings. The truth lies on both sides. The precision and rigour of the linguist's approach should inform literary criticism, but linguistics cannot account for the power of verbal associations, nor explain the peculiar intensity of a poem such as Blake's *Tyger*.

If the language of literature attempts to convey imaginative truth, the language of everyday communication should, among other things, convey factual truth. But what we regard as self-evident may be relative to our society and its institutions; and our belief in it may be governed by its form of representation, or the language in which it is habitually expressed. However, whether or not we can shed these cultural blinkers we are no longer astonished at anything that contemporary propaganda can produce; we accept the formidable alliance of image, music and words to convey messages of dubious veracity, as part of a realm governed not by reason but by technological fantasy. Yet half impressed, half sceptical as we are, we are at the same time continually being made aware of the highly sophisticated verbal and non-verbal modes of message-carrying and persuasion that are now the stock-in-trade of the mass media.

We are also aware that communications, the twentieth century obsession, is having a profound effect on language and on our understanding of its nature. We may marvel at the technology that brings the faces and voices of men on the moon into our homes, but we are also led to realize how astonishing is the commonplace of mere conversation.

Conscious of these currents of popular interest, Miss Jasia Reichardt proposed that the Institute of Contemporary Arts should invite lecturers from various universities and institutes to join in presenting a broad view of the rôle of linguistics in contemporary studies. The venture was a success. And the degree of coherence and corroboration achieved by fourteen lecturers was remarkable. It was also apparent that the broad view has not diminished the importance of linguistics itself. It remains at the point of intersection of the human sciences, and in many ways is at the heart of the proper study of mankind.

As far as possible the lectures are reproduced here as they were delivered. In some cases the force of argument depends on the spoken context, so that references to the audience have not been eliminated in the printed versions. Lecturers have, however, added notes and book references where appropriate, and the editor's notes draw attention to similarities or differences between the points of view expressed. Important topics, and those common to several lectures, are referred to in the index, and the "Further Reading" lists at the end of each lecture provide a comprehensive guide to further study of the whole field.

As chairman of the lectures and editor of this book, I must thank Professor R. H. Robins whose knowledge and advice were most valuable in framing the whole series, and also Jasia Reichardt and her staff at the Institute of Contemporary Arts for their skill in organising the lectures, and for their help with the editorial work.

January 1971

I

The structure of language

R. H. ROBINS

School of Oriental and African Studies, London

INTRODUCTION

Linguistics is quite simply the scientific study of human language in all its manifestations and uses, near and far, present and past, without restriction on time, place, or culture. In this respect linguistics is different from language study, since this latter term is ordinarily used to refer to the study of a particular language, say Latin, French, or German, as a means to reading its literature in the original, or for purposes of written or spoken communication with its speakers in the case of a living language. The linguist, in the sense of the student of linguistics, studies languages, his own and foreign languages, as examples of mankind's faculty of language, to learn more about the way language works and how it may best be described and analysed. An American linguist has put this well: "Linguistic scientists are engaged in developing a sound body of scientific observations, facts, and systematic theory about language in general and languages in particular."[1]

In one way language is too familiar to us all; every normal human being has thoroughly mastered one language in childhood without knowing much about the process, and in areas and in social situations that require and facilitate it many persons of no more than average intelligence and application have a fluent command of two or even more different languages. Just because language is universal and so much taken for granted as part of our lives, its problems and perplexities, but also its incredible fascination to those who take the trouble to examine it for its own sake, often pass unnoticed among otherwise sensitive and percipient persons.

Linguistics as a subject of learning happens to be very much in the news today. Since the Second World War it has more than kept pace with the general expansion of university education over almost the whole world, and one of its ablest and most stimulating scholars, Noam Chomsky, known both for the far-reaching changes he has brought about in almost all aspects of linguistic studies and for his public championing of certain political causes, has been accorded the status of one of the thousand makers of the twentieth century in a recent Sunday newspaper magazine series.

Though as a recognized independent subject linguistics is fairly new, linguistic speculation and the analysis of languages have occupied men's minds from the earliest days of civilization in a number of different cultures. In the history of European civilization linguistic thought, like thought in so many other areas, began in Ancient Greece, under the cover-all title of "philosophy" (philosophía). Pre-Socratic philosophers discussed language, and one of the Socratic dialogues of Plato, the *Cratylus*, is devoted to language. The observations of Plato, Aristotle, and the Stoics on language appear as part of their general exposition of the theory of knowledge and of the principles of logic, though it is to the Stoics that we must attribute the recognition of a specific branch of study relating to the form and function of human speech.

Under the influence of Alexandrian literary criticism, linguistic studies developed some degree of independence in later antiquity, but subsequently other factors promoted close contacts between philosophers and grammarians. This was notably the case with the "speculative grammars" of the later Middle Ages, when scholastic metaphysics and Priscian's Latin grammar (itself a product of Alexandrian literary scholarship) were fused together in a remarkable synthesis of logic, metaphysics, and grammatical theory.[2]

Thereafter empiricism and rationalism made their contributions to the linguistic thinking of Europe in and after the Renaissance; but in addition Europeans were now learning not only about languages spoken outside Europe, but also about the work of linguists in other parts of the world. China, the Jews and the Arabs, and the Sanskrit phoneticians and grammarians of Ancient India have all contributed to our present-day achievements in linguistic science. In particular the excellence of the Indian work and the knowledge gained from it of the Sanskrit language vitally stimulated European linguistics in the early nineteenth century. Sir William Jones, the two Schlegels, Wilhelm von Humboldt, Jakob Grimm, Schleicher, Whitney, Brugmann, and de Saussure are just a few of those who at the end of the eighteenth century and throughout the nineteenth laid the foundations on which we today are still building.

SPEECH

We do well to examine language primarily and principally from the starting point of speech. One is used in literate civilizations like our own to think of languages as systems of writing with a pronunciation; it is better to think of them as systems of oral communication that may in some way be represented in writing. Every normal person speaks, but in many language areas those who can write are few, and everywhere speaking and hearing occupy far more time than writing and reading. Speech is a skill acquired by a child before writing, and in the span of human history writing is very much a newcomer, perhaps three to four thousand years old, while speech is probably coeval with homo sapiens. We may say that it is the conditions of speaking and listening rather than those of writing and reading that have determined the development of language in general and of each particular language. Moreover (and this is one of the more valuable incidental lessons of linguistic studies) the orderliness, complexity, and efficiency of the languages of illiterate peoples, whose cultures are labelled primitive by outside observers, are not inferior (or superior) in quality or degree; nor indeed are the languages of such peoples markedly different in form from languages long studied and familiar as the literate vehicles of world-wide civilizations.

Speaking is essentially making and responding to certain sets of noises by means of which we cooperate in living in and understanding our common world and in regulating our relations with one another therein; the more portentous definition of speech as the expression and communication of thought may be taken as covering a relatively small part of this more general and humdrum activity. The material of speech, sounds emitted from the vocal tract, is limited, but its range and application, nothing less than the entire furniture of earth and heaven and all our doings therein, is unlimited. Yet speaking is only a by-product, an exploitation of waste; with few exceptions, that do not alter the general picture, speaking is simply the noisy interference with expiratory, used, air as it passes up from the lungs through and over the various organs of speech: glottis, tongue, palate, teeth, lips, nasal passage, etc. Breathing out, expiration, is a biologically essential process of ridding the lungs of air charged with carbon dioxide. The energy expended in additionally interfering with it to make a noise, that is, to speak, is minute. In the light of the place taken by language (i.e. by speech) in human life as we know it, one may challenge anyone to name any other use of a spent material that comes anywhere near it in power and significance. Moreover the organs of speech, as they are called, the tongue, the teeth, and so on, are not primarily organs used in speaking, in the way that, for example, the lungs are the organs of breathing and the stomach the organ of digestion; they are organs performing a number of functions in the economy of the human body, and speaking, noisily and purposively interfering with spent breath, is just one function superimposed on them.

Yet this wonderful and complex activity is learned by any normal child in his or her early years. In childhood we master the pronunciation and the grammar of our native, our first or only, language, and its basic vocabulary; grammar and pronunciation are more or less exhaustively acquired for the spoken language in childhood (except in cases of rapid language change, personal dialect replacement, or the like), but our vocabulary goes on changing and enlarging itself all our lives; we learn new words and new uses of old words almost every day, fitting them in to our established pronunciation patterns and grammatical rules.

FORM AND MEANING

We have, then, two sides to language: form and meaning. We can use a range of noises in socially shared patterns to achieve some purpose. Form and meaning are thus in part related as means to end, and both are the proper objects of linguistic science. While other disciplines, such as philosophy, psychology, and literary criticism, all concern themselves with language and with meaning, they do not, rightly from their points of view, hold the whole of language central in their focus of attention, but they are concerned primarily with the place of language in their own fields of enquiry. Some linguists have been almost frightened away from the study of the meaning side of language, because it seems so full of pitfalls and so much less tangible than the forms themselves. One should try to keep both form and meaning within the discipline of linguistics, but one can more easily start with form because it is more readily observable; its field is delimited (sounds and written marks), while that of meaning, if not actually infinite, is certainly unlimited in range. Meaning has in the past been confused with reference or denotation, one aspect of language use, the association of many words, but not of all, in languages with identifiable individual things, persons, processes, and states of affairs, or with classes of them. Too often reference has been universalized by the hypothetizing of "ideas" as the other end of a binary relation between the word and its meaning, though it may be hard to say just what an idea in such a use is except (circularly) that it is the supposed meaning of the word in question. It is probably better to regard meanings as the ways in which words, and types of sentence construction (statement, question, etc.) are used in different situations, or part of the rules for their use, rules known performatively by speakers, acquired by children and second language learners, and made explicit by linguists, especially in their rôle as makers of dictionaries. Referential or denotative use is part of the use to which many words are put, but it is not to be equated with the whole of meaning.

The linguist, then, starts from linguistic form, or from linguistic forms, which he assumes to be meaningful, for that is the main criterion of language as contrasted with babbling or scribbling. But form is not the same as all the sounds spoken or all the symbols written in a language. In studying a language the linguist is not just collecting utterances on tape or on paper and stopping there. Understanding a language means making abstractions from the material, to which the multiplicity of actual utterance can be referred and by which it can be explained. The child does this unconsciously as he learns his language; the linguist does it consciously and makes his work explicit. It involves two things, discovering the relevant facts and framing abstractions to cover them, and stating these in such a way as to make this acquired knowledge available to all comers. Work with languages that do not possess a writing system has taught us a great deal about the techniques of discovery and of statement, essentially speeding up and ordering the work of the language learner anywhere.

Linguistic form, the product of the abstraction process that the linguist applies to his material, covers a familiar field: pronunciation, grammar, and vocabulary, though it deals with this field somewhat differently from traditional pedagogy. In many respects the linguist's abstractions correspond with the intuitions of native speakers themselves on the working of their language. His abstractions fall into general and particular, phonetics, phonology, and grammar on the one hand, and lexicon or vocabulary on the other, the provinces of the grammar book (in its widest sense) and the dictionary respectively. All of this may be considered from two points of view, that of a language as it operates at any one time as a means of communication and without reference to its past or its future, and that of a language as a continuing system that evolves through time, though its speakers are largely unaware of the process. Both these points of view, descriptive linguistics and historical linguistics, as they are called, are equally important in the understanding of human language. At present most attention seems to be devoted to descriptive linguistics; in the nineteenth century the historical point of view predominated, largely under the influence of the discovery of the genetic relations linking Sanskrit with the classical and with most of the modern languages of Europe in the Indo-European family. In England this field of study was often designated "comparative philology", and the term is still in use.

PHONETICS AND PHONOLOGY

If, in line with what was said earlier, we consider language primarily in its spoken form, we see that a double set of abstractions can be made from speech: the virtually infinite number of phonetic differences in people's speech can be assigned to limited sets of units with rules of combination and sequence, and the limitless word stock of a language (limitless because it can always be added to by borrowing or by new creations) can be assigned to limited sets of classes that exhibit limited sets of categories controlling their occurrence in constructions or sentence structures.

The abstractions involved in linguistic form can best be illustrated in the first place at the level of phonology. Phonetics and phonology cover the field rather loosely called "pronunciation" in many textbooks of foreign languages. An abstraction at this level is indeed unconsciously made or assumed whenever we speak of "the English language", "the German language", and so on, with reference to speakers of the standard dialect (or to any other dialect, though in the context of foreign language learning and teaching, the standard dialect is usually taken without comment to represent "the language"). Every person's speech is different from everyone else's; we can distinguish voices over very imperfect channels like telephones; the voices of several speakers of the same age, sex, and locality can be kept distinct throughout a radio play or discussion, though we may never have heard any of the speakers before; and we can recognize the voices of our friends from behind closed doors. Every different feature of these different voices, like every other audible aspect of speech is the product of slightly different shapes, positions, and movements of the vocal organs, resulting in different configurations of the sound waves and in their different impact through the ears on the auditory perceptual centres of the brain of the hearer.

But in listening to what is said, to the message as opposed to recognizing who is talking (and we often do not care, as when we are shopping, travelling, listening to news broadcasts, and the like), we push all this aside and concentrate on certain differences only. The total number of differences which the vocal organs are capable of making and the auditory mechanism is capable of receiving may be virtually limitless (at least one knows as yet no way of setting limits, which probably vary with each individual); but in the ordinary use of our language, or of any language, we seize on distinctive differences, not just any differences. These distinctive differences can largely be located in segments, and this is the basis of alphabetic writing, just one more legacy of Ancient Greek genius. An alphabet does not cover the representation in writing of all and only the distinctive differences in the spoken words of a language; hence the notorious difficulties of English spelling, though most orthographies have similar weaknesses from this point of view; and in all languages there are some non-segmental features, such as stress in English (compare *import* as a noun and as a verb in pronunciation) and intonation, which also can and should be analysed in terms of limited sets of distinctive differences.

For these reasons phonological transcriptions have been devised, partly as the result of years of attempted "spelling reforms". A phonetic transcription represents as far as it can every perceptible difference in what is said; a phonological transcription only employs separate symbols for those segments and other elements that are distinctively different in the language for which it is constructed. In the English word *pin* there are only three such units. *Pin* is minimally distinct from *bin*, from *pen*, and from *pit*. Other audible differences, such as loudness and pitch, do not alter the word you recognize. But such features may be distinctive in the words of other languages; in north Chinese *pin* said on a level tone and *pin* said on a rising tone are different words. Phonetic differences are indefinitely divisible, but the phonological form of a language recognizes only discrete distinctions. I can say the words *pin* and *bin* in all sorts of ways, with more or with less initial aspiration, with heavier or lighter vibration of the vocal cords in the *b*, etc., but as long as you assume that I am talking English you will try to assign what I say to one or the other of the two words. You may think that I am teasing, that I am a bit drunk, that I am a foreigner or a speaker of an unfamiliar dialect, but you will always seek to impose on what I say the pattern of distinctive segments and other elements that you have come to recognize for the English language. *Pin, bin, pen*, and *pit* can differ distinctively at three places only, and there only by the substitution of limited sets of consonants and vowels.

Certain marginal aspects of language are not like this. If I speak softly you will understand that I am being confidential, intimate, or perhaps reassuring; if I shout you assume that I am angry or excited, and the louder I shout the angrier you think I am. We are all familiar with arguments in which each party gets more and more worked up and shouts louder and louder. There are no distinctive jumps here from one unit of loudness to another, but a continuous scale interpreted as such by speaker and hearer. This sort of scalar characteristic of the marginal aspects of speech is found also in non-linguistic ejaculations like screams, but it is not found with the central and specifically linguistic component of the speech signal.

Differences that are not distinctive of one unit from another in a particular language are either ruled out by correct (i.e. a native speaker's) pronunciation, or are irrelevant to the form of the utterance, as are differences in personal voice quality, or are conditioned by the position of the sound unit in relation to neighbouring sounds. Languages differ in their allocation of distinctiveness. English /k/ (the set of sounds heard initially in words like *keep, cut* and *card*) is articulated with a more forward part of the tongue before /i:/, a vowel articulated in the front of the mouth, as in *keep* (/ki:p/), and with a part of the tongue further back before /u:/, a vowel articulated in the back of the mouth, as in *cool* (/ku:l/). These two sorts of /k/ sound are not of themselves distinctive in English, and cannot alone distinguish one word from another; they belong therefore to the same distinctive unit, or phoneme, as such units are technically called. In southern English

/k/ sounds are aspirated (pronounced with a little puff of air) initially, as in *kin*; after an /s/ this is not the case; in *skin* the /k/ is unaspirated, but in view of the different environments in which these two varieties of /k/ sounds occur they are not distinctive, and they are assigned to the same phoneme. But in other languages, where they can stand in the same environment in minimal contrast, an aspirated and an unaspirated *k* sound can constitute separate phonemes, as in Hindi, where /k/ and /kʰ/ distinguish the two words /kana/, one-eyed, and /kʰana/, to eat. We saw that in Chinese the pitch, or tone, of a syllable can by itself distinguish one word from another, and in Chinese one must recognize tone phonemes, varying in their number from four in the north to eight or nine in some varieties of Cantonese in the south.

Thus for each language there are found a limited number of distinctive units, or phonemes, that carry the messages and represent the phonological form of the language. In this connection it is necessary to recognize the various dialects of a language as separate languages as far as their phonological form is concerned. The limited number of phonemes may vary a little as between one description and another according to the precise method used by the linguist, but the principle is the same; from the virtually limitless stock of possible phonetic differences a strictly limited set of phonemes may be abstracted, and it is these that constitute the phonological form of the language and are the bearers of its messages.

Phonemes are limited in number, varying between around fifteen and fifty for different languages. But these limited numbers may be resolved into combinations of even fewer distinctive features. English /p/, /t/, and /k/ differ by their place of articulation only, being bilabial, alveolar, and velar, respectively; they share the features of voicelessness (non-vibration of the vocal cords) and the feature of plosion (complete stoppage of air followed by sudden release). /p/ and /b/, /t/ and /d/, and /k/ and /g/ (as in *get* and *gate*) differ only in respect of voicelessness versus voice (vibration of the vocal cords) in each pair. /m/, /n/, and /ŋ/ (spelled *ng*, as in *sing*) share the three articulatory positions of /p/ and /b/, /t/ and /d/, and /k/ and /g/, respectively, and differ from them only in being nasally released, the air passing out through the nose while they are being articulated. So in this section of English phonology nine distinctive units, nine phonemes, are the product of just six distinctive features, three of place of articulation, and three of manner of articulation; and each of these features, and of all the others likewise involved in the phonological form of any language, depends for its production on the particular configuration of the vocal tract at the time of articulation. Control over such configurations and recognition of the features resulting from them are part of what is familiarly known as learning a language.

Phonological form involves more than the recognition of the phonemes and distinctive features of a language. Consonant and vowel phonemes occur sequentially in syllables, and the possibilities of syllable structure vary greatly from one language to another. In English /h/ cannot occur finally (the letter *h* when final usually indicates a long vowel, not aspiration, as in *hurrah*), and /ŋ/ cannot occur initially in a word. They can in Malay, as in *tengah* (/tǝŋah/), "middle", and *ngaran* (/ŋaran/), "name", words which English speakers find difficult to pronounce, although they contain no non-English consonants, but just non-English arrangements of them. English and German permit far more clustering of consonants before and after a vowel than many languages do; word forms like *strengths* and *sprichst* would be quite impossible in Italian and still more outlandish in Fijian or Hawaiian, where no syllable is closed with a consonant at all (all syllables being open, like English *he* and *to*). In English voiced and voiceless consonants are distinctive initially and finally in words (*pit, bit, cup, cub*), but in German this distinction does not operate finally: *Deich* and *Teich* contrast, but *Bad* and *bat*, though different words and different spellings, are pronounced exactly alike.

Only the main outlines of phonological analysis have been sketched here, but this may be enough to make clear the difference between the gross phonetic repertoire employed by a language and the phonological form of that language. The phoneme theory and phonological theory generally is full of controversies, some of them quite radical, which are not even touched on here. In the study of an unwritten language a phonemic analysis is the prerequisite for a usable transcription, and a subconscious apperception of phonemic principles underlay the Greek adaptation of the Phoenician syllabary to the form of an alphabet.

Phonological form depends not on absolutes, but on contrastive entities defined by their relations with one another in structures within the phonological system of the language. This is why linguistics is frequently called "structural" and why we speak so often of "linguistic systems". System and structure, internal organization, are being opposed to mere aggregations of independent entities, and form is being opposed to substance. One can illustrate how different functions may determine form differently, though the brute facts of substance are the same; in English /b/ contrasts in the bilabial consonants with voiceless /p/ and nasal /m/, and its form and designation is "voiced bilabial plosive", nothing else being distinctively involved; but in Hindi a phonetically identical consonant sound contrasts with /pʰ/ (voiceless aspirated) and /bʰ/ (voiced aspirate) as well as with /p/ and /m/, and it is in consequence designated in Hindi phonology as a "voiced unaspirated bilabial plosive", entering into a different set of immediately contrastive relations.

GRAMMAR

The concept of form in language, which has been explained and illustrated through phonology, is equally valid and essential in grammar, and the distinction of phonetics and phonology gives us only half the picture. Grammar involves a separate level of analysis and description and is no less systematic and structured. Grammatical form is indeed probably the more familiar in the guise of traditional grammar, since both phonetics and phonology have traditionally lain too much under the misleading heading of "the pronunciation of the letters".

Grammar is less dependent on the phonetic substance itself than is phonology; therefore the grammar of a written language (e.g. written English) is similar to, but not the same as, the grammar of a spoken language (e.g. spoken English), and we can study the grammar of a dead language, like Latin or Ancient Greek, without knowing all we would like to about its phonetics (and what we do know is happily ignored by most teachers and students of these languages). In the European grammatical tradition the system of word classes, or "parts of speech", is long established and familiar, and with it the sets of grammatical categories (case, number, tense, person, gender, etc.) that are assigned to the classes and define their membership.

The concept of the word class is a sound one in principle as well as in practice, but the word as a formal unit in grammar cannot be taken for granted, however obvious a sort of unit it appears to us who are familiar with dictionaries and with printed spaces between orthographic words. Formally it must be defined in some way. Very practically, in a newly discovered language where shall we write our spaces in transcribed sentences? We do not hear a pause between most words in connected speech (*a loan* and *alone* are exact homophones), and meanings are a poor guide. *The house* is two words in English, but its translation *huset* is one word in Norwegian; *multiracial* and *consisting of several races* mean much the same, but the former is one word and the latter comprises four words. But what we do find in all languages, written and unwritten, is that sentences consist of sequences of smaller stretches which occur again and again, and which exhibit an internal stability and cohesion together with an external mobility in relation to other such stretches in sentences. *Indefensibility* and *interdenominationalism* keep their syllables in the same order and they cannot be split up by the insertion of other words, but they can appear at almost any point in a sentence. Of course there are marginal cases; it is not easy to decide firmly one way or the other on the status of the unemphatic pronouns in French, which are traditionally written with spaces when they occur before the verb and are hyphenated when they follow it. But the principle is clear, and techniques have been devised for applying it to the grammatical analysis of un-written languages as well as for checking it against the orthographic practice of written ones.

The importance of the word as a formal grammatical unit is partly that on it rests the distinction between morphology, the study of word structure, and syntax, the study of sentence structure, a traditional division within grammar, which despite, or perhaps because of, a good deal of reexamination is still a useful part of the linguist's descriptive apparatus. What is important to reverse is the too frequent attitude that treats morphology as the prime or central part of grammar and syntax as its appendix; from this attitude spring absurd judgments such as "English has less grammar than Latin", or "languages like Chinese have no grammar". The burden of sentence construction and sentence interpretation may be differently divided between word form variation and the grouping and order of words, and languages like Chinese have little of what corresponds to morphological structure in languages like English and German, but no language just strings its words together, and

Chinese syntax can be stated systematically (indeed it must be so stated) no less than the syntax of English or Latin, or of any other language. If anything syntax is the heart and soul of language, with morphology a means of marking syntactic relations employed to varying degrees in different languages.

The phonological form and the grammatical form of a language are interrelated but distinct, and one may approach them from either direction, phonology first or grammar first; and on this there is no lack of controversy. The essential point is that phonology alone does not tell us all we need to know about the sentences of a language, and patterns and structural constraints depending on considerations other than those of phonology force themselves on our attention. *The horse are sleeping* and *the horses is sleeping* are as pronounceable as *the horse is sleeping* and *the horses are sleeping*, but only the last pair is acceptable in standard English. *Horse horses, dog dogs, cat cats*, and *penny pence* are grammatically associated, whereas *fen fence, hen hence*, and *Len lens* are not; and the phonologically very unlike pairs *foot feet, hand hands, mouse mice*, and *rat rats* are grammatically equivalent, and so are *bake baked* and *take took*.

A manifest fact of language is that grammar is more obviously related to meaning than phonology is; the meaning of categories like singular and plural and of their representations in word forms (*cat cat-s*, etc.) is fairly clear, whereas meaning can scarcely be said directly to attach to phonological entities as such, except perhaps for intonation tunes and the use of emphatic stress or the like. Once more it must be admitted that on the exact relationship between grammar and meaning and on the place that meaning should occupy in grammatical analysis there is still a great deal of unresolved argument. Traditional names of grammatical classes and categories are often semantic in origin; *Nennwort, dative case, past tense* are obvious examples. But such names or labels are not necessarily, or even properly, complete definitions; "giving to", however widely interpreted, can hardly cover all the uses of the dative case in Greek, Latin, and German, uses that in fact are somewhat different in each of these languages; and the term *accusative case*, though now devoid of extragrammatical meaning and probably owing its origin to an ancient mistranslation, has survived quite happily. Grammatical number is fairly congruent with singularity and plurality, but gender, which is no less important in several well-known languages as a mark of concord and of syntactic structure, is notoriously out of line as regards animacy and sex differentiation. The relations between grammatical categories and meanings are of great significance in understanding the ways in which languages work, but one can only be on safe ground in working from the forms, which are usually fairly definite, to the meanings, which are much less so, rather than the other way round. A field of grain is a collective, one or many as you may choose to look at it, but *oats* is plural (*the oats are growing well*) and *wheat* is singular (*the wheat is growing well*); *Sunset* is a noun in English, but it would be hard to say whether a sunset is definitely a thing, the usual correlate of nouns, or a process, one of the usual correlates of verbs. It is all very well, and rather charming, to say that in German the compounds of *Mut* are masculine or feminine according to whether the characteristic referred to is masculine or feminine: *Demut*, "humility", and *Anmut*, "grace", are feminine, but *Freimut*, "frankness", and *Übermut*, "arrogance" are masculine.[3] What about *Schwermut*, "sadness"? Is it a masculine characteristic or a feminine one, or neither? But formally we know at once that it is a feminine noun, because a native speaker will put the feminine form of the article in front of it (*die Schwermut*). The forms are there; the meanings are the uses to which the forms are put in discourse.

The logical structure of a proposition and the syntactic structure of a sentence are two different things, though they do, in fact, often correspond with one another; traditional grammar did not really get this distinction clear. But when this has been said, it must be stressed that it remains the ultimate aim of grammatical analysis and description to be able to account formally for every semantic distinction that is carried by the grammatical structure of sentences, as against their lexical content. This aim is now in the forefront of the attention of many present-day linguists, who are developing important insights into the semantic potentialities of grammatical structures.

The elements of grammatical form belong in systems and make up structures. The dative case (or, equivalently, the dative forms of nouns, pronouns, adjectives, etc.) cannot be defined in isolation and identified as the same in different languages. There is certainly some correspondence of use, and therefore some translation equivalence, between the Greek, Latin, and German datives; but the grammatical function and status of each must be different, because in Greek it is a member of a five term system of cases, in

Latin it is a member of a six term system, and in German of a four term system. The Greek and German datives are involved in constructions with prepositions, but the Latin dative does not construct directly with any preposition. Sets of relations like these between the members of grammatical classes and between the constituents of grammatical structures or constructions are what constitute the grammatical form of a language.

LEXICON

In considering phonology and grammar we have stressed that the elements of language are not to be considered as aggregated isolates but as interrelated members of systems and structures. This applies also to the lexical aspect of language. We are familiar with the standard equipment of the language learner, the grammar book, which includes some account of the phonology, and the dictionary. The lexical description of a language, the task of the dictionary, does not cover other material than that which is dealt with by phonetics, phonology, and grammar, but it deals with it from a different point of view. In grammar and phonology we are concerned with what is common to a large and often open-ended number of items: sentence structures, word classes, grammatical categories, syllable structures, phonemes, etc. In the dictionary we are dealing with each word separately, individually focusing attention on what distinguishes it from all other words in the language.[4] Naively one feels that the main province of the dictionary is meaning, the meaning of each word listed, whether the dictionary be unilingual or bilingual; and this is true, just because the meaning of a word, the rules for its use in relation to some aspect or part of the world and of human life therein, must be stated individually. No two words are precisely alike in meaning, absolute synonyms, in all circumstances, and consequently the dictionary must deal with each word in turn. But this does not exhaust its function; grammatical irregularities (like *took* as the past tense of *take* and *men* as the plural of *man*) must also be noted just for their being irregular, outside the general rules for the formations of the word class concerned, and so idiosyncratic to the particular word itself. As Henry Sweet put it, grammar deals with the general facts of a language, lexicology with the special facts.[5]

Because grammar and phonology are concerned with general

features and with classes and the lexicon comprises individual words as separate entities, the lexicon of a language is much more flexible and readily changeable and shows more variation between persons speaking the same dialect of a single language. Probably few persons possess exactly the same word stock at any one time, although, of course, all the commoner words they use will be most likely to be shared. Changes in grammar and in phonology are long term affairs, normally noticeable only over spans of hundreds of years; such changes seriously affect mutual intelligibility, in time producing different languages from a common source, as happened with the development of colloquial Latin into the present day Romance languages. But words can be borrowed from other languages or created anew, and then assigned to existing grammatical classes with no difficulty; consider the great number of technological newcomers in English since the end of the war and the rapid rise and evanescence of the slangs and jargons of advertisers, self-conscious teenagers, and others, all within the abiding frame-work of English grammatical and phonological form. We have ordinarily mastered the pronunciation and the grammar of our native language by mid childhood; inevitably we have to go on learning new words and new ranges of meaning for existing words all our lives.

Though the lexicon of a language is flexible and personally variable, being composed of individual words as individuals, it is still structured, though more loosely than grammar or phonology, and we can legitimately speak of lexical form and lexical structure, and languages differ in their lexical form as they do in other aspects of linguistic form. Vocabulary is indefinitely extensible through the acquisition of loan words and the invention of neologisms, but at any one time the word stock available to a speaker and his hearers is finite. On the other hand the furniture of earth and heaven is infinite, or at least we have no way of asserting an inventory of its components or of the different ways in which it may be considered and examined. This is what the early nineteenth-century philosopher and linguist, Wilhelm von Humboldt, meant when he said that a language makes infinite use of finite resources.[6] We claim to be able to talk about anything and everything, and we can do this because word meanings are not fixed individual relationships between word and thing aggregated into a lexical heap, like so many labels tied to suitcases in a luggage store; word meanings are in part a function of the total number of words and wordlike phrases available for use in a language at a given time. In a sense a sort of "Parkinson's law" applies in vocabulary; the meanings of words expand or contract to fill the available semantic space. We can distinguish as many things as we can name, and we can class them in as many ways as we can use a common term to refer to them. A familiar example of this is in the field of colour recognition.[7] The range of humanly discriminable hues, if not infinite, far exceeds the colour word vocabulary of any known language, and it is well known that different languages make their primary cuts in the colour spectrum at different places; a single colour word in one language has to be translated by two or perhaps more colour words in another language and vice versa. In the learning process it is doubtful if a child learns the main colour words in his language separately (in English, *red*, *green*, *blue*, *yellow*, etc.); each one occupies the place it does in the colour spectrum by virtue of the copresence of the rest of the colour vocabulary. When we need to be more precise than is normally necessary we subdivide the main terms or invent new ones or press other words into technical service: *blush-pink*, *hice green*, *eau-de-nil*, *cream*, etc. The more words there are in a given range the more restricted and exact the function or meaning of each one is. One of the main reasons for the precision of quantitative arithmetical statement as compared with qualitative statement is the infinite extensibility of quantitative terms on the basis of a very small basic lexical stock. According to the degree of exactness required there is always a further term between any two prior terms; thus between 11 and 12 there is $11\frac{1}{2}$ or 11·5, between 11 and $11\frac{1}{2}$ (11·5) there is $11\frac{1}{4}$ (11·25), between 11 and $11\frac{1}{4}$ (11·25) there is $11\frac{1}{8}$ (11·125), and so on indefinitely.

Colour terms are a convenient illustration of the way in which the individual words of a language acquire and are credited with their meanings through their systematic relations with one another in the total vocabulary of the language at any one time and in any one style. If in different styles and in different contexts the system changes, so will the meaning of each word within it, as the words readjust their mutually exhaustive coverage of the whole relevant field of human perception or judgment. If candidates in an examination are graded "good", "fair", "poor", and "fail", then "good" is very good indeed and highly commendable; but if a different system of grading is employed over the same field:

"excellent", "very good", "good", and "fail", then "good" is much lower in rating and less a matter of rejoicing for the candidates so designated. "A good hotel" means a good hotel generally, but we all know the grading system used by some travel agents: "first class", "superior", and "good", and we may do well to avoid those labelled "good".

CONCLUSION

We have, then, the circumscribed but probably unlimited range of actually different vocal sounds, and we have the unbounded and infinite range of the universe of experience. Our social life depends on our use of language, and in language form and structure are imposed in phonology, grammar, and lexicon on these vocal sounds; and through their use form and structure are imposed on our environment, creating indeed what we call our common world. Many traditions treat language as a sacred thing; they are justified in so doing, for it is language that gives order and significance to primal chaos.

NOTES

1 Carroll, J. B.: *The study of language* (Cambridge, Mass., 1953) p. 2.
2 Cf. George Steiner's outline of the rhetorical approach to language in classical antiquity, Lecture 6, pp. 115–16 (Ed.)
3 Wilson, P. G.: *Teach yourself German grammar* (London, 1950) p. 38.
4 The problem of how the lexicographer verifies the precise meaning of words is discussed by Randolph Quirk, Lecture 14, pp. 298–301 (Ed.)
5 Sweet, H.: *Collected papers* (Oxford, 1913) p. 31.
6 "Sie (sc. die Sprache) muss daher von endlichen Mitteln einen unendlichen Gebrauch machen".
Von Humboldt, W.: *Ueber die Verschiedenheit des menschlichen Sprachbaues* (Berlin, 1836, reprinted Darmstadt, 1949) p. 103.
7 See also Stephen Ullmann, Lecture 4, pp. 83–4 and Claire and W. M. S. Russell, Lecture 8, p. 166 (Ed.)

FURTHER READING

ABERCROMBIE, D.: *Elements of general phonetics* (Edinburgh, 1967).

BLOOMFIELD, L.: *Language* (London, 1935). Still unsurpassed as a classic textbook.

CARROLL, J. B.: *The study of language* (Cambridge, Mass., 1953). Valuable survey of the relations of linguistics with other branches of knowledge.

CHOMSKY, N.: *Syntactic structures* (The Hague, 1957). The first public statement of the transformationalist-generative position in linguistics.

CHOMSKY, N.: *Aspects of the theory of syntax* (Cambridge, Mass., 1965).

CHOMSKY, N.: *Topics in the theory of generative grammar* (The Hague, 1966).

FIRTH, J. R.: *Speech* (London, 1930).

JAKOBSON, R. and HALLE, M.: *Fundamentals of language* (The Hague, 1956). Distinctive feature phonology in relation to the phoneme theory.

JONES, D.: *Outline of English phonetics*, sixth edition (London, 1947). Classic account of the phonetics of British English.

LYONS, J.: *Introduction to theoretical linguistics* (Cambridge, 1968). Especially valuable for the coverage it gives to transformational-generative theory and to semantics.

ROBINS, R. H.: *General linguistics: An introductory survey* (London, 1964).

ROBINS, R. H.: *A short history of linguistics* (London, 1967).

SAPIR, E.: *Language* (New York, 1921). One of the most attractively written short introductions to the subject ever produced.

SAPIR, E.: "The status of linguistics as a science", *Language* 5 (1929).

ULLMANN, S.: *Semantics* (1962).

WALDRON, R. A.: *Sense and sense development* (London, 1967).

2

Structural organization of language 1 – phonology

EUGÉNIE J. A. HENDERSON

School of Oriental and African Studies, London

Linguistics—until comparatively recently a Cinderella among the disciplines—is concerned with the scientific study of human language in all its manifestations, as one of the most important aspects of human behaviour, and perhaps the most characteristically human. Phonology, as a branch of linguistics, is concerned with *one* of the manifestations of human language.

Let us consider for a moment just what *are* the ways in which language may be manifested.

WRITTEN AND SPOKEN LANGUAGE COMPARED

Apart from the very small minority of people who claim to have telepathic powers, we human beings, in common with all other living creatures, can only communicate with one another by means of our senses. Written or printed language is only possible as a means of communication because we have eyes to read. Spoken language is directed towards the sense of hearing of the person we wish to communicate with. In the one case we convey our message by means of *visual* symbols—black shapes on paper, or chalk shapes on wood, and so on—in the other by means of *audible* symbols, i.e. speech sounds.

Using my hand and arm muscles, I can produce on a piece of paper with the aid of a pencil a complex black shape, thus:—CAT.

Using a different set of muscles, I can produce the sequence of sounds [kæt]. To all of us here, these two very different physical objects or events, the written shape and the spoken utterance, both relate to a single item in the signalling code we call the English language. We take our linguistic activity so much for granted that we seldom, if ever, reflect upon how utterly different these two types of physical object or event *are*. Apart from the meaning they convey to us, there is no resemblance whatever between them, and yet, despite the physical difference, both the written signal and the spoken signal refer to the same piece of the English language. There is thus a distinction between the language itself and the form in which it is expressed; the same language may be manifested in more than one physical medium. "The language itself" is somehow carried around in the brains of English-speaking people—how we do not yet know, but it seems certain that the code must be one which arranges certain recurrent items in regular patterns. If this were not so, we should not be able to understand each other; we should all be babbling away to ourselves like young babies. It follows, therefore, that the physical media used to convey language must also be capable of arrangement into regular recognizable patterns. The shape on the paper is not a mere scribble—if it were, we should not be able to interpret it. It is made up of three recurrent smaller shapes—C, A, T, which can be combined with other recurrent shapes to form different signals. In the same way, the [k] sound at the beginning of [kæt] recurs in *cap, cut, Jack, kitten,* etc., the [æ] sound in *man, hazard,* etc., and so on. The recurrent items with which we form patterns in the visual medium are *letters,* which are shapes arranged to form patterns in *space;* while the recurrent items in the audible medium are *speech sounds,* which are arranged to form patterns in *time.* Notice that there is not a one-to-one relationship between the recurrent items in the two media; you cannot be sure that wherever you use the letter "C" you will always have the sound [k] in the corresponding pattern in the spoken language. This is why when linguists wish to make a written record of the spoken form of a language they almost always have to use a phonetic notation rather than the traditional orthography. A phonetic notation is one in which—provided you know the rules—there *is* a one-to-one relation between speech sounds and written symbols.

GENERAL PHONETICS AND
FUNCTIONAL PHONETICS

The study of the total range of speech sounds that can be made by human beings is the concern of *general phonetics.* All human beings have substantially the same speech apparatus, so that the total repertory of human sounds is effectively the same for the whole species, but the selection made from this total repertory varies quite considerably from community to community. The study of speech as a universal human phenomenon is *phonetics.* The study of the systematic organization of selected speech sounds in the spoken forms of individual languages has variously been called *functional phonetics, phonemics,* or, more commonly nowadays, *phonology.* The business of phonology is to abstract, describe and classify as neatly as we can the recurrent sound units used to build up the spoken orms of a given language, and to state the rules for their use. Since I assume that I am addressing myself on this occasion principally to those with no previous knowledge of linguistics, I shall try to provide some general notion of what is meant by phonological analysis and of the sort of issues it raises. In order to do so, it will be necessary to oversimplify many issues and to omit mention of many more. Those who wish to pursue the subject further will, however, soon come upon such matters for themselves. I shall also with regret have to exclude all mention of theoretical approaches which, whatever their merits, have on the whole not been in the "mainstream" of development, and are hence unlikely to be encountered by the lay reader in his first acquaintance with the subject.

For the description of phonological units we use terms derived from general phonetics, which describes and classifies speech sounds partly according to the way in which they are articulated, partly according to the way they sound. Consonants, for instance, are described and classified with reference to two main co-ordinates: (1) their manner of articulation, and (2) the place in the mouth at which the articulation takes place. We handle "manner of articulation" in terms of the degree of obstruction or interference with the passage of air from the lungs when we speak, ranging from *stops*, like, *p, t, k, b, d, g*, at one extreme, to vowels at the other—vowels having the minimum amount of interference with the air stream. A third factor is introduced to cover the difference between *p* and *b*, *s* and *z*, etc. which are pairs of consonants made in the same way and at the same place, but differentiated by the action of the vocal cords. In the pronunciation of *b, z, v, d*, etc. the vocal cords vibrate, and these sounds are accordingly said to be *voiced*. In the pronunciation of *p, s, f, t*, etc. the vocal cords do *not* vibrate, hence these sounds are classed as *voiceless*. So that if I talk of a *voiceless bilabial stop* every linguist knows I am talking about a *p*-sound of some kind.

You might at this point wish to ask—What is the difference then, between a phonetic and a phonological description of a language? Is it not possible to devise a framework of phonetic description to cover all the possible sounds human beings can make, and then describe any language that interests us in these terms?

In theory at least, this *is* possible, and for a long time people saw no need to separate phonetics and phonology, believing that all that was required was a sufficient degree of refinement in description to cover all the phonetic variations, major and minor, that might be encountered. A description of a language in these terms could possibly give us a minutely accurate record of its pronunciation but would tell us very little about its structure.

THE PHONEME

About 90 years ago, the great English phonetician, Henry Sweet, the prototype of Shaw's Professor Higgins, devised a system of phonetic notation based upon the Roman alphabet which he described as: "although probably the simplest possible for an accurate analysis of sounds generally, is too cumbrous as well as too minute for many practical purposes." He goes on: "In treating the relations of sounds without going into minute details, and in giving passages of any length in phonetic writing, and especially in dealing with a limited number of sounds, as in treating of a single language—it is necessary to have an alphabet which indicates *only those broader distinctions of sound which actually correspond to distinctions of meaning in language*. (My italics)."[1]

This is the vital point. This embodies already the thinking behind what later became known as the *phoneme concept*, although at the time Sweet was writing the word "phoneme" had not yet been invented. Some examples will clarify what is involved.

Let us take the English *t* sound in *tea* and *two*. In general phonetic terms these are perceptibly different, the one being pronounced without rounded lips, the other with rounded lips. A minutely accurate phonetic transcription would have to record this difference in some way, perhaps by using a subscript *w*, e.g. $[t^w]$ for the rounded *t*, but from the point of view of the structure of spoken English, this is quite a trivial difference for which rules can easily be given and which never corresponds to a "distinction of meaning".

Now let us consider the *t*-sounds in *ton* and *stun*. In my kind of English the *t* of *ton* is slightly aspirated, i.e. there is a clearly perceptible puff of air between the release of the stop and the following vowel. In general phonetic terms we may record this as $[t^h]$.

Now take the *t*-sound in *stun*. Here there is no following aspiration; hence in general phonetic terms we may wish to record this differently, as, for example, $[t'']$.

We find that if we now examine the *t*-sound in *tree*, the tongue contact for this sound is markedly further back on the palate than for the *t*-sound in *tea*. Let us mark the *t* in *tree* with a mark of retraction, thus: [t–].

We find yet another kind of *t*-sound in words like *eighth*. If you compare *eight* and *eighth*, I think you will be able to feel that the point of contact for the tongue is further forward in *eighth* than in *eight*. This fronted kind of *t*-sound we may symbolize thus: [t+].

So we have three different *places of articulation*:—well forward on the teeth as in *eighth*, on the ridge just behind the teeth as in *eight*, or *tea*, and curled back behind this ridge as in *tree*.

We have also observed four different *manners of articulation*:—aspirated as in *ton*, unaspirated as in *stun*, rounded as in *two*, or unrounded as in *tea*.

The rules for the occurrence of one or other of these *t*-sounds are quite regular, however, and can be stated. It is all a matter of context, and no difference in the meaning of words is ever involved.

At the abstract level of the phonological structure of English we are dealing not with several building blocks but with one only, accompanied by certain rules about the way in which it is to be realized in specific contexts. That is to say, the words *tea*, *two*, *ton*, *stun*, *tree*, *eight* and *eighth* all contain the same phonological unit /t/, the rules for the phonetic realization of which in actual speech might be stated as follows:—

(1) Initially in stressed syllables /t/ is realized as [tʰ], i.e. aspirated, except after [s].

(2) After [s], /t/ is realized as [t″], i.e. unaspirated.

(3) Before a following rounded vowel, /t/ is realized as [tʷ], i.e. it is pronounced with rounded lips.

(4) Before a following unrounded vowel, /t/ is realized as [t′], i.e. unrounded.

(5) Before a following interdental sound, /t/ is realized as [t+], i.e. it is pronounced with the tip of the tongue in contact with the upper teeth.

(6) Before a following [r], /t/ is realized as [t–], i.e. the tongue is in contact with the palate behind the teeth-ridge.

(7) Before other sounds and finally, /t/ is realized as [t̪], i.e. the tongue contact is with the teeth-ridge.

A unit of phonological form such as /t/ is what is usually called in linguistics a *phoneme*, and the kind of rules we have been looking at are rules about the non-contrastive or *complementary distribution* of a number of sounds which are different from the general phonetic point of view, but which function together as a single unit in the phonological structure of English. These contextual variations of a phoneme are often called its *allophones*: thus [tʰ], [tʷ], [t+], [t−], etc. are all allophones of the English phoneme /t/. Phonemes themselves are best thought of as abstract units which are realized as speech-sounds in utterances. The term "phoneme" is not a synonym for "speech-sound", though it is sometimes used as such by laymen.

Notice that minor variations between speech sounds that do not correspond to distinctions in meaning in one language may do so in another. The aspiration of the English *t*-sound is non-phonemic, that is to say, it is not used to distinguish English words; but in languages like Chinese, Hindi and Thai (Siamese) the presence or absence of aspiration *does* distinguish words.

e.g. Thai [-tai] *kidney*   [-thai] *Thai*
　　　[-kɔ] *clump, tuft*　[-khɔ] *neck*

The [tʰ] and [kʰ] sounds in these Thai words are to all intents and purposes the same speech-sounds from a general human point of view as the sounds in the words *tie* and *core* in my kind of English. Nevertheless, aspiration plays a very different rôle in the two languages. In English the aspiration of stops is not lexically contrastive but is determined by context, and is therefore non-phonemic, whereas in Thai it is lexically contrastive, and therefore phonemic. Thai [t] and [tʰ] are *not* in complementary distribution. They occur in exactly the same contexts in different words, and it is this contrastive function which justifies their treatment as realizations of two separate phonemes in Thai.

STRESS AND PITCH

The kind of phonemes we have been considering so far have been entities that may be thought of as constituting, or as corresponding to, successive segments in the stream of speech. But such segments are not the only distinctive units of speech. Features such as stress and pitch may also play a contrastive rôle, and may therefore also be regarded as phonemic in certain languages.

Think of the Spanish words: *término* "end", *termíno* "I finish", *terminó* "he finished".

We should say here that the succession of vowel and consonant phonemes is the same; the contrast lies in the placement of the stress. Stress placement is thus phonemic in this instance. Compare also pairs of English words like *ímport* (noun) and *impórt* (verb), in which stress is not only lexically contrastive but plays a grammatical rôle too.

What about pitch in English?

If I say *Yes* with sharply falling pitch, [ˋ], or *Yes* with low rising pitch, [ˏ], or *Yes* with a fall in pitch followed by a rise, [ˇ] the differences you hear certainly correspond to distinctions in meaning of some sort, but nevertheless we feel that *Yes* itself is the "same word" in each case. The differences in pitch are to be related not to the meaning of the word as such, but to the meaning of the whole utterance. Using what are from the point of view of the structure of English the same pitch patterns, I can say:—

I don't want to	[_–ˋ_]	(with falling pitch on *want*)
or *What did you say?*	[__–ˊ]	(low rise, beginning on *what*)
or *It wasn't raining*	[__–ˇ]	(fall-rise on *raining*)

Here the pitch patterns affect whole sentences. This kind of exploitation of pitch is contrastive, but not *lexically* contrastive, and so is not generally regarded as phonemic. Contrast the use of pitch in the following sets of words from Thai and Igbo (language of Nigeria):—

THAI

Mid pitch	Low pitch	Falling pitch	High pitch	Rising pitch
-kha	_kha	ˋkha	^kha	ˊkha
"thatch grass"	(name of a tribe)	"price"	"to trade"	"leg"

IGBO

Low pitch on both syllables	High pitch on both syllables	High followed by low pitch	Low followed by high pitch
àkwà	ákwá	ákwà	àkwá
"bed"	"cry"	"cloth"	"egg"

In languages such as these the very meanings of the words, in the usual lexical sense, depend upon the pitches used. Languages exploiting pitch variation in this particular way are referred to as *tone languages*,[2] and the tones may be regarded as phonemes, realized not as consonant and vowel sounds but as pitch patterns.

THE TASK OF THE PHONOLOGIST

The task of the phonologist is to discover just what is the possible range of contrasts in the spoken forms of the language he is investigating, whether these are contrasts of pitch or stress, or of consonant and vowel sounds only.

By comparing sets of words such as:—

pin	*pin*	*pin*
tin	*pen*	*pit*
bin	*pan*	*pick*
din	*pun*	*pill*
thin	*pawn*	*pig*
kin		*pip*
gin		*pith*
sin		
fin		

he establishes the system of phonemes operating at the different places in the structure of English monosyllables. The vertical axes give the *systems* of phonemic contrasts, the horizontal axes the *structure* of the word being examined. Here the structure is the simple one: Consonant-Vowel-Consonant, or CVC. This would seem to be a pretty simple procedure and in practice it works well most of the time. Nevertheless, theoretical and practical problems are encountered from time to time, and to borrow a metaphor used in the discussion after last week's lecture, the theory sometimes "leaks a bit".

PROBLEMS

Let us, for example, look at the principle of *complementary distribution*, which is one of the foundation stones upon which phoneme theory is built. The English [h] sound in *hat* and the nasal [ŋ] sound in *king, sing, bring*, etc., are in non-contrastive or complementary distribution. That is to say, at whatever place in structure you find the one, you will never find the other. They are mutually exclusive. In syllable initial position we find [h], in syllable final position and before another consonant we have [ŋ]. Never the other way round. Are they then to be regarded as allophones of the same phoneme, and if not, why not? There is no theoretical reason why they shouldn't be, if complementary distribution is the criterion. Even more disturbing to some people is the fact that consonants and vowels are often in complementary distribution: are they too to be regarded as allophonic variants of a single phonological unit of some kind?

Many linguists have shrunk from such a solution, and to help them out a further criterion of "phonetic similarity" was recognized. It was held that two sounds could only be regarded as realizations of the same phoneme *if* they were in complementary distribution *and* were phonetically similar. But how is one to determine phonetic similarity? Just how similar must two sounds be before they can be regarded as realizations of the same phoneme?

This leads straight on to a further problem. If a given sound Y is in one context taken as a realization of phoneme X, must the same sound Y be regarded as a realization of phoneme X in all the other contexts in which it occurs? The English nasals are a case in point. Contrasting sets of words like *son, some, sung* lead us to establish three nasal phonemes occurring in word-final position. Initally we have only two, /m/ and /n/, as in *main, name*, but not *ngame. There is no serious problem here, merely a difference between a system of two and a system of three. But when we come to words like *bank, hump, hunt, hand* and so on, in which nasal consonants occur before a stop consonant in the same word,[3] we find there is no nasal contrast here at all, since the kind of nasal sound that occurs is always predictable from the sound that follows: before [k] it will be [ŋ], the nasal made in the same place as [k]; before [p] it is always [m]; and before [t] or [d] it is always [n]; i.e. the nasal is always made at the same place of articulation as the following stop. Phonetically speaking, then, we have three separate nasal sounds, the same three that we have in *some, son, sung*, but with this difference: there is no question here of a contrast corresponding to a change in meaning. There is no three-term nasal phoneme system operating in words like *tank, ink, bank*; only one nasal sound is permissible. So what does the phonologist do about it? Those who set great store by the criterion of phonetic similarity will say that since the sounds [n], [m], and [ŋ] are the realizations of three separate phonemes elsewhere in the language, they must be interpreted in the same way when they are found before a stop, even though there is no significant contrast in this environment.

Once a phoneme always a phoneme. This is not an entirely satis-factory solution, however. There is clearly some redundancy here. Why talk of phonemes at all when there is no possibility of a contrast linked to a change of meaning? Is one perhaps concerned with a different sort of unit altogether, a unit which one could only specify as "Nasal"? If we were to write such a unit as "N", spellings such as *haNd*, *hiNt*, *laNp*, *baNk*, would all be perfectly unambiguous.

Notice that in Italian, which has /n/ and /m/ phonemes but no contrastive use of the velar nasal [ŋ], there is, nevertheless, a velar nasal sound in words like *banco* [baŋko]. In this case, however, phonologists do not regard the [ŋ] sound as the realization of a phoneme /ŋ/, because nowhere in the language is the sound in contrast with [n] or [m]. What they must do is regard it as an allophone of either /n/ or /m/, the favoured choice being /n/, per-haps partly on account of the spelling.

DISTINCTIVE FEATURES

Recently many linguists have been inclined to believe that these problems and many others like them are easier to handle if one does not regard the phoneme as an unanalysable entity. Phonemes were for many years regarded by the majority of linguists as the ultimate, smallest phonological units—as unsplittable linguistic atoms, so to speak. It is popular nowadays to regard the phoneme as analysable into its component contrastive features—the features which account for the distinctions between phones—and to regard these distinctive component features themselves as the ultimate, smallest phono-logical units.

To set about the analysis of a language into these phonological distinctive features one makes use once more of sets of words which appear to be minimally distinct from each other, and one tries to systematize the distinctions. Let us take as our starting point the following series of English words:—

| *mill* | *bill* | *pill* | *fill* |
| *nil* | *dill* | *till* | *sill* |

We clearly have a system of initial phonemes: /m, n, b, d, p, t, f, s/. What are their distinctive features?

bill is contrasted with *pill* by the presence or absence of *voice*, i.e. the vibration or lack of vibration of the vocal cords, in the first consonant. Otherwise these two words are articulated in essentially the same way. So we assign the distinguishing feature "+voice" to the phoneme /b/, and the feature "−voice" to /p/.

With the pair *bill* and *dill* the distinction is one of place of articulation, *labial:dental*. Otherwise both initial consonants are voiced, both are stops. So we assign "+labial" to /b/ and "+dental" to /d/. Since *bill* is to *dill* as *pill* is to *till*, i.e. distinguished by labial place of articulation as contrasted with dental place of articulation, we assign the features "+labial" and "+dental" to them too.

With the pair *dill/till* the distinctive feature is "+voice", as with *bill/pill*. It is important to note that although we know that the *d* of *dill* is *phonetically* a voiced sound, we don't regard "+voice" as a *phonologically* distinctive feature until we have found a pair of words distinguished solely by the presence or absence of voice. Looking at *pill* and *fill*, we find the distinction is one of *manner* of articulation, i.e. stop as contrasted with fricative. Phonetically speaking, there is also a difference in the place of articulation; [p] is articulated with the two lips, [f] with the upper teeth against the lower lip. This difference is, however, not phonologically distinctive, since there are no words distinguished solely by the contrast between bilabial and labiodental articulation. The English phonemes /p/ and /f/ are therefore regarded as both having the feature "+labial", as contrasted with /t/ and /s/, which are both "+dental". /t/ and /s/ are distinguished from each other by the same *stop:fricative* contrast which distinguishes /p/ and /f/.

This leaves the two words *mill* and *nil* to be considered. The initial consonants in *mill* and *bill* are both voiced and both labial, those in *nil* and *dill* both voiced and both dental. The distinction here lies in the contrast *nasal:non-nasal*.

The words we have been considering form only a very small part of the total number of English monosyllables, but I think you can see how one can begin to build up a picture of each phoneme as a group or bundle of phonologically distinctive features, viz:—

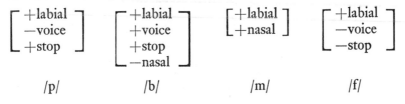

$$\begin{bmatrix} +\text{labial} \\ -\text{voice} \\ +\text{stop} \end{bmatrix} \qquad \begin{bmatrix} +\text{labial} \\ +\text{voice} \\ +\text{stop} \\ -\text{nasal} \end{bmatrix} \qquad \begin{bmatrix} +\text{labial} \\ +\text{nasal} \end{bmatrix} \qquad \begin{bmatrix} +\text{labial} \\ -\text{voice} \\ -\text{stop} \end{bmatrix}$$

/p/　　　　　　/b/　　　　　　/m/　　　　　　/f/

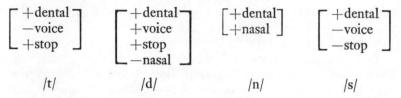

$$\begin{bmatrix} +\text{dental} \\ -\text{voice} \\ +\text{stop} \end{bmatrix} \quad \begin{bmatrix} +\text{dental} \\ +\text{voice} \\ +\text{stop} \\ -\text{nasal} \end{bmatrix} \quad \begin{bmatrix} +\text{dental} \\ +\text{nasal} \end{bmatrix} \quad \begin{bmatrix} +\text{dental} \\ -\text{voice} \\ -\text{stop} \end{bmatrix}$$

$$/\text{t}/ \qquad\qquad /\text{d}/ \qquad\qquad /\text{n}/ \qquad\qquad /\text{s}/$$

Phonetic features which are not distinctive do not appear in the bundles. This is why the feature "+voice" does not appear in the feature-bundles for /m/ and /n/. There is no *voice:voiceless* contrast in nasal sounds in English. Similarly, the aspiration of the stop in *till* and *pill* is interpreted as part of the phonetic relization but not as a distinctive feature. It could be argued that we should mark /p/ and /t/ as "+aspiration" and /b/ and /d/ as "−aspiration", and regard the presence or absence of voice as non-distinctive. What is clear is that in the phonetic realization there is some redundancy— we commonly have both the aspiration contrast *and* the voice contrast to help us. But the rules of distinctive feature phonology demand that you choose one or other as the relevant feature. In the case of English, it would probably work all right to take "±aspiration" as the distinctive feature contrast in the stops, but what of pairs like *seal/zeal*, *fine/vine*, and so on? We might end up with two contrasts in complementary distribution, e.g. "±voice" for fricatives, "±aspiration" for stops. This suggests that we ought to group them together under a single heading if we possibly can, and this is what I have done here in suggesting "±voice" as the relevant contrast in both cases.

Let us now turn to the question of the stops in words like *spill*, *skill*, *still*.

The phoneme /p/ in *pill* is, as we have seen, a bundle of distinctive features, namely

$$\begin{bmatrix} +\text{labial} \\ -\text{voice} \\ +\text{stop} \end{bmatrix}$$

But there is no voice contrast in *spill*, so that the presence or absence of voice is no longer a distinctive feature of the p-segment in this context. We thus have a phonological unit in this word which is not a bundle of three features but of two only: "+labial", to distinguish it from *skill* and *still*, and "+stop" to distinguish pairs like *spell*, *smell*, etc. We might write this unit /B/, to distinguish it from the phonemes /b/ and /p/ in words like *bill* and *pill*. A unit of this very generalized kind is sometimes called an *archiphoneme*, and we say that the phonological contrast between the presence and absence of voice is neutralized in this particular context.

We can now see a possible solution in these terms to the problem posed by words like *bank, hand, hunt, hump, lamp,* etc. in which the place of articulation of the nasal is not contrastive. The only distinctive feature of the segment before the stop is "+nasal". We thus have in this environment an archiphoneme, which we can write /N/ to distinguish it from the phonemes /n/, /m/ and /ŋ/.

What about another of our problems, that of the complementary distribution of consonants and vowels? Can distinctive features help us towards a solution here too?

Distinctive feature phonology postulates two major phonological contrasts: "±vocalic" and "±consonantal". These give rise to four main types of units:—

Vowels, which are "+vocalic" and "−consonantal".
Liquids, i.e. *l* and *r* sounds, which are "+vocalic" and "+consonantal". That is to say, they exhibit both consonantal and vowel-like features (as, for example, the way in which they may be syllabic in words like *kettle* in English).
Consonants are for the distinctive feature phonologist "−vocalic" and "+consonantal". Included under this head are most of what we are accustomed to call consonants, e.g. stops, fricatives, nasals, but excluding liquids.

There is also a fourth type of unit, the *glides,* which are both "−vocalic" and "−consonantal". Examples are *h* and the glottal stop.

By definition, therefore, a unit which is $\begin{bmatrix} +\text{vocalic} \\ -\text{consonantal} \end{bmatrix}$ can never be the same as one which is $\begin{bmatrix} -\text{vocalic} \\ +\text{consonantal} \end{bmatrix}$ The "complementary distribution" of vowels and consonants doesn't enter into it any more. The "problem" no longer exists.

You may or may not be convinced by the foregoing brief exposition that the distinctive feature concept stops up some of the leaks in the earlier phoneme theory. Be that as it may. Distinctive feature phonology is much in vogue at the present time, and in a somewhat more sophisticated form is the favoured approach of Chomsky and his followers.

PHONOLOGY IN A GENERATIVE GRAMMAR

I will conclude this evening with a brief look at the rôle of phonology in what Chomsky calls *generative grammar*.

For Chomsky such a grammar has three components:—
    (1) a syntactic component
    (2) a phonological component
and (3) a semantic component.

The phonological component provides the rules for the conversion of the words and other elements of the language into their spoken forms.

Note that for Chomsky phonology and semantics are both a part of grammar. This is contrary to the view held by the majority of structural linguists from about 1935 onwards, who regarded grammar, phonology, and semantics as three separate and independent levels of language.

The aim of a grammar, according to Chomsky, should be to "embody the speaker's competence in and knowledge of his language",[4] and we should assess the worth of a grammatical description and the linguistic theory behind it by the degree of success it attains on the way to this goal.

To see what this means for phonology, let us take a very simple example:[5]

We have in English a noun *brick*, but no nouns *blick*, *bnick* or *ftick*.

Written phonemically, using an asterisk for the non-existent forms, we have:—

    1. /brik/   2. /*blik/   3. /*bnik/   4. /*ftik/.

The traditional way of handling this situation is simply to note the form that exists and to ignore those that don't. This may be stated in the form of a rule to the effect that /brik/ is a realization of the grammatical category *noun*. We can express this rule thus:—

Noun → /brik/

This is a true statement and all right as far as it goes, but Chomsky says it doesn't go far enough. It does *not* embody the English speaker's competence in and knowledge of his own language.

Any speaker of English intuitively knows that although there is no such word as /blik/, /blik/ is an admissible form in a sense in which /bnik/ or /ftik/ are not. Someone may tomorrow produce a detergent called "Blick", but not one called "Bnik" or "Ftik". (Note that this distinction is not a matter of universal phonetics: there are languages in the world in which *bn-* and *ft- do* occur as initial clusters.) An adequate grammar of English must, says Chomsky, distinguish /brik/ and /blik/ as admissible forms from /bnik/ and /ftik/ as inadmissible forms, thus making explicit what English speakers know, unconsciously, to be true.

Let us look at a rule which would do this:—

$$\text{Initial } C_1C_2 \rightarrow sC_2$$

That is to say, where C_2 is a true consonant in the sense of being $\begin{bmatrix} -\text{vocalic} \\ +\text{consonantal} \end{bmatrix}$, C_1 is always [s]. This rule specifically excludes the possibility of /bnik/ and /ftik/ and a whole lot of other impossible forms like *vnig, tsaim, gnait*, etc., but it does not exclude /blik/, since /l/ is not a consonant, $\begin{bmatrix} +\text{consonantal} \\ -\text{vocalic} \end{bmatrix}$, but a liquid, $\begin{bmatrix} +\text{consonantal} \\ +\text{vocalic} \end{bmatrix}$, in Chomsky's phonological model. So /blik/ would thus be recognized as an accidental gap in English, but still a phonologically permissible form.[6]

ORDERED RULES

We have just had an example of a very simple phonological rule of the kind used in generative grammar. There is perhaps time to mention briefly a further important aspect of this approach by rule, which is that the rules must be applied in sequence in a given order. The statements I made earlier about allophones were also rules of a sort, but they were not *ordered* rules. They were, if you like, *simultaneous* rules. It doesn't make the slightest bit of difference whether you first say that /t/ before /θ/ is fronted and then that /t/ before /r/ is retracted, or whether you reverse the order of statement. In generative phonology, however, the order in which the rules are applied is important.

Here is a simple example of the operation of ordered rules in a variety of Canadian English.[7]

In this kind of English such words as *high, find, knives, how, houses* are pronounced with diphthongs [ai] and [au], just as in Southern British English. Words like *white, knife, shout, house*, on the other hand, are regularly pronounced with diphthongs beginning with a vowel sound rather like the *a* in the word *about*, i.e. [əi], [əu]. The rule is that [əi] and [əu] are used before a following voiceless consonant, while [ai] and [au] are found finally and before a following voiced consonant. A further feature of the kind of Canadian English we are examining is that between vowels *t* is voiced, i.e. *letter* is pronounced [ledər]. We have therefore two rules, which I shall label X and Y:—

> Rule X /a/ → [ə] in diphthongs followed by voiceless
> consonants.
> Rule Y /t/ → [d] between vowels.

There are, however, two dialects of this type of English, which I shall label A and B.

Dialect A pronounces *typewriter* as [təiprəidər], dialect B pronounces *typewriter* as [təipraidər]. It is assumed that in both dialects the phonemic form of the word is /taipraitər/, and that the difference in realization is to be accounted for by the application of the rules already given. If you consider the facts for a moment, you will readily see that the difference between the two dialects lies in the *order* in which Rules X and Y are applied to the underlying phonemic form.

In dialect A, /taipraitər/ is first converted by Rule X to [təiprəitər], and then by Rule Y to [təiprəidər].

In dialect B, the order of application is reversed. /taipraitər/ is first converted by Rule Y to [taipraidər], and then by Rule X to [təipraidər].

NOTES

1 Sweet, H.: *Handbook of Phonetics*, p. 102–3.
2 See also Claire and W. M. S. Russell, Lecture 8, pp. 176–7 (Ed.)
3 Notice that I am using "word" here to mean a grammatically indivisible unit. I am excluding forms like *hanged* which structurally speaking consist of a word plus a grammatical formative.
See John Lyons, Lecture 3, pp. 61–2 (Ed.)
4 Chomsky, N.: "Current Issues in Linguistic Theory" in Fodor and Katz: *The Structure of Language*, p. 60.

5 This problem has been handled at various times and in various ways by both Chomsky and Halle:
  (5a) See Chomsky, N.: "Current Issues in Linguistic Theory" in Fodor and Katz: *The Structure of Language*, p. 64.
  (5b) and Halle, M.: "Phonology in Generative Grammar" in *The Structure of Language*, pp. 340–2.
6 This rule only works for people who do not pronounce the initial *p* in words like *psychology* or *ptarmigan*.
7 Joos, M.: "A phonological dilemma in Canadian English", *Language* 18, No. 2, pp. 141–4.
  Chomsky, N. and Halle, M.: *The Sound Pattern of English*, pp. 342–3.
  Halle, M.: "Phonology in Generative Grammar" in *The Structure of Language*, pp. 343–4.

FURTHER READING

ABERCROMBIE, D.: *Elements of General Phonetics* (Edinburgh, 1967), especially Chapters 1 and 5.

GIMSON, A. C.: *An Introduction to the Pronunciation of English* (London), especially Chapters 1 and 5.

GLEASON, H. A.: *An Introduction to Descriptive Linguistics* (New York), Chapter 16–21 inclusive.

HALLE, M.: "Phonology in generative grammar" (in Fodor and Katz: *The Structure of Language*, New York, 1964), pp. 334–54.

HARMS, R. T.: *Introduction to Phonological Theory* (New York).

JAKOBSON and HALLE: *Fundamentals of Language* (The Hague, 1956).

JONES, D.: *The Phoneme: its nature and use* (Cambridge).

MARTINET, A.: *Phonology as Functional Phonetics* (Oxford).

PIKE, K.: *Phonemics: a technique for reducing languages to writing* (Michigan).

ROBINS, R. H.: *General Linguistics: an introductory survey* (London, 1964), Chapter 4.

3

Structural Organization of language 2 – grammar

JOHN LYONS

University of Edinburgh

WHAT IS GRAMMAR?

Let me begin by explaining in what sense I shall be using the term "grammar". The word derives ultimately from Greek and originally meant nothing more than "the art of reading and writing". Quite early in the history of Greek scholarship, however, it came to be used as a general term for the investigation and description of language; and, when we use the phrase "traditional grammar", it is usually this sense of the word "grammar" that we have in mind. Professor Robins has traced the history of traditional grammar in the first lecture of this series. All I need to do here is to emphasize the fact that, in traditional usage, the word "grammar" carried a number of implications that the majority of linguists today would not wish to accept. I will mention just two.

I have said that the word "grammar" comes from a Greek word meaning "the art of reading and writing". Its origin and subsequent extension reflect the fact that the Greek grammarians (from the Hellenistic period, at any rate) were primarily concerned with the language of literature, and gave relatively little attention to the everyday spoken language. Nowadays, most linguists would say that speech is the natural and primary medium in which language is manifest and that the written language is secondary. (This does not mean that the written language is unimportant; nor does it imply that the written language is in all respects parasitic upon speech.[1]) One of the consequences of the traditional grammarian's concentration upon the written language, and more particularly upon the language of literature, is that many people tend to think of grammar as being something that is taught formally at school, like reading and writing, and do not always appreciate that the spoken language is regulated by grammatical rules, which we learn as children, for the most part long before we go to school, and to which we unconsciously conform thereafter whenever we speak the language. Let me stress, therefore, that this is so. Languages that have never been committed to writing are no less subject to grammatical description than languages that have long been used for literature.

A second implication commonly associated with the word "grammar" is that it must be prescriptive in orientation and purpose: that the grammarian's task is to formulate the rules of "correct" speech and writing. There is of course considerable support for this view in the practice of grammarians throughout the centuries. But grammar need not be seen in this light. Just as one can draw a distinction between descriptive and prescriptive ethics, let us say, so one can distinguish between descriptive and prescriptive grammar. In other words, we can define grammar to be the study, and subsequent description, of the way in which people actually speak rather than as the prescription of how, in our or anyone else's view, they ought to speak.

I have mentioned these two implications of the word "grammar" in order to forestall any possible confusion. Let me now go on to say that, although the term "grammar", is used by some linguists in the rather comprehensive sense in which it has been employed in the past, it tends to be interpreted somewhat more narrowly in a good deal of modern linguistic theory. In this narrower sense it is opposed, on the one hand, to phonology and, on the other, to semantics; and this is the sense in which I am using the term. For those who are familiar with traditional terminology, let me say that grammar, in the narrower interpretation, covers *syntax, accidence* and *word-formation*; or, to use more modern terms, *syntax, inflexion* and *derivation*. What I mean by these terms I will explain presently. For the moment (taking for granted the validity of the notions "word" and "sentence"), we can say that grammar is that part of the systematic description of language which accounts for the way in which words are combined to form sentences.

FORMAL GRAMMAR

Modern grammatical theory is often described, by contrast with traditional grammar, as being "formal" rather than "notional"; and I now want to explain what is meant by this. (Professor Robins has said something about it in the opening lecture of the series.) In this context, the word "formal" implies two rather different though related, characteristics: on the one hand, "not based on meaning", and, on the other, "explicit" or "precise". The first of these implications rests upon the distinction between form and meaning; and the sense of "formal" that derives from this distinction is comparable with the sense in which it is used in such phrases as "formal logic". The second implication is more important, and we shall return to it later in our discussion of generative grammar: for the present, it will be sufficient to say that a formal theory (in the second sense of the term "formal") is one that has been made mathematically precise—one that has been *formalized*—typically, as a deductive system with axioms, rules of inference and theorems (or "conclusions") provable within the system.

There is a historical, if not logical, connexion between the two senses of "formal". Many linguists believe that the analysis of meaning is the weak point in the study of language and cannot yet be made objective and precise; and that, for this reason, if for no other, grammar should be independent of semantics. This was the point of view taken by the great American linguist Leonard Bloomfield; and it has been tremendously important in the development of modern linguistic theory.[2] There is no necessary connexion, of course, between the two senses of "formal" that I have distinguished. If the analysis of meaning can be made objective and precise, then semantics is no less amenable to formalization, in principle at least, than is grammatical theory; and there is at the present time considerable interest among linguists in the possibility of constructing a theory of formal semantics. Professor Ullmann will be referring to this in his lecture: I need say no more about it here.

The "Bloomfieldian" view of the relationship between grammar and semantics, though based upon a quite false conception of meaning and an unnecessarily limited notion of grammatical analysis, was on balance a beneficial, rather than a harmful, influence in the development of linguistics. This is a personal opinion that not all linguists would share, and I will not attempt to justify it here. I mention it because it undoubtedly colours my whole approach to linguistics; and in a lecture like this I should perhaps declare my prejudices in advance. For the rest of this lecture I will assume that by "grammar" we mean "formal grammar"; and, for simplicity, I will make the further assumption that "formal" includes both of the two senses I have distinguished above.[3]

GRAMMATICAL UNITS

Traditional grammar recognized four different kinds of grammatical units: sentences, clauses, phrases and words. Of these four, *sentences* and *words* may be described as primary, and *clauses* and *phrases* as secondary. Clauses and phrases are secondary in the sense that they are defined with reference to some prior definition of words and sentences. Let me explain what I mean. Both phrases and clauses are said to be sequences of words operating as units within the grammatical structure of sentences: they therefore presuppose some prior notion of what is a word and what is a sentence. The difference between clauses and phrases is a little hazy in practice. It is commonly said, for example, that a clause has its own subject and predicate, whereas a phrase does not: but it is not always clear when a sequence of words "has" a subject and a predicate. Part of the reason for this uncertainty lies in the fact that traditional grammar made a more or less liberal appeal to the notion of covert elements (words or sequences of words) which, though not actually present in an utterance were to be "understood" as grammatically relevant. Since "having a subject and predicate" was one of the principal defining characteristics of the sentence in traditional grammar, we can say that the difference between clauses and phrases lies in the difference between "sentencelike" and "non-sentencelike" sequences of words. (This difference can be formalized within modern generative grammar in terms of the operations of "conjoining" or "embedding" sentences.) So much then by way of an overview of the traditional list of grammatical units and of the relations between them. I now want to draw your attention to certain distinctions which, though not particularly subtle or difficult to understand, have often been neglected both in traditional grammar and in modern linguistics.

The first is the distinction between the sentence and the utterance. By an *utterance* we mean any continuous stretch of speech or writing from a single source.[4] (It is inconvenient that the word "utterance" is restricted in normal usage to the spoken language and "text" to the written language.) For example, the following, we will assume, might occur as English utterances in some appropriate context:

(1) *Got a bit of a hangover, have you?*
(2) *The prisoner ate a hearty breakfast.*
(3) *It looks like rain. I don't suppose there'll be any play this afternoon. We may as well stay at home.*

Of these three utterances, only the second is normally described as a sentence. The first is grammatically incomplete, or elliptical (that is to say, it is only part of a sentence) and the third is a sequence of three sentences. So utterances and sentences are not coterminous. This is a point that is stressed in many handbooks of linguistics.

But there is a more important difference between the sentence and the utterance, which is not so commonly emphasized by linguists. This is a difference of theoretical status: the sentence is more "abstract" than the utterance. Sentences, as such, do not occur —they are not bits of "language behaviour" or stretches of speech. They are theoretical constructs, postulated by the linguist in order to account for the grammatical structure of utterances. Whether the sentence is to be taken as primitive or as definable in terms of other notions within grammatical theory is a question we need not go into here. We will assume an intuitive knowledge of what is and of what is not a sentence. We can now go on to define the language as the set of sentences postulated by the linguist in order to describe, indirectly, the utterances produced by members of a speech-community—their "language behaviour". (It will be observed that I have defined the language as a set of sentences and not as a set of utterances. This conforms to the distinction drawn by Ferdinand de Saussure between "langue" and "parole".)

We defined grammar, it will be recalled, as "that part of the systematic description of language which accounts for the way in which words are combined to form sentences". But what do we mean by "word"? This is a highly equivocal term. At least three senses of "word" must be distinguished if we want to make use of it in talking about the grammatical structure of sentences. Consider first of all a conventional dictionary of English, which contains, in the ideal, all the "words" in the language (as well as various idioms and phrases, which do not concern us here). Now consider the following sentence: *The horses jumped over the fence*. It contains six "words". Not all of them, however, will be found in a standard dictionary of English, despite the fact that it contains, as we have said, all the "words" in the language! We will not find *horses* or *jumps* in our dictionary. Why not? Because they are formed by regular grammatical processes from *horse* and *jump*: there is therefore no need to list them separately. One of the ambiguities latent in the term "word" should now be obvious enough. From one point of view *horse* and *horses*, or *jump*, *jumps*, *jumping* and *jumped*, are different "words"; from another point of view, they belong to the same "word". Let us keep these two senses of "word" apart, both terminologically and notationally, by saying that *horse* and *horses* are different *word-forms* associated with the same *lexical word* HORSE (I am using small capitals to refer to lexical words).

Let us now pass on to the second ambiguity. Consider the "word" *sent* in *I sent my brother a letter* vs. *I have sent my brother a letter*. If we substitute the lexical word WRITE for the lexical word SEND, we find that there is now a difference in the associated word-forms that occur in the contexts *I . . . my brother a letter*, on the one hand, and *I have . . . my brother a letter*, on the other. In the former context we have *wrote*, and in the latter *written*. They would be traditionally described as "the past tense of WRITE" and "the past participle of WRITE", respectively. Let us now introduce a distinction between the *grammatical word* and the *word-form*, saying that *wrote* is the word-form that realizes the grammatical word "past tense of WRITE" and *written* is the word-form that realizes the grammatical word "past participle of WRITE". In terms of this distinction we can say that *sent* in *I have sent my brother a letter* is from one point of view the same "word" as *sent* in *I sent my brother a letter*—it is the same word-form. But from another point of view it is a different "word"— it realizes a different grammatical word.

I have distinguished, then, three kinds of "words": lexical words, grammatical words and word-forms; and, in distinguishing between grammatical words and word-forms, I have made use of the important notion of *realization*, by means of which we can relate the two levels of grammar and phonology (or, in the case of the written language, of grammar and orthographic representation): grammatical units are realized by complexes of phonological (or orthographic) units.

So far, it will be observed, I have not mentioned the *morpheme*, which many linguists would regard as a more basic grammatical unit than the word. I do not in fact share the common view that morphemes are "basic", in a way that words are not; but I will not argue that point here. We shall come to morphemes in a moment.

MORPHOLOGY AND SYNTAX

A distinction is often drawn, within grammar, between *morphology* and *syntax*, morphology being defined as the study of the internal structure of words and syntax as the study of the way in which words combine with one another to form phrases, clauses and sentences. This would seem to be in conflict with our provisional definition of grammar as that branch of the description of languages which accounts for the way in which words combine to form sentences. What I mean is that our definition of grammar seems to leave no place for morphology. But this contradiction, or discrepancy, is only apparent; it rests upon the ambiguity of the term "word". Syntax specifies the permissible combinations of *grammatical words*; and morphology describes the internal structure of each of the corresponding *word-forms*.

The distinction between morphology and syntax is not equally important in all languages. It is less important, for example, for the description of English than it is for the description of Latin or Russian; and, in the opinion of certain linguists at least, the distinction cannot be drawn at all with respect to the so-called "analytic", or "isolating", languages like Vietnamese. We will not go into this question.

To illustrate from English. The word-form *unbelievable* has an obvious internal structure ("obvious", I mean, to anyone who knows English and demonstrable by systematically comparing *unbelievable* with a host of other word-forms). It is composed of three segments: *un*, *believe*, and *able*; and the three segments are *morphemes*. (Some linguists would say that they are morphs, rather than morphemes. I will come back to this point.) There is of course a deliberate connexion between the terms "morpheme" and "morphology" (as there is between "phoneme" and "phonology"): and the term "morphology", derived from the Greek word meaning "form" or "shape", was introduced into linguistics in the nineteenth century (from biology) to refer to the study of the "form" of words (i.e. of word-forms).

The example I have given falls under the heading of *derivation* (or *word-formation*); and it is a matter of dispute whether derivation comes wholly within the scope of grammar, and, if it does, precisely how it relates to syntax. (It will be noted that I have deliberately confined my remarks on derivation to the internal structure of words as word-forms. I have not committed myself on the question whether *unbelievable* and *believe* are forms of the same lexical word BELIEVE or whether they are to be referred to two distinct lexical words. The latter view is more traditional, and underlies the practice of our standard dictionaries of English.)

The relationship between syntax and *inflexion* (or *accidence*) is

universally admitted to be one that should be handled within the
theory of grammar, although linguists are by no means agreed about
the way in which this should be done. Let me just illustrate the kind
of phenomena that are covered by the term "inflexion". I said
earlier that *jump*, *jumps*, *jumping* and *jumped* were different forms of
the same lexical word JUMP; it is this fact that defines them as
inflexional. Inflexion then has to do with the formation of the
appropriate word-forms realizing different grammatical words
associated with the same lexical word. For example, *jumped* is
formed by adding the suffix *-ed* to the stem *jump*. But what about
the form *went*, which realizes the past tense of GO? There is no way
in which we can form *went* from *go*. As a word-form *went* is
morphologically unanalysable. The grammatical word realized by
went, however, is no less readily analysed into its component parts,
or factors, than is the grammatical word realized by *jumped*. The
difference between the two cases can be brought out by drawing
upon the distinction between morpheme and morph that is made
by a number of linguists. In terms of this distinction we can say
that the suffix *-ed* is a *morph* which in the form *jumped*, though
not in the form *went*, realizes the past tense morpheme. I will
say no more about morphology here.[5] We will now move on to
syntax.

FORM CLASSES

The term "form class" has been used in a variety of senses in
linguistics. One common interpretation of the term might run as
follows: A *form class* is any set of forms (word-forms, morphs, etc.)
that have the same distribution throughout the sentences of the
language. (By "having the same distribution" is meant "occurring
in the same range of environments". It is assumed that a distinction can be drawn between grammatically well-formed ("grammatical") and semantically well-formed ("meaningful") sentences;
and that "sentences" in the definition of "form class" refers to
grammatically well-formed sentences, which may or may not be
meaningful. This is now, and has long been, a controversial
distinction.[6])

According to this definition, it will be observed, form classes are
related to, but do not coincide with, the parts of speech of
traditional grammar. Apart from anything else, the parts of speech

group together classes of lexical words rather than classes of word-forms. (When we say, for example, that *went* is a verb we mean that it is one of the forms of the lexical word GO and that GO is a verb.) For simplicity of exposition, however, I will talk from now on in terms of the traditional parts of speech ("noun", "verb", "adjective", etc.) In doing this, I am making two assumptions: I am assuming, first of all, that the conventional classification of English words as "nouns", "verbs", "adjectives", etc., is, on the whole, justifiable within the framework of modern formal grammar and, secondly, that all the necessary morphological rules could be added to the grammar and integrated satisfactorily with the syntax. These are big assumptions, to say the least! But they do not affect the general principles.

We are now in a position to construct a very simple formal grammar, which, you will note, has associated with it a *lexicon* (or dictionary). Every grammar presupposes a lexicon; and, conversely, every lexicon, or dictionary, presupposes a grammar. I will explain the various symbols that have been used in the grammar in a moment.

GRAMMAR: (1) S → Det $\vdash$ N + V + Tense + Det + N
(2) S → Det + N + Cop + Tense + A
LEXICON: Det = {*the*, ...}
N = {MAN, BOOK, DOOR, ...}
V = {READ, OPEN, ...}
Tense = {Present, Past}
Cop = {BE}
A = {GOOD, INTERESTING, ...}

This, as I said, is a very simple formal grammar: it describes only two very simple sentence-types, exemplified by *The man opened the door* or *The book is interesting*. I am assuming that there will be morphological rules, (whatever might be their form) to account for the fact that BE + Present is a grammatical word realized as *is*, that READ + Past is realized as *read* (pronounced like the form *red*), whereas OPEN + Past is realized as *opened*, and so on.

The arrow which appears in the two grammatical rules is to be interpreted as "is composed of". Rule (1), therefore, means that a sentence (S) may be composed of a sequence of elements, of which the first belongs to the class of Determiners (Det), the second to the class of Nouns (N), the third to the class of Verbs (V), the

3

fourth to a class of elements subsumed under the category of Tense, the fifth to the class of Determiners and the sixth to the class of Nouns.

Rule (2) means that a sentence may be composed of a Determiner and a Noun followed by the "copula" (Cop)—i.e. "the verb TO BE"—a Tense and an Adjective (A).

Clearly, this grammar will not take us very far in the description of English sentences. But it will serve to illustrate the general points I have been making so far; and it brings us naturally to the subject of generative grammar, which has been one of the most exciting developments in linguistics recently.

GENERATIVE GRAMMAR

What does the term "generative" mean in this context? The answer is that it has two rather different senses, both of which are included when we talk of generative grammar in connexion with the description of natural languages. First of all, it means "precise" or "explicit" (i.e. it has one of the senses of "formal" that we distinguished earlier). It should be noted that this is close to the sense in which we talk of "generating" a series in mathematics. For example, we say that the function $2x + 1$ generates the series $1, 3, 5, 7, 9, \ldots$, when x takes one of the values $0, 1, 2, 3, 4, \ldots$. In much the same sense, we can say that the simple formal grammar illustrated above *generates* a particular set of sentences: *The man opened the door*, *The book is interesting*, etc. (Note that this set will also include a large number of semantically ill-formed sentences: e.g., *The door opened the man*.) The sentences the grammar generates are thereby defined to be grammatical and the sentences it fails to generate are thereby defined to be ungrammatical. It may be worth pointing out that this sense of "generate" is very abstract. There is no necessary connexion between generative grammar and the use of computers or any other kind of "hardware". The mathematics involved can be applied to all sorts of physical systems and operations. But a generative grammar is not of itself a mechanical or electronic device for the production of sentences.

The second sense of "generative" has to do with the fact that human languages are "open-ended". Any native speaker of a language is able to produce and understand an indefinitely large number of utterances that he has never previously encountered. It is this ability that Chomsky has referred to as "rule-governed creativity". The fact that human beings have this ability and draw upon it in their everyday use of language is one of the things that most sharply distinguishes language from systems of animal communication. A generative grammar, in the second sense of the term "generative", is one that mirrors this property of "rule-governed creativity" by generating an indefinitely large number of sentences. The simple grammar illustrated above is not of course generative in this sense.

What is it then that makes a grammar generative in this second sense? The answer is that the grammar must contain rules that can be applied indefinitely many times within the boundaries of the same sentence. Such rules are called *recursive*. A simple example of a recursive rule would be the following:

$$S \rightarrow Det + N + V + Tense + Det + N\ (+\ and\ +\ S).$$

It will be observed that this rule differs from rule (1) given above in just one respect. It contains an optional occurrence of *and* + S on the right-hand side (the fact that the addition of *and* + S is optional is indicated by the parentheses). This means that the same rule can be applied again to the S that has been introduced into the sentence by the previous application of the rule. At some point in the application of the rule we must of course bring the sentence to an end by failing to select the optional *and* + S: if it were not optional, the result would be an infinite "loop". This simple recursive rule that I have just constructed may be interpreted as saying that a sentence may contain within it an indefinitely large number of smaller sentences (or clauses) joined together by *and*. Within the limits of the conception of grammatical structure that we have been operating with so far, this is quite a reasonable way of generating compound sentences in English. But we must extend our conception of grammatical structure.

IMMEDIATE CONSTITUENTS

So far we have been assuming that sentences can be fully described, as far as their grammatical structure is concerned, as sequences of words. We must now modify that assumption.

Consider the following sentence: *The old man at the bus stop has been standing there for half an hour*. It consists of fifteen word-forms arranged in a particular order. We will refer to this sequential arrangement of the constituent word-forms as the *linear structure* of the sentence. Over and above its linear structure (and to some degree, perhaps, independent of it), the sentence has another kind of syntactic structure, which may be described as *hierarchical*. By this is meant the fact that various groups of words within the sentence form intermediate units (some of which at least may be identified as phrases, in the traditional sense). One such intermediate unit is *the old man at the bus stop*: another is *has been standing there* and a third is *for half an hour*. Furthermore, *the old man at the bus stop* is not just a sequence of words, but consists of two smaller intermediate units: *the old man* and *at the bus stop*. What I have been calling "intermediate units" are commonly referred to as *immediate constituents*. We say (assuming that this is in fact the correct analysis from this point of view) that our model sentence consists of three immediate constituents: *the old man at the bus stop*, *has been standing there* and *for half an hour*. Each of these has its own immediate constituents: for example, *the old man at the bus stop* consists of the immediate constituents *the old man* and *at the bus stop*; and at yet a lower level *the old man* can be analysed into the immediate constituents *the* and *old man*. And so on.

There is nothing revolutionary in this notion of constituent structure. It has its equivalent in traditional grammar. But it is only recently that linguists have attempted to handle it within a system of generative rules.[7]

TRANSFORMATIONAL GRAMMAR

In principle all sorts of different kinds of generative grammar are possible; and the construction and comparison of different kinds of generative grammar is an important and highly-specialized field of research at the present time, initiated as far as linguistics is concerned by the work of Chomsky in the early 1950s. We will now look very briefly, and informally, at that model of generative grammar which Chomsky calls *transformational*.[8]

Let us begin by taking a traditional example of *grammatical ambiguity*. (I have used this example in my *Theoretical Linguistics*, and elsewhere. There is some doubt as to how precisely it would be handled in Chomsky's model of transformational grammar. Chomsky himself in his most recent work has tended towards what he calls the "lexicalist" position.[9] The problem in question has to do with the status of derivational morphology in transformational grammar. This raises a number of complex issues, which we will not go into here. For the sake of the present discussion we may assume that the noun *love* is transformationally related to the verb LOVE i.e., like *loved*, *loving*, etc., it is a form of LOVE.) The phrase *the love of God* is ambiguous (though of course in most contexts it will support only one of the two interpretations it bears). It may mean "the love that God feels" or "the love that is felt for God".

Let us now grant that, as far as the constituent-structure of the phrase goes, its potential ambiguity is not reflected in its syntactic analysis. For in both cases we can say that *the love of God* is a noun phrase composed of two immediate constituents, *the love* and *of God*, the first of which is a noun phrase (NP) and the second of which, let us say, is an adjectival phrase (AP) composed of a preposition, *of*, and a noun, *God*. This rather *ad hoc* analysis in terms of immediate constituents may be represented by means of the "tree diagram" in Figure 1. One way of generating phrases of

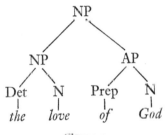

Figure 1

this type might be by means of the following rules:

(1) NP → NP + AP
(2) NP → Det + NP
(3) AP → Prep + N

These are what are called *phrase-structure rules*. The way in which they assign the appropriate hierarchical structure to the sentences that they generate will be evident from the tree diagram.

I have deliberately taken what I described as "a traditional example of grammatical ambiguity". This is often referred to in terms of a distinction between the "subjective" (or "active") and "objective" (or "passive") interpretation of the "possessive". Let me quote from a standard Latin grammar: "When the substantive on which the genitive depends contains the idea of an action . . ., the possession may be *active* or *passive*. Hence the division into: 1. The Active or Subjective Genitive: *amor Dei, love of God, . . .* (God loves); . . . 2. Passive or Objective Genitive: *amor Dei, love of God, . . .* (God is loved)."[10] We might note in passing that this account of the phenomenon we are concerned with makes use of the rather vague phrase "contains the idea of an action" in order to refer to a class of nouns related to a particular subclass of transitive verbs. Unless one can specify more precisely the membership of the classes of nouns and verbs involved, one cannot account for the distinction between the subjective and the objective "possessive" in a generative grammar. We will assume that a precise specification of the kind required is in principle possible. How then do we describe this construction within the framework of generative grammar? More particularly, how is it described in Chomsky's system of transformational grammar?

Chomsky's system assigns to every sentence that it generates two distinct, but related, syntactic analyses: a "deep" analysis and a "surface" analysis. Each of these may be represented by means of a constituent-structure tree-diagram of the kind illustrated in Figure 1. And the two levels of syntactic structure are related (through a series of intermediate structures) by what are called *transformational rules* (not to be identified, let me add, with phrase-structure rules of the kind illustrated above: transformational rules differ in format and in their mode of operation). The surface-structure analysis of the phrase *the love of God* is defined to be something like that represented in Figure 1. This is not assigned directly, however, by phrase-structure rules, but rather by transformational rules operating in sequence upon one or other of two different "underlying" analyses. A rough indication of the form these "deeper" analyses might take is given in Figures 2 and 3. It is the former of these that accounts for the subjective interpretation of *the love of God* (by deriving it from the structure underlying sentences like *God loves/loved men,*); and it is the latter that accounts for the objective interpretation (by deriving it from the structure underlying sentences like *Men love/loved God*).

Transformational grammar is a highly technical subject, and it would be impossible to give any real indication of its scope and

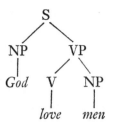

Figure 2

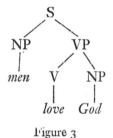

Figure 3

nature in less than a full series of lectures. What I have done is simply to take one kind of grammatical ambiguity, well recognized in traditional grammar, and to say, informally, how Chomsky's model of transformational grammar handles this. I should not wish to give the impression that transformational grammar has been developed solely, or even primarily, for this purpose. The case for transformational grammar rests on many other considerations too. But at this point I must refer you to the now very extensive literature.

PHILOSOPHICAL AND PSYCHOLOGICAL IMPLICATIONS

No one can even raise the question of the philosophical and psychological implications of grammatical theory these days without making reference to the views of Chomsky. He more than anyone else is responsible for the fact that a number of philosophers and psychologists are now interested in linguistics, and more particularly in generative grammar. Chomsky's views have received a good deal of publicity; and I will assume that they are sufficiently familiar. (Chomsky's *Language and Mind*[11] is the most accessible and the most authoritative statement of his current position. But it can hardly be understood without some knowledge of the technicalities of transformational grammar.) Let me merely say that it is Chomsky's conviction that the similarity in the grammatical structure of all languages is so striking, as also is the speed with which the child learns to manipulate the formal operations involved in constructing sentences and relating them to one another, that the structure of human language must be peculiarly congenial to the human mind and that a knowledge of the principles of universal grammar must be innate.

I will not comment on this hypothesis here. To attempt to do so in the space available would be impertinent. I will merely say that I do not myself believe that the evidence that Chomsky appeals to is as strong as he makes out. On the other hand, I do believe that Chomsky's hypothesis is worthy of serious consideration; and, at the very least, he has shown that certain more fashionable alternatives are untenable.[12]

I will conclude by making explicit reference to the great change that has taken place in grammatical theory in the last few years. I started, it will be recalled, by explaining what I understood by the term "formal grammar"; and I said that a formal grammar, in addition to being precise, was "not based on meaning". But I introduced the subject of transformational grammar by means of what I called a "grammatical" ambiguity. Actually, there is no inconsistency here. It might be the case that a particular syntactic analysis was arrived at, or at least justified, independently of semantic considerations and then found to have, as a "bonus" as it were, the advantage that it also gave a "natural" explanation of some identity or difference of meaning. It might also be the case that of two possible syntactic analyses, equally satisfactory from the point of view of formal grammar, one allowed for a more systematic explanation or description of some semantic phenomenon than the other: in which case, we would select the semantically more satisfactory grammatical analysis. One might argue that in neither of the two cases we have envisaged would the grammar have been *based* on semantic considerations. Grammar and semantics have been integrated, to the extent that this is possible, after a prior independent analysis of both.

I have just given in outline the kind of argument which, I believe, the majority of linguists interested in transformational grammar would have given, if challenged on this point, even two or three years ago. The situation is now strikingly different.

A significant number of "transformationalists" have now adopted the view that there is no level of "deep" syntactic structure distinct from and independent of semantic representation. Some of them have suggested that Chomsky's attempt to establish such a level of analysis derives from the "Bloomfieldian" origins of transformational grammar, and should be abandoned. The relationship between grammar and semantics is still, as it has always been, a highly controversial topic. It is too early to predict the outcome of the present controversy within the "transformationalist" camp. All I can do is to refer you to some of the literature and encourage you to look at it.

NOTES

1 For a fuller discussion of this point see my *Introduction to Theoretical Linguistics* (London and New York: Cambridge University Press, 1968), pp. 38–42.

2 R. H. Robins: *A Short History of Linguistics* (London: Longmans, 1967).

3 For some discussion of this point see my *Introduction to Theoretical Linguistics*, Chapter 4.

4 Cf. Peter Strawson's definition of an utterance in philosophical description, Lecture 5, p. 92 (Ed.)

5 For a summary of recent work see P. H. Matthews: "Morphology" in J. Lyons (Ed.) *New Horizons in Linguistics* (Harmondsworth: Penguin, 1970).

6 See my *Theoretical Linguistics*, Chapter 4, for some discussion.

7 Ibid., Chapter 6.

8 For a fuller, though still quite informal, treatment reference may be made to my book on *Chomsky* (London: Fontana and New York: Viking, 1970); and for some discussion of more recent work to my chapter on "Generative grammar" in *New Horizons in Linguistics*.

9 See his "Remarks on nominalization" in R. Jacobs and P. S.

3*

Rosenbaum: *Readings in English Transformational Grammar* (Boston: Ginn).
10 B. L. Gildersleeve and G. Lodge: *Latin Grammar*, 3rd edition (London: Macmillan, 1895) § 363.
11 N. Chomsky: *Language and Mind* (New York: Harcourt, Brace & World, 1968).
12 See my book on *Chomsky*.

FURTHER READING

BOLINGER, D.: *Aspects of Language* (New York).
CRYSTAL, D.: *What is Linguistics?* (London, 1968).
LYONS, J.: *Chomsky* (London and New York, 1970).
LYONS, J. (Ed.): *New Horizons in Linguistics* (Harmondsworth, 1970).

4

Semantics

STEPHEN ULLMANN

Trinity College, Oxford

The word *semantics* comes from the Greek *sēma* "sign", which is also found in *semaphore*. As a technical term denoting one of the divisions of linguistics, the study of meaning, *semantics* was first used in 1883 by the French philologist Michel Bréal, though the need for such a discipline had already been recognized about sixty years earlier. In the course of time a certain terminological confusion has arisen around the term. This is due to a double ambiguity. Firstly, the use of the word *semantics* is not confined to linguistics. There is also a "philosophical semantics" which constitutes one of the branches of the general theory of signs and is concerned with relations between signs and what they stand for. Philosophical semantics also has a practical extension, the "general semantics" of Korzybski, Chase, Hayakawa and others who seek to eliminate the indiscriminate use of abstractions and other abuses of language. The present essay will deal exclusively with linguistic semantics.

Secondly, the term *semantics* is highly ambiguous even within linguistics itself. This is due to the fact that meaning is not restricted to words but exists both below and above the word level: below it, at the level of inflexions, suffixes, prefixes and other non-independent but significant elements (so-called "bound morphemes"); above it, at the level of phrases, clauses, sentences and even larger units of discourse. Semantics *tout court*, however, usually refers to the study of word-meanings, and it is in this sense that the term will be used in this paper.

In the first half-century of its existence, semantics was a purely historical discipline. Interest centred upon changes of meaning, their classification, their causes as well as the "laws" underlying their general movement. Since the early 1930s, a remarkable revolution has occurred in this field: emphasis has shifted to descriptive semantics, to the part which words play in the structure of language at a given moment, irrespective of their antecedents. Although there is still a certain amount of interest in historical processes, present day semantics is dominated by a purely descriptive, "synchronic" orientation and in particular by two basic approaches: the conception which regards words as *signs*, as units endowed with a symbolic function, and the view of language as an integrated system, a *"structure"* whose elements, including words, are interdependent and help to delimit each other.

A · WORDS AS SIGNS

This conception raises two fundamental problems: (1) relations between the form and the meaning of a word; (2) the fact that the same form can have more than one meaning.

I. Form and meaning: transparent and opaque words

Without going here into the vexed question of the "meaning of meaning", we may start from the obvious fact that every word has a formal side (its phonetic and graphic structure) and a semantic side (the information conveyed by the form). The founder of structural linguistics, Ferdinand de Saussure, called these two sides the *signifiant* and the *signifié*, and various other terms have been proposed; I shall call them, as I have done elsewhere, the "name" and the "sense", and shall reserve "meaning" for the relation between name and sense. In practice, however, there will be no harm in using "sense" and "meaning" as interchangeable synonyms wherever this does not lead to any ambiguity.

The nature of the relationship between name and sense was already a controversial issue in Greek philosophy. There were two opposing theories: the "naturalists" believed that there is an intrinsic correspondence between form and meaning, whereas the "conventionalists" argued that the relation is purely arbitrary and traditional: "that which we call a rose By any other name would smell as sweet." The debate was reopened by Saussure's re-affirmation of the conventionalist doctrine at the beginning of the present century. The controversy flared up again in 1939, and in the discussion which ensued, various important aspects of the problem were clarified. We now know, for example, that every language contains two types of words: transparent, "motivated" ones as well as those which are entirely opaque and unmotivated. The existence of totally different names for the same object in various languages is an obvious sign of opaqueness and lack of motivation, as for example in the series: English *book*, French *livre*, Greek *bíblos*, Russian *kniga*, Hungarian *könyv*, etc. Transparency, on the other hand, may result from three different types of motivation:

(1) Onomatopoeic words like *splutter, sizzle, growl* are *phonetically motivated*: the sounds imitate the meaning. Not very surprisingly, such terms tend to be similar in different languages even where there are no genetic connexions between them: thus we have English *cuckoo*, French *coucou*, German *Kuckuck*, Greek *kókkyx*, Russian *kukushka*, Hungarian *kakuk* and other forms showing the same phonetic pattern.

(2) A derivative like *dreamer* and a compound like *shoe-lace* are *grammatically motivated*: they are perfectly transparent and self-explanatory to anyone familiar with their components. It has been suggested that this type of motivation is purely relative since the components themselves—the verb *dream*, the suffix *-er*, the nouns *shoe* and *lace*—are opaque, unanalysable units. This is no doubt true but does not affect the status of the compounds and derivatives which obviously belong to the transparent section of the vocabulary.

(3) Figurative expressions like *live wire, wire-puller, crossing of wires, a wiry person* owe their transparency to *semantic motivation*: they are metaphors based on some kind of similarity between these phenomena and a wire in the physical sense.

Recent investigations have also shown that languages—or even successive periods in the history of the same idiom—may differ characteristically in their preference for the transparent or the opaque type and for the various forms of motivation. Grammatical structure in particular has provided useful criteria for "semantic typology". It has been found that German has a marked predilection for grammatically motivated words and French for opaque terms, whereas English stands between the two but behaves on the whole more like French in this respect. Thus we find simple, unmotivated English and French words corresponding to transparent German compounds which are sometimes based on a metaphor, thus combining grammatical with semantic motivation:

glove, gant	*Handschuh*	(hand + shoe)
thimble, dé	*Fingerhut*	(finger + hat)

Elsewhere, English and French will have a classical compound or derivative where German uses a formation made up of elements already in the language: *hippopotamus* (Greek *híppos* horse + *potamós* river)—German *Nilpferd* (Nile + horse), *semantics*—*Bedeutungslehre* (meaning + lore), and many more. It should be noted, however, that there are cases where an opaque form in French corresponds to a transparent one in English: *semaine, hebdomadaire—week, weekly*; *suie, fuligineux—soot, sooty.*

The contrast between motivated and unmotivated words has important pedagogical and socio-linguistic implications. A language with many transparent compounds and derivatives and numerous formal connections between words will obviously be taught differently from one where opaque, unanalysable, monolithic terms abound. In idioms like English and French, where so many ordinary words are made up of Greek or Latin elements, or even a mixture of the two, there exists what has been called a "language bar" between speakers with and without a classical education: many Graeco-Latin formations will be perfectly transparent to the former and entirely opaque to the latter.

II. One form with several meanings: semantic ambiguity

Semantic ambiguity ought to be clearly distinguished from ambiguity due to grammatical factors. There are two cardinal types of semantic ambiguity, though the boundary between them is not always clear-cut:

(1) Multiple meaning or "*polysemy*", where one word has two or more senses: thus, *volume* can mean "bulk, mass", "tome", "strength or power of sound", etc.

(2) *Homonymy*, where two or more different words have the same form. This has three varieties:

(a) *Homophones*: words pronounced alike but spelt differently: *write—rite—right—wright.*

(b) *Homographs*: words spelt alike but pronounced differently: *lead* (noun)—to *lead.*

(c) *Homonyms* in the strict sense: words both spelt and pronounced alike: *bear* (noun)—to *bear.*

Among the various aspects of ambiguity on which research has been done are the frequency of the different types and the conflicts to which they may give rise. In English and French, homonymy is particularly widespread because of the large number of mono-syllabic words in these languages. This is no doubt one of the reasons which led to the retention of a non-phonetic, historically based mode of spelling which distinguishes between homophones at least on the written or printed page. In the field of polysemy, there seems to be some connection between the frequency of a word and the number of meanings it has. The late G. K. Zipf even tried to formulate these fluid phenomena with mathematical precision when he suggested that "different meanings of a word will tend to be equal to the square root of its relative frequency (with the possible exception of the few dozen most frequent words)":

$$m = F^{\frac{1}{2}}$$

The two types of semantic ambiguity are obviously of very unequal importance. Polysemy is not a defect but an essential feature of language; the alternative would be to have separate words for any possible subject we may wish to talk about. Homonymy, on the other hand, is in no way essential, except to the punster: a language without homonyms is perfectly conceivable, and would in fact be a more efficient vehicle of communication. Under normal circumstances, neither polysemy nor homonymy is likely to lead to any serious ambiguity: the context will usually suffice to eliminate all irrelevant meanings. There are, however, cases where two or more senses of the same word, or two or more homonymous terms, may occur in the same context, and if this happens frequently, the ambiguity may result in the disappearance of some of the conflicting elements. In the case of polysemy, it is usually sufficient to discard one or more of the incompatible senses, without sacrificing the word as a whole. Thus the adjective *cunning* originally meant "learned, intelligent, skilful"; Shakespeare still wrote in *Twelfth Night*, Act III, scene 4: "I thought he had been valiant, and so *cunning* in fence." Towards the end of the XVIth century, *cunning* began to be employed in the sense of "crafty, artful, sly", and this led to the disappearance of the more favourable meaning. Similarly, when *undertaker* came to be used, at first as a euphemism, in its present sense, it was no longer suitable in the wider meaning of "contractor", "one who embarks on some business enterprise."

Clashes between homonyms, and the subsequent elimination of one of the terms involved, have been studied in great detail by linguistic geographers. A famous example is the conflict between the words for "cock" and "cat" in part of South-West France. In that area, word-final [-ll] has become [-t], so that Latin *gallus* "cock" has given *gat* and has thus coincided with the local name of the cat, *gat*, from Vulgar Latin *cattus*. This produced a homonymic clash in the course of which *gat* "cock" disappeared and was replaced by local words for "pheasant" and "curate" or "provost".

In the same way, two Old English verbs, one meaning "leave, allow", the other "hinder", fell together in the form *let*. As a result, *let* "hinder" was eliminated though it still survives in two combinations: a "*let* ball" and "without *let* or hindrance". The old noun *near* "kidney" (cf. German *Niere*) has had to be abandoned because of the confusion between *a near* and *an ear*; in some areas, however, *near* was retained and *ear* was replaced by *lug*.

Not all homonymic clashes are due to genuine ambiguity. Sometimes a word is avoided merely because its similarity to another term would call forth undesirable associations, as happened in the case of an orchestra with a group of six players which was called a *quintet* because *sextet* would have been too suggestive.

B · STRUCTURAL RELATIONS BETWEEN WORDS

Structural linguistics regards language as a highly organized totality where the various elements are interconnected and derive their significance from the system as a whole. Language has been pictured as a chess-board where no item can be added, removed or displaced without affecting the general pattern. This approach can be more easily applied to phonological and grammatical structures, consisting of relatively few and closely integrated elements, than to the vocabulary which is made up of a vast number of loosely organized items. According to one estimate, there are 44 or 45 phonemes in English, as against nearly 415,000 words in the *Oxford Dictionary*. In spite of these difficulties, "structural semantics" has already succeeded in identifying some significant patterns at three distinct levels: that of individual words, that of conceptual spheres, and that of the vocabulary as a whole.

I. Single words

Every word is surrounded by an "*associative field*", a network of associations based on relations between names, between senses or between both. To take again an example mentioned in the previous section, the verb *write* is involved in three associative series:

(a) Formal associations between names (homonymy): *write—rite, right, wright*.

(b) Semantic associations between senses (synonymy and various other relations): *write—scribble, scrawl, read, say, speak, pen, paper,* etc.

(c) Formal and semantic associations with members of the same family: *write—writer, writing, rewrite, underwrite, writ*.

Experimental evidence suggests that type (a) is marginal in normal subjects but becomes more prominent in mentally retarded children, and also as a result of fatigue, headaches and influenza.

Although associative fields are subjective, variable and unstable structures, some of their elements are so widespread that they can permanently alter the form or meaning of a word. To take but one example, Latin *scribere* became *escrivre* in Old French, but this was subsequently changed to *écrire*, under the influence of two verbs in the same associative field: *lire* and *dire*.

II. Conceptual spheres

Some conceptual spheres are organized into so-called "*lexical fields*": closely integrated sectors of the vocabulary, in which a particular sphere is divided up, analysed and evaluated in a unique manner. In this way, lexical fields reflect, and hand down to future generations, a whole *Weltanschauung*, a scale of values and philosophy of life. In this respect, one ought to distinguish between concrete and abstract fields and, among the concrete ones, between continuous and discrete phenomena.

(1) Concrete fields:

(a) *Continuous elements.*—One such field which has been thoroughly investigated in a variety of languages is the system of colours.[1] Since the spectrum of colours is a continuous band, there is a multiplicity of possible solutions, and the number and nature of distinctions may vary from one idiom to another, as is seen for example from the following table—taken from L. Hjelmslev's *Prolegomena to a Theory of Language*—of colour terms in English and Welsh:

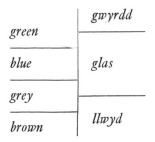

green	gwyrdd
blue	glas
grey	
brown	llwyd

It is interesting to note that the Navaho, an American Indian tribe, have a single term for "grey" and "brown", and also for "blue" and "green"; on the other hand, they distinguish between two kinds of blackness, one referring to the black of darkness, the other to the black of such objects as coal. It is also relevant that patients suffering from colour amnesia have been found to react erratically to colour tests: having forgotten the words, they have lost the key to the underlying conceptual system.

(b) *Discrete elements.*—A great deal of research has been done on the organization of kinship terms, with particular reference to American Indian languages. There are, however, remarkable variations even between European idioms. In Hungarian, for example, there was no single word for "brother" or "sister" until the first half of the XIXth century; instead, there were, and still are, separate and totally different terms for "elder brother", "younger brother", "elder sister" and "younger sister". In Swedish, there is a distinction between *farfar* "father's father" and *morfar* "mother's father", and similarly between *farmor* and *mormor*; in the same way, the Romans distinguished between *patruus* "father's brother" and *avunculus* "mother's brother", and also between *amita* "father's sister" and *matertera* "mother's sister", whereas in English only the two middle terms have survived as *uncle* and *aunt*.

(2) *Abstract fields.*—The rôle of lexical fields in the organization of human experience is even more obvious in the sphere of abstract concepts. In a famous treatise on intellectual terms in German, J. Trier showed as early as 1931 that the Middle High German system was quite different from the modern one. Around 1200, the key-words in this lexical field embodied two principles: feudalism and universality. The former imposed a strict distinction between courtly and non-courtly knowledge, whereas the latter provided a global term for the whole range of human wisdom, theological as well as mundane. With the disintegration of feudalism, the former distinction became meaningless, and this and other factors led to a complete restructuring of the system.

More recently, intellectual terms have been studied on very different lines by J. Lyons, in his book on Plato (cited in the bibliography) and in his *Introduction to Theoretical Linguistics* (1968). Lyons is particularly interested in the semantic relations between terms belonging to the same lexical field: synonymy, subordination, incompatibility, "oppositeness" of meaning, etc.

III. The structure of the vocabulary

In present-day semantics, the difficult and complex problems raised by the structure of the vocabulary are being approached from two main directions. Some scholars are interested in a general classification of concepts, a kind of modernized Roget's *Thesaurus*, which would provide a unified yet flexible framework for the study of different authors, periods or languages. One such scheme, devised by Hallig and Wartburg, divides concepts into three broad categories, each of them with numerous subdivisions: "the Universe", "Man", and "Man and the Universe". The adoption of this, or some other, classification in a series of specialized monographs would have obvious practical advantages: it would be easy to compare the results and to detect any characteristic differences, any significant enrichment, impoverishment or shift of emphasis.

The other approach, which has become very popular during the last few years, has been described as "*componential analysis*" since it seeks to break down meaning into its smallest components. The best-known experiment of this kind is the scheme put forward in 1963 by two of Noam Chomsky's collaborators, J. J. Katz and J. A. Fodor, and subsequently reprinted in their book cited in the bibliography. This scheme, which is designed to form part of the "semantic component" of a transformational-generative grammar, distinguishes between two kinds of elements in the meaning of a lexical item: "semantic markers", which occur in other words as well, and "semantic distinguishers", which are peculiar to the term in question. The components are arranged in hierarchical order, proceeding from the general to the particular. A very simple example may illustrate the method. The meaning of the English word *boy* may be analysed as a combination of the following components: "noun—animate—human—male—young." *Girl* would have the same components, except for "female" instead of "male". If a word has more than one meaning, each of these would have a different "path", a different set of components, so that the method can also serve as a device for the removal of ambiguities.

The Katz-Fodor scheme, which has many complexities that cannot be mentioned here, has since been considerably modified by J. J. Katz himself. It has been widely discussed and strongly criticized by several linguists (cf. e.g. Weinreich's treatise mentioned in the bibliography. Meanwhile, European semanticists have been analysing the structure of the vocabulary on rather different lines (cf. Greimas's book cited in the bibliography), though they too are primarily interested in identifying the smallest components—they call them "semes"—of which meaning is made up.

Three general impressions emerge from this rapid and selective survey of some current trends in semantics:

(1) Semantics is no longer under a cloud, as it was for a number of years following the publication of L. Bloomfield's influential book, *Language*, in 1933. Some twenty years later, a leading American linguist, C. C. Fries, still complained: "For many linguistic students the word *meaning* itself has become almost anathema". Now the pendulum has swung to the opposite extreme and semantics has become one of the growing-points of linguistic study.

(2) What is of paramount importance for the future of semantics is that it should develop into a more balanced discipline. As has been noted, semantics was once an exclusively historical study; more recently, it has become predominantly descriptive. Both approaches are legitimate: what is needed is a better balance between the two. The same is true of the respective rôles of theory and practice in this field. Present-day semantics leans too much towards theoretical speculation: it is time some of the ambitious schemes which have been put forward concerning semantic "universals" and other features were tested in the light of empirical evidence.

(3) Semantics is at the point of intersection of many interests: linguistics, philosophy, psychology, anthropology, information theory, stylistics and various other studies are all concerned with different aspects of meaning. It is this central position which makes semantics one of the most stimulating and most educative branches of linguistic science.

NOTES

1 See also R. H. Robins, Lecture 1, p. 31 and Claire and W. M. S. Russell, Lecture 8, p. 166 (Ed.)

FURTHER READING

1. Linguistic Semantics

ANTAL, L.: *Content, Meaning and Understanding* (The Hague, 1964).
ANTAL, L.: *Questions of Meaning* (The Hague, 1963).
BALDINGER, K.: *Teoría Semántica* (Madrid, 1970).
BRÉAL, M.: *Essai de sémantique* (Paris, 1897).
CARNOY, A.: *La Science du mot. Traité de sémantique* (Louvain, 1927).
FODOR, J. A. and KATZ, J. J. (Eds.): *The Structure of Language* (Englewood Cliffs, 1964).
GUIRAUD, P.: *La Sémantique* (Paris, 1955).
KOZIOL, H.: *Grundzüge der englischen Semantik* (Vienna, 1967).
KRONASSER, H.: *Handbuch der Semasiologie* (Heidelberg, 1952).
LEECH, G. N.: *Towards a Semantic Description of English* (London, 1969).
LYONS, J.: *Structural Semantics. An Analysis of Part of the Vocabulary of Plato* (Oxford, 1963).
STERN, G.: *Meaning and Change of Meaning. With Special Reference to the English Language* (repr. Bloomington, 1964).
ULLMANN, S.: *The Principles of Semantics* (2nd ed., Oxford, 1963 impr.).
ULLMANN, S.: *Semantics. An Introduction to the Science of Meaning* (Oxford, 1962).
WALDRON, R. A.: *Sense and Sense Development* (London, 1967).
WEINREICH, U.: "Explorations in Semantic Theory" in *Current Trends in Linguistics*, vol. III (The Hague, 1966)

2. Philosophical Semantics

CARNAP, R.: *Introduction to Semantics* (Cambridge, Mass., 1942).
CHRISTENSEN, N. E.: *On the Nature of Meanings* (Copenhagen, 1961).
COHEN, L. J.: *The Diversity of Meaning* (2nd ed., London, 1966).
GREIMAS, A. J.: *Sémantique structurale* (Paris, 1966).
OGDEN, C. K. and RICHARDS, I. A.: *The Meaning of Meaning* (8th ed., London, 1946).
PARKINSON, G. H. R. (Ed.): *The Theory of Meaning* (Oxford, 1968).
SCHAFF, A.: *Introduction to Semantics* (Oxford, 1962).
ZIFF, P.: *Semantic Analysis* (Ithaca, 1960).

5

Meaning, truth and communication

P. F. STRAWSON

Magdalen College, Oxford

What is it for anything to have a *meaning* at all, in the way, or in the sense, in which words or sentences or signals have meaning? What is it for a particular sentence to have the meaning or meanings it does have? What is it for a particular phrase, or a particular word, to have the meaning or meanings it does have? These are obviously connected questions. Any account we give of meaning in general (in the relevant sense) must square with the account we give of what it is for particular expressions to have particular meanings; and we must acknowledge, as two complementary truths, first, that the meaning of a sentence in general depends, in some systematic way, on the meanings of the words that make it up and, second, that for a word to have a particular meaning is a matter of its making a particular systematic contribution to the meanings of the sentences in which it occurs.

I am not going to undertake to try to answer these so obviously connected questions. That is not a task for one lecture; or for one man. I want rather to discuss a certain conflict, or apparent conflict, more or less dimly discernible in current approaches to these questions. For the sake of a label, we might call it the conflict between the theorists of communication-intention and the theorists of formal semantics. According to the former, it is impossible to give an adequate account of the concept of meaning without reference to the possession by speakers of audience-directed intentions of a certain complex kind. The particular meanings of words and sentences are, no doubt, largely a matter of rule and convention; but the general nature of such rules and conventions can be ultimately understood only by reference to the concept of communication-intention. The opposed view, at least in its negative aspect, is that this doctrine simply gets things the wrong way round or the wrong way up, or mistakes the contingent for the essential. Of course (the upholders of this opposed view would say) we may expect a certain regularity of relationship between what people intend to communicate by uttering certain sentences and what those sentences conventionally mean. But the system of semantic and syntactic rules, in the mastery of which knowledge of a language consists—the rules which determine the meanings of sentences—is not a system of rules *for* communicating at all.[1] The rules can be exploited for this purpose; but this is incidental to their essential character. It would be perfectly possible for someone to understand a language completely—to have a perfect linguistic competence—without having even the implicit thought of the function of communication; provided, of course, that the language in question did not contain words explicitly referring to this function.

A struggle on what seems to be such a central issue in philosophy should have something of a Homeric quality; and a Homeric struggle calls for gods and heroes. I can at least, though tentatively, name some living captains and benevolent shades: on the one side, say, Grice, Austin and the later Wittgenstein; on the other, Chomsky, Frege and the earlier Wittgenstein.

First, then, as to the theorists of communication-intention. The simplest, and most readily intelligible, though not the only way of joining their ranks is to present your general theory of meaning in two stages: first, present and elucidate a primitive concept of *communication* (or communication-intention) in terms which do not presuppose the concept of *linguistic meaning*; then show that the latter concept can be, and is to be, explained in terms of the former.[2] For any theorist who follows this path, the fundamental concept in the theory of meaning is that of a speaker's, or, generally, an utterer's, *meaning something by* an audience-directed utterance on a particular occasion. An utterance is something produced or executed by an utterer; it need not be vocal; it could be a gesture or a drawing or the moving or disposing of objects in a certain way.[3] What an utterer means by his utterance is incidentally specified in specifying the complex intention with which he produces the utterance. The analysis of the kind of intention in question is too complex to be given in detail here, so I shall confine myself to incomplete description. An utterer might have, as one of his intentions in executing his utterance, that of bringing his audience to think, that he, the utterer, believes some proposition, say the proposition that *p*; and he might intend this intention to be wholly overt, to be clearly recognized by the audience. Or again he might have the intention of bringing his audience to think that he, the utterer, wants his audience to perform some action, say *a*; and he might intend this intention of his to be wholly overt, to be clearly recognized by the audience. Then, provided certain other conditions on utterer's intention are fulfilled, the utterer may be said, in the relevant sense, to mean something by his utterance: specifically, to mean that p, in the declarative mode, in the first case and to mean, in the imperative mode, that the audience is to perform action a in the second case. Grice, for one, has given us reason to think that, with sufficient care, and far greater refinement than I have indicated, it is possible to expound such a concept of communication-intention or, as he calls it, utterer's meaning, which is proof against objection and which does not presuppose the notion of linguistic meaning.[4]

Now a word about how the analysis of linguistic meaning in terms of utterer's meaning is supposed to proceed. Here again I shall not go into details. The details would be very complex. But the fundamental idea is comparatively simple. We are accustomed, and reasonably, to think of linguistic meaning in terms of rules and conventions, semantic and syntactic. And when we consider the enormous elaboration of these rules and conventions—their capacity, as the modern linguists stress, to generate an infinite number of sentences in a given language,—we may feel infinitely removed from the sort of primitive communication situation which we naturally think of when trying to understand the notion of utterer's meaning in terms which clearly do not presuppose linguistic meaning. But rules or conventions govern human practices and purposive human activities. So we should ask what purposive activities are governed by these conventions. What are these rules rules for doing? And the very simple thought I spoke of which underlies the suggested type of analysis is that these rules are, precisely, rules for communicating, rules by the observance of which the utterer may achieve his purpose, fulfil his communication-intention; and that this is their *essential* character. That is, it is not just a fortunate fact that the rules allow of use for this purpose; rather, the very nature of the rules concerned can be understood only if they are seen as rules whereby this purpose can be achieved.

This simple thought may seem too simple; and in several ways. For it is clear that we can, and do, communicate very complicated things by the use of language; and if we are to think of language as, fundamentally, a system of rules for facilitating the achievement of our communication-intentions, and if the analysis is not to be circular, must we not credit ourselves with extremely complicated communication-intentions (or at least desires) independently of having at our disposal the linguistic means of fulfilling those desires? And is not this absurd? I think this is absurd. But the programme of analysis does not require it. All that the analysis requires is that we can explain the notion of conventions of communication in terms of the notion of pre-conventional communication at a rather basic level. Given that we can do this, then there is more than one way in which we can start pulling ourselves up by our own linguistic boot-straps. And it looks as if we can explain the notion of conventions of communication in terms of the notion of pre-conventional communication at a rather basic level.

We can, for example, tell ourselves a story of the analytic-genetic variety. Suppose an utterer achieves a pre-conventional communication success with a given audience by means of an utterance, say x. He has a complex intention vis-a-vis the audience of the sort which counts as a communication-intention and succeeds in fulfilling that intention by uttering x. Let us suppose that the primary intention was such that the utterer *meant* that p by uttering x; and, since, by hypothesis, he achieved a communication-success, he was so *understood* by his audience. Now if the same communication-problem presents itself later to the same utterer in relation to the same audience, the fact, known to both of them, that the utterer meant that p by uttering x before, gives the utterer a reason for uttering x again and the audience a reason for interpreting the utterance in the same way as before. (The reason which each has is the knowledge that the other has the knowledge which he has.) So it is easy to see how the utterance of x could become established as between this utterer and this audience as a means of meaning that p. Because it has worked, it becomes established; and then it works *because* it is established. And it is easy to see how this story could be told so as to involve not just a group of two, but a wider group. So we can have a movement from an utterer pre-conventionally meaning that p by an utterance of x to the utterance-type x conventionally meaning that p within a group and thence back to utterer-members of the group meaning that p by a token of the type, but now *in accordance with the conventions*.

Now of course this explanation of conventional meaning in terms of utterer's meaning is not enough by itself. For it only covers the case, or only obviously covers the case, of utterance-types without structure—i.e. of utterance-types of which the meaning is not systematically derived from the meanings of their parts. But it is characteristic of linguistic utterance-types to have structure. The meaning of a sentence is a syntactic function of the meanings of its parts and their arrangement. But there is no reason in principle why a pre-conventional utterance should not have a certain complexity—a kind of complexity which allowed an utterer, having achieved one communication-success, to achieve another by repeating one part of the utterance while varying the other part, what he means on the second occasion having something in common with, and something which differentiates it from, what he means on the first occasion. And if he does thus achieve a second success, the way is open for a rudimentary *system* of utterance-types to become established, i.e. to become conventional within a group.

A system of conventions can be modified to meet needs which we can scarcely imagine existing before the system existed. And its modification and enrichment may in turn create the possibility of thoughts such as we cannot understand what it would be for one to have, without supposing such modification and enrichment to have taken place. In this way we can picture a kind of alternating development. Primitive communication-intentions and successes give rise to the emergence of a limited conventional meaning-system, which makes possible its own enrichment and development which in turn makes possible the enlargement of thought and of communication-needs to a point at which there is once more pressure on the existing resources of language which is in turn responsive to such pressure. . . . And of course there is an element of mystery in this; but so there is in human intellectual and social creativity anyway.

All the foregoing is by way of the roughest possible sketch of some salient features of a communication-intention theory of meaning and of a hint as to how it might meet the obvious objection that certain communication-intentions presuppose the existence of language. It has all been said before, and with far greater refinement. But it will serve, I hope, as a sufficient basis for the confrontation of views that I wish to arrange.

Now, then, for the at least apparently opposed view, which I have so far characterized only in its negative aspect. Of course the holders of this view share some ground with their opponents. Both agree that the meanings of the sentences of a language are largely determined by the semantic and syntactic rules or conventions of that language. Both agree that the members of any group or community of people who share knowledge of a language—who have a common linguistic competence—have at their disposal a more or less powerful instrument or means of communicating, and thereby of modifying each other's beliefs or attitudes or influencing each other's actions. Both agree that these means are regularly used in a quite conventional way, that what people intend to communicate by what they say is regularly related to the conventional meanings of the sentences they utter. Where they differ is as to the relations between the meaning-determining rules of the language on the one hand and the function of communication on the other: one party insists, and the other (apparently) refuses to allow, that the general nature of those rules can be understood only by reference to this function.

The refusal naturally prompts a question—namely: What *is* the general character of those rules which must in some sense have been mastered by anyone who speaks and understands a given language? The rejected answer grounds their general character in the social function of communicating, e.g., beliefs or wishes or instructions. If this answer is rejected, another must be offered. So we ask again: What is the general character of these meaning-determining rules?

It seems to me that there is only one type of answer that has ever been seriously advanced or developed, or needs to be seriously considered, as providing a possible alternative to the thesis of the communication-theorist. This is an answer which rests on the notion of truth-conditions. The thought that the sense of a sentence is determined by its truth-conditions is to be found in Frege and in the early Wittgenstein, and we find it again in many subsequent writers. I take, as an example, a recent article by Professor Davidson. Davidson is rightly concerned with the point that an adequate account of the meaning-rules for a language L will show how the meanings of sentences depend on the meanings of words in L; and a theory of meaning for L will do this, he says, if it contains a recursive definition of truth-in-L. The "obvious connexion", he says, between such a definition of truth and the concept of meaning is this: "the definition works by giving the necessary and sufficient conditions for the truth of every sentence, and *to give truth-conditions is a way of giving the meaning of a sentence*. To know the semantic concept of truth for a language is to know what it is for a sentence

—any sentence—to be true, and *this amounts, in one good sense we can give to the phrase, to understanding the language.*"[5]

Davidson, in the article I quote from, has a limited concern. But the concern finds its place inside a more general idea; and the general idea, plainly enough, is that the syntactic and semantic rules together determine the meanings of all the sentences of a language and do this by means, precisely, of determining their truth-conditions.

Now if we are to get at the root of the matter, to isolate the crucial issue, it seems to me important to set aside, at least initially, one class of objections to the adequacy of such a conception of meaning. I say one class of objections; but it is a class which admits of subdivisions. Thus it may be pointed out that there are some kinds of sentences—e.g. imperatives, optatives and interrogatives—to which the notion of truth-conditions seems inappropriate, in that the conventional utterance of such sentences does not result in the saying of anything true or false. Or again it may be pointed out that even sentences to which the notion of truth-conditions does seem appropriate may contain expressions which certainly make a difference to their conventional meaning, but not the sort of difference which can be explained in terms of their truth-conditions. Compare the sentence "Fortunately, Socrates is dead" with the sentence "Unfortunately, Socrates is dead". Compare a sentence of the form "*p* and *q*" with the corresponding sentence of the form "*p* but *q*". It is clear that the meanings of the members of each pair of sentences differ; it is far from clear that their truth-conditions differ. And there are not just one or two expressions which give rise to this problem, but many such expressions.

Obviously both a comprehensive general theory of meaning and a comprehensive semantic theory for a particular language must be equipped to deal with these points. Yet they may reasonably be regarded as peripheral points. For it is a truth implicitly acknowledged by communication-theorists themselves[6] that in almost all the things we should count as sentences there is a substantial central core of meaning which is explicable either in terms of truth-conditions or in terms of some related notion quite simply derivable from that of a truth-condition; e.g. the notion, as we might call it, of a compliance-condition in the case of an imperative sentence or a fulfilment-condition in the case of an optative. If we suppose, therefore, that an account can be given of the notion of a truth-condition itself, an account which is indeed independent of reference

4

to communication-intention, then we may reasonably think that the greater part of the task of a general theory of meaning has been accomplished without such reference. And by the same token, on the same supposition, we may think that the greater part of the particular theory of meaning of a particular language L can also be given, free of any such, even implicit, reference; for it can be given by systematically setting out the syntactic and semantic rules which determine truth-conditions for sentences of L.

Of course, as already admitted, something will have to be added to complete our general theory and to complete our particular theories. Thus for a particular theory an account will have to be added of the transformations that yield sentences with compliance-conditions or fulfilment-conditions out of sentences with truth-conditions; and the general theory will have to say what sort of thing, semantically speaking, such a derived sentence in general is. But this, though yielding a large harvest in sentences, is in itself a relatively small addition to either particular or general theory. Again, other additions will be necessary in connexion with the other objections I mentioned. But, heartened by his hypothesized success into confidence, the theorist may reckon on dealing with some of these additions without essential reference to communication-intention; and heartened by his hypothesized success into generosity, he may be happy to concede rights in some small outlying portion of the de facto territory of theoretical semantics to the theorist of communication-intention, instead of confining the latter entirely to some less appetizing territory called theoretical pragmatics.

I hope it is now clear what the central issue is. It consists in nothing other than the simple-seeming question whether the notion of truth-conditions can itself be explained or understood without reference to the function of communication. One minor clarification is called for before I turn to examine the question directly. I have freely used the phrase "the truth-conditions of sentences" and I have spoken of these truth-conditions as determined by the semantic and syntactic rules of the language to which the sentences belong. In such a context we naturally understand the word "sentence" in the sense of a "type-sentence". (By a sentence in the sense of a type I mean the sense in which there is just one English sentence, say, "I am feeling shivery" or just one English sentence, say, "She had her sixteenth birthday yesterday", which one and the same sentence may be uttered on countless different occasions by different people and with difference references or applications.) But for many type-sentences, such as those just mentioned, the question whether they, the *sentences*, are true or false is one that has no natural application: it is not the invariant type-sentences themselves that are naturally said to be true or false, but rather the systematically varying things that people say, the propositions they express, when they utter those sentences on different particular occasions. But if the notion of truth-*values* is in general inappropriate to type-sentences, how can the notion of truth-*conditions* be appropriate? For presumably the truth-conditions of something are the conditions under which it is true.

The difficulty, however, is quite easily resolved. All that needs to be said is that the statement of truth-conditions for many type-sentences—perhaps most that are actually uttered in ordinary conversation—has to be, and can be, relativized in a systematic way to contextual conditions of utterance. A general statement of truth-conditions for such a sentence will then be, not a statement of conditions under which that sentence is a truth, but a general statement of a type of conditions under which different particular utterances of it will issue in different particular truths. And there are other more or less equivalent, though rather less natural, ways of resolving the difficulty.

So now, at last, to the central issue. For the theorists of formal semantics, as I have called them, the whole weight, or most of the weight, both of a general theory of meaning and of particular semantic theories, falls on the notion of truth-conditions and hence on the notion of truth. We agree to let it rest there. But we still cannot be satisfied that we have an adequate general understanding of the notion of meaning unless we are satisfied that we have an adequate general understanding of the notion of truth.

There is one manoeuvre here that would completely block all hope of achieving adequate understanding; and, if I am not mistaken, it is a manoeuvre which has a certain appeal for some theorists of formal semantics. This is to react to a demand for a general explication of the notion of truth by referring us back to a Tarski-like conception of truth-in-a-given-language, L, a conception which is elucidated precisely by a recursive statement of the rules which determine the truth-conditions for sentences of L. This amounts to a refusal to face the general philosophical question altogether. Having agreed to the general point that the meanings of the sentences of a language are determined, or largely determined, by rules which determine truth-conditions, we then raise the general question what sort of thing truth-conditions are, or what truth-conditions are conditions *of*; and we are told that the concept of truth for a given language is defined by the rules which determine the truth-conditions for sentences of that language.

Evidently we cannot be satisfied with this. So we return to our general question about truth. And immediately we feel some embarrassment. For we have come to think there is very little to say about truth *in general*. But let us see what we can do with this very little. Here is one way of saying something uncontroversial and fairly general about truth.[7] One who makes a statement or assertion makes a true statement if and only if things are as, in making that statement, he states them to be. Or again: one who expresses a supposition expresses a true supposition if and only if things are as, in expressing that supposition, he expressly supposes them to be. Now let us interweave with such innocuous remarks as these the agreed thoughts about meaning and truth-conditions. Then we have, first: the meaning of a sentence is determined by those rules which determine how things are stated to be by one who, in uttering the sentence, makes a statement; or, how things are expressly supposed to be by one who, in uttering the sentence, expresses a supposition. And then, remembering that the rules are relativized to contextual conditions, we can paraphrase as follows: the meaning of a sentence is determined by the rules which determine *what* statement is made by one who, in uttering the sentence in given conditions, makes a statement; or, which determine *what* supposition is expressed by one who, in uttering the sentence in given conditions, expresses a supposition; and so on.

Thus we are led, by way of the notion of truth, back to the notion of the *content* of such speech acts as stating, expressly supposing and so on. And here the theorist of communication-intention sees his chance. There is no hope, he says, of elucidating the notion of the content of such speech acts without paying some attention to the notions of those speech acts themselves. Now of all the speech acts in which something true or false may, in one mode or another, be put forward, it is reasonable to regard that of statement or assertion as having an especially central position. (Hot for certainties, we value speculation primarily because we value information.) And we cannot, the theorist maintains, elucidate the notion of stating or asserting except in terms of audience-directed intention. For the fundamental case of stating or asserting, in terms of which all variants must be understood, is that of uttering a sentence with a certain intention—an intention wholly overt in the sense required by the analysis of utterer's meaning—which can be incompletely described as that of letting an audience know, or getting it to think, that the speaker has a certain belief; as a result of which there may, or may not, be activated or produced in the audience that same belief. The rules determining the conventional meaning of the sentence join with the contextual conditions of its utterance to determine what the belief in question *is* in such a primary and fundamental case. And in determining what the belief in question is in such a case, the rules determine what statement is made in such a case. To determine the former *is* to determine the latter. But this is precisely what we wanted. For when we set out from the agreed point that the rules which determine truth-conditions thereby determine meaning, the conclusion to which we were led was precisely that those rules determined what statement was made by one who, in uttering the sentence, made a statement. So the agreed point, so far from being an alternative to a communication theory of meaning, leads us straight in to such a theory of meaning.

The conclusion may seem a little too swift. So let us see if there is any way of avoiding it. The general condition of avoiding it is clear. It is that we should be able to give an account of the notion of truth-conditions which involves no essential reference to communicative speech acts. The alternative of refusing to give any account at all—of just resting on the notion of truth-conditions—is, as I have already indicated, simply not open to us if we are concerned with the philosophical elucidation of the notion of meaning: it would simply leave us with the concepts of meaning and truth each pointing blankly and unhelpfully at the other. Neither would it be helpful, though it might at this point be tempting, to retreat from the notion of truth-conditions to the less specific notion of correlation in general; to say, simply, that the rules which determine the meanings of sentences do so by correlating the sentences, envisaged as uttered in certain contextual conditions, with certain possible states of affairs. One reason why this won't do is that the notion of correlation in general is simply too unspecific. There are many kinds of behaviour (including verbal behaviour)—and many more kinds could be imagined—which are correlated by rule with possible states of affairs without its being the case that such correlation confers upon them the kind of relation to those possible states of affairs that we are concerned with.

Another reason why it won't do is the following. Consider the sentence "I am tired". The rules which determine its meaning are indeed such as to correlate the sentence, envisaged as uttered by a particular speaker at a particular time, with the possible state of affairs of the speaker's being tired at that time. But this feature is not peculiar to that sentence or to the members of the class of sentences which have the same meaning as it. For consider the sentence "I am not tired". The rules which determine its meaning are also such as to correlate the sentence, envisaged as uttered by a certain speaker at a certain time, with the possible state of affairs of that speaker's being tired at that time. Of course the kinds of correlation are different. They are respectively such that one who uttered the first sentence would normally be understood as affirming, and one who uttered the second sentence would normally be understood as denying, that the state of affairs in question obtained; or again they are such that one who utters the first sentence when the state of affairs in question obtains has made a true statement and one who utters the second sentence in these circumstances has made a false statement. But to invoke these differences would be precisely to give up the idea of employing only the unspecific notion of correlation in general. It is not worth labouring the point further. But it will readily be seen not only that sentences different, and even opposed, in meaning are correlated, in one way or another, with the same possible state of affairs, but also that one and the same unambiguous sentence is correlated, in one way or another, with very many different and in some cases mutually incompatible states of affairs. The sentence "I am tired" is correlated with the possible state of affairs of the speaker's being at the point of total exhaustion and also with the state of affairs of his being as fresh as a daisy. The sentence "I am over 40" is correlated with any possible state of affairs whatever regarding the speaker's age; the sentence "Swans are white" with any state of affairs whatever regarding the colour of swans.

The quite unspecific notion of correlation, then, is useless for the purpose in hand. It is necessary to find some way of specifying a particular correlation in each case, viz. the correlation of the sentence with the possible state of affairs the obtaining of which would be necessary and sufficient for something *true* to have been said in the uttering of the sentence under whatever contextual conditions are envisaged. So we are back once more with the notion of truth-conditions and with the question, whether we can give an account of this notion which involves no essential reference to communicative speech acts, i.e. to communication-intention.

I can at this point see only one resource open, or apparently open, to the theorist of meaning who still holds that the notion of communication-intention has no essential place in the analysis of the concept of meaning. If he is not to swallow his opponent's hook, he must take some leaves out of his book. He sees now that he cannot stop with the idea of truth. That idea leads straight to the idea of *what is said*, the content of what is said, when utterances are made; and that in turn to the question of what is being *done* when utterances are made. But may not the theorist go some way along this path without going as far along it as his opponent? Might it not be possible to *delete* the reference to communication-intention while *preserving* a reference to, say, belief-expression? And will not this, incidentally, be more realistic in so far as we often voice our thoughts to ourselves, with no communicative intention?

The manoeuvre proposed merits a fuller description. It goes as follows. First: follow the communication-theorist in responding to the challenge for an elucidation of the notion of truth-conditions by invoking the notion of, e.g. and centrally, statement or assertion; (accepting the uncontroversial point that one makes a true statement or assertion when things are as, in making that assertion, one asserts them to be). Second: follow the communication-theorist again in responding to the challenge for an elucidation of the notion of asserting by making a connexion with the notion of belief; (conceding that to make an assertion is, in the primary case, to give expression to a belief; to make a true assertion is to give expression to a correct belief; and a belief is correct when things are as one who holds that belief, in so far as he holds that belief, believes them to be). But third: part company with the communication-theorist over the nature of this connexion between assertion and belief; deny, that is, that the analysis of the notion of asserting involves essential reference to an intention, e.g., to get an audience to think that the maker of the assertion holds the belief; deny that the analysis of the notion of asserting involves *any* kind of reference to audience-directed intention; maintain, on the contrary, that it is perfectly satisfactory to accept as fundamental here the notion of simply voicing or expressing a belief. Then conclude that the meaning-determining rules for a sentence of the language are the rules which determine *what* belief is conventionally articulated by one who, in given contextual conditions, utters the sentence. As before, determining what this belief is, is the same thing as determining what assertion is made. So all the merits of the opponent's theory are preserved while the reference to communication is extruded.

Of course, more must be said by this theorist, as by his opponent. For sentences which can be used to express beliefs need not always be so used. But the point is one to be made on both sides. So we may neglect it for the present.

Now will this do? I do not think it will. But in order to see that it will not, we may have to struggle hard against a certain illusion. For the notion of expressing a belief may seem to us perfectly straightforward; and hence the notion of expressing a belief in accordance with certain conventions may seem equally straightforward. And yet, in so far as the notion of expressing a belief is the notion we need, it may borrow all its force and apparent straightforwardness from precisely the communication-situation which it was supposed to free the analysis of meaning from depending on. We may be tempted to argue as follows. Often we express beliefs with an audience-directed intention; we intend that our audience should take us to have the belief we express and perhaps that that belief should be activated or produced in the audience as well. But then what could be plainer than this: that what we can do with an audience-directed intention we can also do without any such intention? That is to say, the audience-directed intention, when it is present, is something added on to the activity of expressing a belief and in no way essential to it—*or* to the concept of it.

Now what a mixture of truth and falsity, of platitude and illusion, we have here! Suppose we reconsider for a moment that analysis of utterer's meaning which was roughly sketched at the beginning. The utterer produces something—his utterance *x*—with a complex audience-directed intention, involving, say, getting the audience to think that he has a certain belief. We cannot detach or extract from the analysis an element which corresponds to his expressing a belief with no such intention—though we could indeed produce the following description and imagine a case for it: he acts *as if* he had such an intention though as a matter of fact he has not. But here the description depends on the description of the case in which he has such an intention.

What I am suggesting is that we may be tempted, here as else-where, by a kind of bogus arithmetic of concepts. Given the concept of Audience Directed Belief Expression (ADBE), we can indeed think of Belief Expression (BE) without Audience Direction (AD), and find cases of this. But it does not follow that the concept of ADBE is a kind of logical compound of the two simpler concepts of AD and BE and hence that BE is conceptually independent of ADBE.

Of course these remarks do not show that there is no such thing as an independent concept of belief-expression which will meet the needs of the anti-communication-theorist. They are only remarks directed against a too simple argument to the effect that there is such a concept.

This much is clear. If there is such an essentially independent concept of belief-expression which is to meet the need of the analysis of the notion of meaning, we cannot just stop with the phrase "expressing a belief". We must be able to give some *account* of this concept, to tell ourselves some intelligible story about it. We can sometimes reasonably talk of a man's actions or his behaviour as expressing a belief when, e.g., we see those actions as directed towards an end or goal which it is plausible to ascribe to him in so far as it is also plausible to ascribe to him that belief. But this reflection by itself does not get us very far. For one thing, on the present programme, we are debarred from making reference to the end or goal of communication an essential part of our story. For another, the sort of behaviour we are to be concerned with must be, or be capable of being, formalized or conventionalized in such a way that it can be regarded as subjected to, or performed in observance of, rules; and of rules, moreover, which regulate the behaviour precisely in its aspect as expression of belief. It will not do to say simply: we might suppose a man to find *some* satisfaction (unspeci-fied) or some *point* (unspecified) in performing certain formalized (perhaps vocal) actions on some occasions, these actions being systematically related to his having certain beliefs. For suppose a man had a practice of vocalizing in a certain way whenever he saw the sun rise and in another, partly similar, partly different, way whenever he saw it set. Then this practice would be regularly re-lated to certain beliefs, i.e. that the sun was rising or that it was setting. But this description gives us no reason at all for saying that

4*

when the man indulged in this practie he was *expressing the belief* that the sun was rising or setting, in accordance with a rule for doing so. We really have not enough of a description to know *what* to say. As far as we could tell, we might say, he just seems to have this ritual of *saluting* the rising or the setting sun in this way. What need of his it satisfies we don't know.

Let us suppose, however—for the sake of the argument—that we can elaborate some relevant conception of expressing a belief which presupposes nothing which, on the present programme, we are debarred from presupposing; and that we draw on this concept of expressing a belief in order to give an account, or analysis, on the lines indicated, of the notion of linguistic meaning. Then an interesting consequence ensues. That is, it will appear as a quite contingent truth about language that the rules or conventions which determine the meanings of the sentences of a language are public or social rules or conventions. This will be, as it were, a natural fact, a fact of nature, in no way essential to the concept of a language, and calling for a natural explanation which must not be allowed to touch or modify that concept. There must be nothing in the *concept* to rule out the idea that every individual might have his own language which only he understands. But then one might ask: why should each individual observe his own rules? or any rules? Why shouldn't he express any belief he likes in any way he happens to fancy when he happens to have the urge to express it? There is one answer at least which the theorist is debarred from giving to this question, if only in the interests of his own programme. He cannot say: Well, a man might wish to *record* his beliefs so that he could refer to the records later, and then he would find it convenient to have rules to interpret his own records. The theorist is debarred from giving this answer because it introduces, though in an attenuated form, the concept of communication-intention: the earlier man communicates with his later self.

There might be one way of stilling the doubts which arise so rapidly along this path. That would be to offer possible natural explanations of the supposed natural fact that language is public, that linguistic rules are more or less socially common rules; explanations which successfully avoided any suggestion that the connexion of public rules with communication was anything but incidental and contingent. How might such an explanation go? We might say that it was an agreed point that the possession of a language enlarges the mind, that there are beliefs one could not express without a language to express them in, thoughts one could not entertain without a rule-governed system of expressions for articulating them. And it is a fact about human beings that they simply would not acquire mastery of such a system unless they were exposed, as children, to conditioning or training by adult members of a community. Without concerning ourselves about the remote origins of language, then, we may suppose the adult members of a community to wish their successors to have this mind-enlarging instrument at their disposal—and evidently the whole procedure of training will be simplified if they all teach the same, the common language. We may reasonably suppose that the learners, to begin with, do not quite appreciate what they will ultimately be doing with language; that it is for them, to begin with, a matter of learning to do the right thing rather than learning to say the true thing; i.e. a matter of responding vocally to situations in a way which will earn them reward or avoid punishment rather than a matter of *expressing their beliefs*. But later they come to realize that they have mastered a system which enables them to perform this (still unexplained) activity whenever they wish to; and *then* they are speaking a language.

Of course it must be admitted that in the process they are liable also to acquire the *secondary* skill of communicating their beliefs. But this is simply something added on, an extra and conceptually uncovenanted benefit, quite incidental to the description of what it is to have mastered the meaning-rules of the language. If, indeed, you pointedly direct utterances, of which the essential function is belief-expression, to another member of the community, he will be apt to take it that you hold whatever beliefs are in question and indeed that you intend him to take this to be so; and this fact may give rise, indeed, it must be admitted, does give rise, to a whole cluster of social consequences; and opens up all sorts of possibilities of kinds of linguistic communication other than that which is based on belief-expression. This is why, as already acknowledged, we may have ultimately to allow some essential reference to communication-intention into outlying portions of our semantic theory. But this risk is incurred only when we go beyond the central core of meaning, determined by the rules which determine truth-conditions. As far as the central core is concerned, the function of communication remains secondary, derivative, conceptually inessential.

I hope it is clear that any such story is going to be too perverse and arbitrary to satisfy the requirements of an acceptable theory. If this is the way the game has to be played, then the communication-theorist must be allowed to have won it.

But must the game, finally, be played in this way? I think, finally, it must. It is indeed a generally harmless and salutary thing to say that to know the meaning of a sentence is to know under what conditions one who utters it says something true. But if we wish for a philosophical elucidation of the concept of meaning, then the dictum represents, not the end, but the beginning, of our task. It simply narrows, and relocates, our problem, forcing us to inquire what is contained in the little phrase ". . . says something true". Of course there are many ways in which one can say something which is in fact true, give expression, if you like, to a true proposition, without thereby expressing belief in it, without asserting that proposition: e.g. when the words in question form certain sorts of subordinate or co-ordinate clauses, and when one is quoting or play-acting and so on. But when we come to try to explain in general what it is to say something true, to express a true proposition, reference to belief, or to assertion (and thereby to belief) is inescapable. Thus we may harmlessly venture: Someone says something true if things are as he says they are. But this "says" already has the force of "asserts". Or, to eschew the "says" which equals "asserts", we may harmlessly venture: Someone propounds, in some mode or other, a true proposition if things are as anyone who believed what he propounds would thereby believe them to be. And here the reference to belief is explicit.

Reference, direct or indirect, to belief-expression is inseparable from the analysis of saying something true (or false). And, as I have tried to show, it is unrealistic to the point of unintelligibility—or, at least, of extreme perversity—to try to free the notion of the linguistic expression of belief from all essential connexion with the concept of communication-intention.

Earlier I hinted that the habit of some philosophers of speaking as if "true" were a predicate of type-sentences was only a minor aberration, which could readily enough be accommodated to the facts. And so it can. But it is not a simple matter of pedantry to insist on correcting the aberration. For if we are not careful, it is liable to lead us totally wrong. It is liable, when we inquire into the nature of meaning, to make us forget what sentences are *for*. We connect meaning with truth and truth, too simply, with sentences; and sentences belong to language. But, as theorists, we know nothing of human *language* unless we understand human *speech*.

NOTES

1 See John Lyons' outline and discussion of surface and deep structure rules, Lecture 3. (Ed.)

2 Not the *only* way; for to say that a concept θ cannot be adequately elucidated without reference to a concept Ψ is not the same thing as to say that it is possible to give a classical analysis of θ in terms of Ψ. But the *simplest* way; for the classical method of analysis is that in terms of which, in our tradition, we most naturally think.

3 Cf. Lyons' definition of an utterance in grammatical description, Lecture 3, p. 60 (Ed.)

4 Grice: "Meaning", *Philosophical Review* (1957).
"Utterer's Meaning, Sentence-Meaning and Word-Meaning", *Foundations of Language* (1968).
"Utterer's Meaning and Intentions", *Philosophical Review* (1969).

5 Davidson: "Truth and Meaning", *Synthese* (1967), p. 310.

6 This acknowledgement is probably implicit, though not very clearly so, in Austin's concept of *locutionary meaning* (see *How to Do Things with Words*, Clarendon Press, Oxford, 1962); it is certainly implicit in Grice's distinction between what speakers *actually say*, in a favoured sense of "say", and what they imply (see "Utterer's Meaning, Sentence-Meaning and Word-Meaning"); and again in Searle's distinction between the *proposition* put forward and the illocutionary mode in which it is put forward (see *Speech Acts*, Cambridge University Press, 1969).

7 Cf. The pragmatist's notion of truth. Colin Cherry, Lecture 13, pp. 279–80 (Ed.)

FURTHER READING

Austin: *How to Do Things with Words* (Oxford, 1962).

PARKINSON, G. H. R. (Ed.): *The Theory of Meaning* (Oxford, 1968).
SEARLE: *Speech Acts* (Cambridge, 1969).
STRAWSON (Ed.): *Philosophical Logic* (Oxford, 1967).
WITTGENSTEIN: *Blue and Brown Books* (Oxford, 1958).
WITTGENSTEIN: *Philosophical Investigations* (Oxford, 1953).
WITTGENSTEIN: *Tractatus Logico-Philosophicus* (London, 1922 and 1961).

6

Linguistics and Literature

GEORGE STEINER

Churchill College, Cambridge

The naked truism that "all literature is language" states both the self-evidence and great difficulty of my argument. *All* literature—oral or written, lyric or prosaic, archaic or modern—is language in a condition of special use. *Every* literary form—the incantation of the Bushman or a *nouveau roman*, a rhyming doggerel on the lavatory wall or St. John of the Cross' "Songs of the soul in rapture at having arrived at the height of perfection, which is union with God by the road of spiritual negation", *King Lear* or *The Mousetrap*—is no more and no less than a language act, a combination of linguistic units. There can, conceivably, be language without literature (artificial or computer languages may satisfy this negative condition): there can be no literature without language. Mallarmé's dictum that poems are made not of ideas but of *words*, cuts deep.

Literature is "language in a condition of special use". Here our difficulties begin. What is that condition? No articulate statement, one might almost say, no phonetic act or inscription but is susceptible of communicating emotion and, in a sustaining context, of conveying beauty. All signals we emit are potentially resonant with values and intensities beyond those of bare information. Zola made gross but memorable art of an inventory of cheeses; Joyce could, I imagine, spin music off a random page in the telephone directory. In short: we cannot, *a priori*, point to any language act or element and say· this is excluded from all literary employ. Indeed, in the precise sense figured in Borges's allegory of the Library at Babel, that "library which others call the universe", all literature—Aeschylus and Dante, Shakespeare and Tolstoy, as well as the masters not yet born—is extant, is latent life, in the mere aggregate of language. It is a certain combination of words, potentially available as are *all* combinations, in the total vocabulary and grammatical sets of a given tongue.

Yet, in some vital measure, this combination is realized according to criteria different from, or at the least not wholly corresponding to, criteria of immediate speech (we have to be very careful here because it is precisely the criteria of immediate, unselected speech that certain literary genres of naturalism or *verismo* seek to simulate). The poet, the "maker of literature" chooses his linguistic material from the totality of available expressive means. So, of course, does anyone formulating a sentence or even a monosyllabic outcry. But the poet's selection occurs at a special level of deliberation. It stems from a special intensity of conscious focus. Many, in fact most, of the pertinent indicators are common to the poet and to anyone in his society who would speak with clarity, force, personal stress and a minimal elegance. *All* good speech has in it energies which are poetical. In poetry, save at the extreme limits of esoteric or nonsense verse, the main strengths are those of common expressiveness. But the literary *intent* is, at its obscure but primary root, different. Literature is language freed from a paramount responsibility to information ("paramount" is necessary because much great literature, from Hesiod's *Works and Days* to Solzhenitsyn's *The First Circle* is meant to inform in ways entirely comparable to those of a treatise on agronomy or of a newspaper article). The paramount responsibilities of literature, its ontology or *raison d'être*, lie outside immediate utility and/or verifiability. But note how difficulties bristle: the immense moral, psychological "utility" of literature is a commonplace—though one which I personally feel needs re-examining—and the "truths" discovered and communicated by great art are among the best we hold. Thus I mean something more banal: the poem or the novel may prove of extraordinary use to the community; the propositions it puts forward about life may be authentic and of the deepest truth. But these benefits will, as it were, be ancillary. We do not turn to literary form at the first brute need of communication; there is always a simpler way of saying things than that of the poet. Perhaps speed is relevant here: literature is more prodigal of time than is unpremeditated statement. Like music, it moves in temporal co-ordinates which are, in some tangible but difficult to define way, proper to itself. Both the prolixities and concisions of literary language have metronome markings which differ from those of the routine and largely indiscriminate currents of common verbal exchange. Hence, I believe, the profound, obsessive striving of the poet after survival: literature is language in some degree outside ordinary time and thus will survive time better, says Ovid, than marble or bronze. And the truths which it states, while being no less rigorous, no less important, no less radical than those stated by an historical document or mathematical theorem, are not subject to quite the same modes of proof. When literature is most itself, the sum of truth and information which is inherent in it cannot be abstracted, cannot—or only very imperfectly—be paraphrased. That truth and information are indivisible from the exact combination of formal expressive devices, from the unique enacted or executive form (R. P. Blackmur's term) of the given ode, sonnet, drama or fiction. In common speech, a major proportion of linguistic material is contingent, superfluous, merely conventional; neighbouring or roughly analogous counters can be substituted and little will be lost. Ideally—and there is much that approaches the ideal in Dante, in Keats, in a paragraph by Proust—a single alteration will transform or destroy the literary text. It will change the meaning. A poetic form *acts out* its meaning, and is as inseparable from the complete formal means of that action as is, in Yeats's famous query, the dancer from the dance.

Let me go back to the start. Literature is language, but language in a condition of special use: that condition being one of total significance, and of a significance which is—for every true poem or piece of literary prose—unique. No replacement of any semantic element, however small (consider the rôle of typography in Mallarmé, in e. e. cummings) will do. These two criteria—significance as the exact, determined sum of all linguistic means employed, and non-substitutability of any of these means by some unit brought in "from outside"—seem to me to allow a rough, working definition of the distance between literature and the language-world or lexical and syntactic context from which it is drawn.

LITERATURE AS LANGUAGE

But even as literature is at every moment and by very definition drawn from the history and currency of the relevant language, so our understanding of literature is, in essence, linguistic.

To classical antiquity this was a truism. So far as antiquity conceived of "literature" at all (and whether and how early it did so remains a moot point), it saw the métier of the poet or tragedian as being one of special appliance: language applied, in a perfectly deliberate and analysable fashion, to the job of persuasion or ornamentation or dissimulation, as the case might be. Poetics came under the heading of rhetoric; both were patently of the realm of the grammarian and teachers of eloquent discourse. In political societies in which the arts of government and public management were very largely those of persuasive formulation, the poet was supreme exemplar of *efficient speech*. In Homer a man might find tags to organize for himself, in terms unmatched for economy and musical memorability, almost any posture of civic, military and domestic experience. Out of Euripides on rage, or eros, or the coming of a storm, the speaker in the city would learn how to align most effectively the tonal, plastic and grammatical resources of daily usage. The grammarian parsing the *Iliad* to generations of school boys, the scholiast on Sophokles, were, in the fullest sense, applied linguists, "pointers out" of the joints and bevels with which the master-carpenters of the language put together notable linguistic artifacts. That there might be, as Plato argued in the *Ion*, mysterious, daemonic sources of impulse at work in the poet's creative frenzy did not in any way subtract from the essentially rhetorical, rationally demonstrable anatomy of his product. At only one major point did the classical view of poetry and drama touch on genuinely fundamental issues of the nature of language. This was in the conflict between the Platonic theory of *mimesis* and the Aristotelian model of *katharsis*. The Platonic notion of the capacity of language, particularly when joined to music, to elicit imitative action, his insight into the possibility that verbal fictions weaken or corrupt our grasp on what Freud was to call "the reality principle", his attempt to distinguish negatively between verifiable and poetic truths—all these raise linguistic issues of final importance. Aristotle's rejoinder is based on a far less penetrating sense of language and inclines to a cursory identification of form with explicit content. Nevertheless, in the *Poetics* no less than in the *Ion* and the *Republic*, questions are posed or, at least, intimated regarding the operations of language which have not, until now, been resolved.

But for the rest, the poetics of antiquity are, resolutely, a branch of the study of grammar and public discourse. Via Cicero and Quintilian, this classification obtains throughout medieval and scholastic study of the written word.

Hugues de Saint-Victor's *Didascalicon*, with its significant sub-title *De studio legendi* ("an art of reading"), dating from the first half of the XIIth century, is a well-known case in point. The commanding rubric is that of *logica*, the study both analytic and heuristic of the proper laws and effective conventions of human speech, when that speech is purged of the randomness and anarchy of vulgate usage. The analysis of grammar leads to that of argument (*logica dissertiva vel rationalis*), demonstration, dialectic and invention being the natural aims of thoroughly mastered, organized linguistic structures. *Rhetorica* is a sub-species of this threefold division, as literature and secular eloquence are special cases of persuasive and ornamented dialectic.

These neo-Aristotelian or post-Hellenistic taxonomies may strike us as arbitrary or imperceptive. But they brought with them a scruple and strength of actual linguistic practice which constitutes one of the real, and all but extinct, glories of the western inquisitive tradition. Exegetists from the XIIth century to Scaliger possessed a knowledge of prosodic forms, a feel for the live and technical fibres of grammar, a familiarity with the syntactic sources of pathos, violence and sublimity, which we can hardly pretend to equal. They may have worked at the surface of language but it was a surface intricately mapped—and far more literature than romantic theory would have us suppose *is* surface, conventionally impelled and publicly construed. Scholastic and renaissance grammarians knew that whatever else he may be, the great writer is a technician, an artisan exhibiting profound but ultimately public, understandable skills. The great grammarians of Port Royal in the XVIIth century who are so much invoked in current debate on transformational grammars, were the direct heirs of this tradition of scholastic rhetoric.

Why the XVIIIth century should have been so largely indifferent to the linguistic structures underlying literature is a problem which, to the best of my knowledge, has been little looked into. The reasons are probably far reaching. The XVIIIth century ideal was, fundamentally, one of lucid paraphrase: the lyric or dramatic genre being an elevation, an embellishment of a content which could, in turn, be extracted from the poem and laid out in everyday prose. Those criteria of intelligibility, robust clarity and ordered sequence which give the finest of neo-classic and Augustan writing its distinctive urbane force, were, in the best sense, prosaic. Moreover that universal civility which the XVIIIth century strove for—the notion that almost the entirety of felt and thought life could be articulated in elegant but unobtrusive French—militated against any warier, more penetrative view of the limits or local depths of language. To these factors we must add a characteristic vein, which will run ever-broadening through the Victorian and modern periods, of

Horatian-Christian moralizing. The work of literature was to be judged not as a linguistic artifact, defining its own stylized, extra-territorial standards of truth and relevance: it was to be seen for its explicit ethical content, and judged accordingly. Dr Leavis's judgement of Samuel Johnson's Shakespeare criticism can stand for an essential trait of the entire Augustan age:

> Not really appreciating the poetry, he cannot appreciate the dramatic organization; more generally, he cannot appreciate the ways in which not only Shakespeare's drama but all works of art *act* their moral judgements. For Johnson a thing is stated, or it isn't there.

Or to put it otherwise: the XVIIIth century values great literature *in spite of* rather than *because of* the language in which it has what is to us its unique, determining life.

But it was precisely in the late XVIIIth century, with Sir William Jones's famous paper on Sanskrit and its relations to Greek and Latin of 1786, that comparative linguistics in the modern sense gets under way. By the 1820's many of what we now recognize as the essential, deep problems in the study of language had been clearly posed.

That August Wilhelm von Schlegel should, at the same time, be a literary critic of major importance, one whose stress on the organic nature of a work of art exercised great influence on the entire romantic movement, *and* Professor of Sanskrit in Bonn, aptly illustrates the new mood. It is from the early XIXth century on that technical linguistics, the philosophy of language and the study of literature will engage in a joint—though often interrupted and mutually suspicious—collaborative enterprise. And they will do so with an awareness of complexities and a sense of discriminations between possible disciplines very different from the confident classifications of literature and rhetoric made by ancient and medieval grammarians.

In Coleridge almost every aspect of the modern note is struck at once and with a resonance reaching to our own day. I have in mind chapters xv through xxii of the *Biographia Literaria*, texts in which a poetic and a linguistic sensibility conjoin with a perceptive acuity, breadth of exact inference and consciousness of the orders of difficulty involved which I would still judge unsurpassed. Coleridge's presiding notion is plain: "For language is the armoury of the human mind; and at once contains the trophies of its past, and the weapons of its future conquests." Crucially, there lies behind this statement a conviction, possibly derived from Kant and Schelling, that language is less a passive mirror than an intensely-energized beam of light, shaping, placing and organizing human experience. We "speak the world" and the poet does so with exceptional reach and steadiness of focus. From this conviction derive the marvellous delicacies and re-creative precisions of Coleridge's practical criticism of Shakespeare and Wordsworth. Consider this passage on the effects of metre (Chapter xviii):

> As far as metre acts in and for itself, it tends to increase the vivacity and susceptibility both of the general feelings and of the attention. This effect it produces by the continued excitement of surprise, and by the quick reciprocations of curiosity still gratified and still re-excited, which are too slight indeed to be at any one moment objects of distinct consciousness, yet become considerable in their aggregate influence. As a medicated atmosphere, or as wine during animated conversation; they act powerfully, though themselves unnoticed. Where, therefore, correspondent food and appropriate matter are not provided for the attention and feelings thus roused, there must needs be a disappointment felt; like that of leaping in the dark from the last step of a stair-case, when we had prepared our muscles for a leap of three or four.

It is not only the manifold incisiveness of the passage that calls for comment and reflection: it is the unobtrusive but undeniable anticipation of those directions of thought which, today, are designated by semantics, the contrastive study of stress, psycho- and even bio-linguistics. Or take the definition—no less rigorous for being itself imaged—of the special excellence of Wordsworth's representations of nature: "Like a green field reflected in a calm and perfectly transparent lake, the image is distinguished from the reality only by its greater softness and lustre." And note, finally, the control of what Coleridge himself termed "speculative instruments", the firmness of critical vocabulary which informs the stricture that there is in some of Wordsworth's poetry "an approximation to what might be called *mental* bombast, as distinguished from verbal".

That the avenues opened by Coleridge's "linguistic poetics" were not followed up during the course of the XIXth century—some of

Baudelaire's critical writings being an exception, though an exception directed most trenchantly toward art rather than literature—is, in part, an accident of the availability or absence of personal genius. There are respects in which Coleridge had no immediate successor but Newman. But more emphatically, the two great energies of XIXth century literary study were moralizing—the tradition which leads from Dr Johnson to Matthew Arnold and, ultimately, to Leavis—and historicist. With such representative critics as Sainte-Beuve and Taine (in this case Edmund Wilson is the modern heir), the study of literature was made resolutely historical-sociological. Comparative linguistics, with its brilliant successes in establishing the genetics and morphology of Indo-European languages, ran parallel to the understanding of literature. Mutual contacts were few and superficial.

But it is Coleridge's presence which stands most vivid and premonitory when the modern "language revolution" gets under way at the turn of our century.

THE LANGUAGE REVOLUTION

As I have sought to show elsewhere, this revolution had many congruent sources. That re-examination of the foundations of mathematical logic which we associate with Hilbert, Frege and the early work of Russell, led both to the development of modern symbolic logic and to the key recognition that such logic, no less than mathematics itself, was a code, an information structure, with dilemmas and potentialities relevant to the understanding of language. The work of Cassirer on the essentially symbolic nature of human expression (work ultimately rooted in Vico and Coleridge) touched at more than one point on that of the symbolic and mathematical logicians. Though initially unaware of the fact, even resistant to it, the psychoanalytic movement was, fundamentally, an exploration of language habits, of the verbal gestures of consciousness; the raw material of the psychoanalytic process is inevitably linguistic. The insights of psychoanalysis into the neurophysiology of mental life remain conjectural; its disclosures in the realm of linguistic usage and taboo, of semantic ambivalence and pathology are firmly established. Correlative to this movement we may cite the methodical study of the evolution of speech in children as it is found in Piaget. These several currents of thought were clearly parallel to those at work in philosophy: behind Wittgenstein's proposition that philosophy is essentially "speech therapy", behind his insistence that the philosopher's natural and pre-eminent job is the elucidation of men's uses of syntax, lies a far-reaching mutation of attitude. Linguistic philosophy, which has since Carnap, Wittgenstein and Austin been so dominant in our very sense of the philosophic enterprise, represents a reaction against the confident architectures of total meaning, of total history or metaphysics that mark Hegel, Comte and the XIXth century. But it also represents the belief that any true examination of meaning is, first and perhaps also in the final analysis, an examination of the relevant grammar, of the instrumentalities of language by and through which man argues and experiences possible models of reality.[1] This belief, and its enactment in philosophy, literature and art are, I think, directly concordant with a profound crisis of confidence in language brought on by the ruin of classic humanist values after 1914. The investigations of silence, of the limits of language in the face of extreme human need which characterize the work of Wittgenstein, of Kafka, of Rilke, of the Dada movement, which have reached to the near-silent music of Webern and the voids of stillness in Beckett—these are of a piece. Having become dubious of the powers and humane values of language, logicians, writers and artists returned to language with a sharpened, wary consciousness.

It is precisely from this period that we can date that collaborative interaction of linguistics and poetics foreshadowed in medieval rhetoric and in Coleridge.

The main facts are well known. In 1915 a group of students at Moscow University founded the Moscow Linguistic Circle. A year later, a number of young philologists and literary historians founded the Petersburg Society for the Study of Poetic Language. From the outset, these associations were characterized by an exceptionally intimate collaboration of poets, technical linguists, and historians of Russian language and literature. At the famous occasion when Roman Jakobson read his paper on "Xlebnikov's Poetic Language" —a paper which foreshadowed almost the whole development of the current linguistic analysis of literature—Majakovskij was present. Poets such as Gumilev and Axmatova were in close touch with the linguistic analyses of poetic syntax undertaken in Petersburg by Viktor Sklovskij and Boris Ejxenbaum. With the publication, in 1916, of a joint volume of *Studies in the Theory of Poetic Language*, the modern movement is fully under way. The mere titles of such papers as L. Jakubinskij's "The Accumulation of Identical Liquids in Practical and in Poetic Speech" or of Ejxenbaum's "How Gogol's 'Overcoat' is Made" (with its profoundly original study of cadence, phrasings and image clusters in a piece of narrative prose), define a scheme of work which is only now being fully realized. Through his knowledge of Slavonic philology, of poetics and of the new theories of language being developed by Saussure, Jakobson united in his own work the principal energies of the Formalist or linguistic-poetic approach. His treatise *On Czech Verse*, published in 1923, may be seen as the first instance of a methodical application of modern semantic (or, as they are more technically called, semasiological) criteria to a comparative analysis of the structure and effects of metrical patterns. The choice of language was no accident. With the increasing Marxist attacks on Formalism and Jakobson's own departure from the Soviet Union, the focus of linguistic poetics had shifted to Prague.

Certain Czech scholars would trace the beginnings of the linguistic school of Prague back to 1911; what is certain is that the Prague Linguistic Circle held its first meeting in October 1926, and that it rapidly became an influential centre for the examination of literature in the light of linguistics. The contribution to current sensibility made by Jakobson, by N. S. Trubetzkoy, by J. Mukarovsky, would be difficult to overestimate. It is here that those concepts of structualism and semiology which are now so modish were first set out, and set out with a responsiveness to the genius of poetry and the demands of exact philology which current imitations, particularly in France, do not always match. It is in the Prague manifesto that concepts which are today banal were first formulated: language is "a coherent whole in which all parts interact upon each other"; "only poetry enables us to experience the act of speech in its totality and reveals to us language not as a ready-made static system but as creative energy"; "everything in the work of art and in its relation to the outside world . . . can be discussed in terms of sign and meaning; in this sense, esthetics can be regarded as a part of the modern science of signs, semasiology." Or to put it quite simply: the study of a poem is an attempt to register exhaustively the semantic elements or signal-structure of which that poem is made and through which, alone, it reaches our consciousness.

The Conference on Style held at the University of Indiana in 1958 (like the conference on linguistics and anthropology held at the same place six years earlier) was calculated to summarize forty years of work already accomplished, and to map future progress. It was here that Roman Jakobson summed up what are to be the main effects of the language revolution on our understanding of literature. First, an admonition:

> The poetic resources concealed in the morphological and syntactic structure of language, briefly the poetry of grammar, and its literary product, the grammar of poetry, have been seldom known to critics and mostly disregarded by linguists but skillfully mastered by creative writers.

And then the programmatic statement:

> All of us here, however, realize that a linguist deaf to the poetic function of language and a literary scholar indifferent to linguistic problems and unconversant with linguistics methods are equally flagrant anachronisms.

WHAT HAVE LINGUISTICS CONTRIBUTED?

How far have these aims and recognitions, first argued in Petersburg and Prague half a century ago been fulfilled?

Any attempt at a comprehensive answer would, necessarily, become a bibliography. It would have to include an analysis of the special branch of linguistic and poetic practical criticism represented by the instigations of C. K. Ogden and the actual writings of I. A. Richards and William Empson. It would examine the fragmentary but formidably suggestive "hermeneutic" criticism of Walter Benjamin, with its endeavour to combine a linguistic with a sociological methodology in the reading of baroque drama and of Baudelaire. It would want to say a good deal (though so far as I am concerned, critically) of the "semiotics", "semiology" and "structural grammatology" presently flourishing in France. It would invite close valuation of a number of key texts: Josephine Miles's "More Semantics of Poetry" (1940), John Crowe Ransom's "Wanted: An Ontological Critic" (1941), Christine Brooke-Rose's *A Grammar of Metaphor* (1958), I. A. Richards's "Poetic Process and Literary Analysis" and Jakobson's "Linguistics and Poetics" (both in 1960), Samuel R. Levin's "Poetry and Grammaticalness"

(1964). Professor Stephen Ullmann's studies of the syntax of the French novel would be highly relevant as well as Donald Davie's two incisive books on energy and structure in English verse. One would want to look closely at the fascinating analyses of coding, information patterns and narrative structure in primitive or archaic folk songs and oral recitation, made by T. A. Sebeok and Tzvetan Todorov. Already the terrain is very large and impossible to chart according to any one single criterion of intent or success.

Nevertheless, the charge that all this deployment of linguistic resources, of philosophic intelligence, of trained sensibility to the poetic life of language has not really contributed all that much to our reading of a poem, cannot be ignored. Time and again, it will be said, the application of sophisticated semantic categories, the quasi-mathematical dismemberment of a literary text, the lexical and syntactic elaboration of its armature, produce conclusions that are either unconvincingly esoteric or platitudinous. Surely we had no need of Jakobson or Saussure to tell us that the juxtaposition of Anglo-Saxon with Latinate words in a Shakespearean line makes for dramatic contrast, or that the stressed array of sharp vowel sounds in a poem by Mallarmé—the letter *i* for example—makes for distinct effects of brittle whiteness and chill. And, above all, what have linguistics, semiology, psycholinguistics contributed to the root wonder of invention, to our understanding of the process whereby certain human beings find words which are profoundly new yet somehow occasion in the reader of the poem a mystery of immediate recognition?

To plead the exceeding difficulty of the whole business is no evasion. It turns out that a complete formal analysis of even the most rudimentary acts of speech, poses almost intractable problems of method and definition. Even the existence or rigorous designation of morphemes as "the smallest individually meaningful elements in the utterances of a language" is not universally accepted, and there have been recent attempts to define the atomic parts of speech in terms even more restrictive or more grammatically active (i.e. the use of the notion of "sememes"). A glance at any current work in transformational generative grammar shows what intricate operations and philosophically or psychologically conjectural presuppositions are enlisted in the normative description of the simplest three- or four-word sentences and phrase-units. Dr Leavis's admonition, though I regard it as ultimately mistaken or over-simplified, that "language, in the full sense, in the full concrete reality . . . eludes the cognizance of any form of linguistic science" is worth keeping in mind. Indeed, whether there is, as yet, a genuine "linguistic science" as distinct from a body of preliminary hypotheses and partial empirical *données*, is highly arguable.

Translate these difficulties into what is, nearly by definition, the most complex of all semantic phenomena, a poem, a major literary text, and the fantastic complication of the job becomes obvious. Each of the elements of the act of communication which linguistics seeks to define and formalize assumes, in literature, an exponential force and intricacy. In decoding or analysing formally simple messages, linguistics and semiology come up against obstinate problems of context. How far back must the computer or human recipient read in order to be certain of the right sense of the particular phrase or even single word? In a poem, perhaps even in a work of the length of a novel by Flaubert, the relevant context is total. Every single verbal and syntactic building block bears on the meaning of any particular passage. Between that passage or line of verse and the sum of the work reciprocal qualifications, illuminations, ironic or supporting undercurrents are operative. Our sense of the given phrase or paragraph alters the live shape of the book and is, in turn, transmuted by it. The organic, self-informing nature of a literary text makes formal analysis of single semantic units or moments extremely vulnerable. The same is true of such notions as "tone", "stress", "valuation", "register", each of which is decisive to the significance of any element in the poem. Yet it is precisely these notions, even where they occur in the most conventional of daily speech forms, that have, until now, defied accurate linguistic classification. That language is polysemic—i.e. that the same word can mean very different things and articulate this diversity simultaneously—has been known since the day when Odysseus used a pun to rout the Cyclops. In poetry, and in much literary prose, polysemy, with all its devices of word-play, *double-entendre*, ambiguity and phonetic echo, is constant. A great poet is one around whose use of any individual word is gathered a live cluster of resonance, of overtones and undertones. When the Ghost tells Hamlet that the secrets of Purgatory would make his hair stand on end "Like quills upon the fretful porpentine", the phrase strongly suggests an heraldic crest. This suggestion has been prepared for, mutedly, by Horatio's previous description of the Ghost as "Armed at point exactly, cap-a-pe". Now the intimation and associated family of images is developed: the Ghost admonishes Hamlet that the dread truths of Purgatory must not be *blazoned* forth. Originally, *blazon* signified a painted shield; by derivation it comes to signify the act of disclosure, of identification, which is the object of heraldry. But the mere sound of the word, here the echo being simpler and deeper than that of a pun, makes us apprehend the *blaze*, the cleansing fires in which the Ghost is doomed, for a time, to dwell. Shakespeare did not "know" that modern philology ascribes a remote, common origin to the two words. That knowledge was active and implicit in his total use of all valuations and tonalities of language. Or take the Fool's prophecy in *Lear* that his master shall be treated *kindly* by Regan. Terrible queries and ironies lie in that little word. Is there *kindness* in our human *kind*; what if each man deal after his *kind*? And did Shakespeare, with his ultimate responsiveness to the manifold life of language, implicate the common etymological stem which makes of *Kind* the German word for "child"?

How is linguistics, labouring as it does with the "deep structure" analysis of such pronouncements as "John loves Mary" to cope?

Yet a good deal *has* been achieved, especially in regard to attitude and in regard to an awareness of the orders of difficulty which are involved. Serious readers of literature *do* read differently since, say, Jakobson and I. A. Richards. The sense of the ways in which a poem defines its own semantic sphere, in which the criteria of significance are internalized, has been sharpened. We deal far more prudently than did Dr Johnson or Matthew Arnold with the matter of poetic truth, with the supposition that metaphoric language has verifications and consistencies that are internal, and whose verification has a logic, properly speaking, a *symbolic logic* of its own. Our perceptions of the means of syntactic dislocation used in poetry, of the specific determinations generated for the ear by certain phonetic and phonological sequences, are more responsible than those available to XIXth century and to impressionistic criticism. An understanding of the combinatorial nature of prosody, of the manner in which the graphic scheme of a line of poetry can either accord or conflict with phonemic patterns, has already produced solid results in the study of XVIth century and modern verse. A statistical analysis that segmental sound effects in Pope are likely to correspond to lexical meanings whereas in Donne, probably intentionally, sound effects rarely coincide with syntactic and semantic units, is more than ingenuity: it implies fundamental insights about the differences in the uses of feeling and expressive means as between Metaphysical and Augustan poetics. The doors opened in 1921 by Sklovskij's famous essay on *Tristram Shandy* as a parodistic form of narration, analysable by precise linguistic tools, will not soon be closed. Above all, it is our awareness of complication that has deepened. We know, as never before, that if literature of some kind is a universal phenomenon, if the contrivance of a language-world, related to but also profoundly distinct from that of sensory fact, is general and spontaneous to man—the product is special and fiercely difficult to interpret fully. We know a little more than previous cultures about the anti- or counter-worlds of the poet, and about the intensely circumscribed freedom within which they operate. We are drawing near, albeit by very small steps, to grasping the scandalous wonder whereby a set of oral or written signals can create characters more "real" and assuredly more lasting than are our own and the lives of their creators. What enigma of the autonomous vitalities of language lies in Flaubert's bitter outcry that he lay dying whilst Mme Bovary, the petty creature of his verbal labours, would endure. In brief: our concepts of literature grow richer and more provisional. T. S. Eliot's celebrated dictum about something "having happened to the mind of England" between the time of Donne and that of Tennyson not only strikes one today as portentously unverifiable: it embodies the style of judgement of what may well prove to have been the last major literary critic almost wholly innocent of a training in and interest for modern linguistics.

But rather than draw a balance-sheet, I should like to list some of the principal problems and possibilities that lie ahead of linguistic poetics.

PROBLEMS AND PROSPECTS

That study of the special linguistic nature of poetry begun with the discussions on *epitheta ornantia* in the Moscow Linguistic Circle fifty years ago, must carry forward. We want to know more about the suspensions of common causality and logical dependence in poetic discourse. We want more exact knowledge (the question was already posed by Plato) of the "kinetic" working of different metres and stanzaic patterns, of the ways in which stress, accentuation, rhyme, repetition, assonance, enjambement affect our nervous receptors and trigger emotions often concordant with, but at times directly subversive of, the manifest content of the poem. I. A. Richards was confident that this "rhetoric of effects" lay within analytic reach; it has, in fact, proved elusive. We need to know a good deal more than we do about the epistemological tactics whereby a poem (Wallace Stevens's "Anecdote of the Jar" being the great exemplar of this theme) divides itself from reality, yet, if the poet's authority be sufficient, insinuates into reality new possibilities of order and relation:

> The wilderness rose up to it,
> And sprawled around, no longer wild.
> The jar was round upon the ground
> And tall and of a port in air.
>
> It took dominion everywhere.
> The jar was gray and bare.
> It did not give of bird or bush,
> Like nothing else in Tennessee.

Where, as it happens, a formal, syntactical analysis of the last two lines will encounter difficulties that lead straight to the secret genius of the poem.

Consisting, as it does, of large units and being, apparently, so diffuse in structure, prose has proved strongly resistant to close analysis. Saintsbury's *History of English Prose Rhythm* now impresses one as over-simplified and often doctrinaire. But it is becoming clear that the linguistic elements which go into the creation of a major prose style—say that of Tacitus, of Swift, of Joyce—are no less accidental and no less susceptible of formal investigation than are those of verse. The frontier zone, so much exploited since the 1880's, in which prose-poetry and poetic prose meet, is, from a linguistic point of view, particularly revealing. But great prose—Diderot's *Neveu de Rameau*, Kafka's *Metamorphosis*—has a music of its own, and one for which we do not, as yet, have adequate notation.

The typology of literary genres and conventions of style is still at a rudimentary stage. The habits of memory, of narrative unfolding, of formulaic description in an heroic epic reflect a congeries of social, economic, psychological and linguistic factors. The history of the sonnet, from Petrarch to Berryman, is the history of a very special, yet perennially formative, contour of statement; a sonnet organizes the world in a way which numerous poets have found indispensable, but whose deep-lying rationale is not yet completely understood. The career of the ode is that of a certain cast of emphatic, public feeling. There are fundamental but obscure inter-relations between the rise of the novel and the changes occasioned in men's experience of time by the growth of science and industrial technology. Language anticipates and enacts the altering pulse of material life. In what ways has the *accelerando* of modern communication—the lightning sparsities of telephone and telegraph—militated against those habits of elaboration, of adjectival richness, of verbal ceremony, which underlay verse drama? What correlations can be shown between changes in sexual life and changes both in actual verbal taboos and in the cadence of contemporary prose? In what respect do changes now occurring in our speech habits lead one to suppose that new and different genres will follow on the decline of the novel?

We possess scarcely the rudiments of a theory of translation, of any model of how the mind operates when it passes from one language to another. Speaking of the attempt to transfer into English a Chinese philosophic concept, I. A. Richards remarked: "We have here indeed what may very probably be the most complex type of event yet produced in the evolution of the cosmos." But what kind of event is it? Are we dealing, as the Sapir-Whorf hypothesis argues, with a situation in which each of the more than four thousand languages now current on the earth articulates a specific, ultimately irreducible segmentation of reality? Are different languages radically diverse modes of structuring and experiencing reality? In which case, even the best of translations is a species of mimetic approximation or illusory transfer? Or are the foundations of all languages a finite set of innate universals—this being the view of Zelig Harris, Chomsky, and transformational grammar? If this is so, the possibility of genuine translation follows, and the deep-structure analogues of human tongues will be found to outweigh the surface disparities. These are some of the questions I am now working on. And in this domain the language revolution has crucial bearing. Being a search for underlying patterns of essential significance, the problem of translation has affinities with symbolic logic and the study of language itself as a combinatorial code. Considerable labour and expense is going into the matter of

5

machine translation. This, in turn, being a special branch of the uses of computers for linguistic analysis. Let me say at once that I am sceptical. I suspect that even the most sophisticated computers furnish models of phrasing which are far too elementary, far too schematic, to throw real light on human linguistic competence and performance. Particularly in regard to determinations of meaning and of implication, judgements that are based on a grasp of the entire relevant context, the ten to the fourteenth power electro-chemical cells and synapses in the human brain operate at a speed and at a level of selective finesse which, I would suppose, lies totally beyond the reach of mechanical computation. I am sceptical also with respect to the potentialities of machine translation. Here there is widespread confusion. The construction of giant special glossaries is definitely possible. Such glossaries may indeed speed up dramatically the laborious process of the translation of scientific and technological documents. But such electronic glossaries, however refined, are no more than super-dictionaries; they are aids *to* human translation. They do not, in any true sense, translate a body of normal linguistic matter into a parallel body in another language. The summation put forward by Dr Yngve in the *Proceedings of the American Philosophical Society* in 1964, seems to me unassailable: "Work in mechanical translation has come up against a semantic barrier . . . We have come face to face with the realization that we will only have adequate mechanical translation when the machine can 'understand' what it is translating and this will be a very difficult task indeed." And so far no evidence has come in to contradict the conclusion of the so-called ALPAC report issued in Washington in 1966: "there is no immediate or predictable prospect of useful machine translation." None the less, the lines of investigation which have led to these negative conclusions are of the greatest linguistic interest. Through them we are learning a great deal about the nature and limits of language, about the concepts—hitherto so largely impressionistic—of what is meant by the possibility or impossibility of ordinary and of poetic translation. In certain strictly defined areas, moreover, such as the statistical determination of the relations between the literary and the vulgate vocabulary at any given period of history, such as the accurate description of the rates of mutual interpenetration or absorption of different languages, or in the analytic mapping of lexical and grammatical habits in a particular author or body of anonymous work (the Pauline epistles, the Junius letters), computers *do* have a useful rôle. Indeed it is exactly at the point where they fail that they may tell us most of the singular genius of language and of the "language animal".

Beyond all these questions, immensely difficult as they are, lie even deeper queries and possibilities of study. Are certain languages more apt to literature than others? All societies of which we have knowledge devise and perform music. By no means all have a literature, except in the most rudimentary and vaguely expanded sense of the term. Are the primary factors social, economic, geographic? Or is there in the very structure of certain languages a latency of poetic invention? Was there that in ancient Hebrew and Greek which generated lasting forms of symbolic statement, whereas neighbouring cultures, Egypt for example, produced ritual texts, but not the free, non-utilitarian play of fiction? Man is a primate who can lie, who can make counter-factual statements. What quality in the fabric of certain languages has transmuted this strange capacity into literature? Are certain tongues more anchored in the material truths of reality than are others? What of the poetics and metaphysics of the future tense, that scandalous marvel whereby the human mind pre-empts a tomorrow which the living speaker will not experience and whose very existence is a piece of syntactic inference? Is poetry, in some deep sense, always part remembrance and part prophecy—the very reality of past and future being mainly a convention of language? Do certain so-called primitive tongues, whose tense and case systems are far more ramified than those in, say, Greek, French or English, inhibit the development of literature just because they have affixed to reality too numerous and too precisely divisive labels?

And there is the profoundly disturbing question of linguistic entropy. Do great languages "run down", do they lose their speed and accuracy of creative reflex? Do they close windows in their community rather than open them? Is there in languages—Hebrew and Chinese being the most interesting exceptions—a life cycle of rich growth, confident maturity and gradual decline? Are the critical elements behind the fact that XXth century English literature, with the exception of D. H. Lawrence, is the product of American and Irish poets, novelists, playwrights, essayists, of an economic, political, social or linguistic nature? Does the presence of a Shakespeare (or, analogously, of a Dante, Cervantes or Goethe) in a language inhibit the development of later resources? To an un-biased observer, it is very nearly an unavoidable conclusion that English as it is spoken and written in England today is an enervated, tired version of the language as compared with the almost Eliza-bethan rapacities and zest of American English and of the breathless signals it is sending into the world. Which is cause, which is effect? Somewhere ahead of us lies a discipline of socio-linguistics, a collaborative inquiry by literary critics, linguists, sociologists and psychologists, of which we have, as yet, only indistinct premoni-tions. But the root question is of the utmost importance: it may well be that cultures and societies die when their uses of language atrophy.

Problematic and, in many ways, scarcely defined as so many of these questions are, I confidently predict that the serious study of literature will have to engage them. This means that the separation between literary and linguistic studies still prevalent in so many universities, especially in this country, must be reviewed. To regard oneself as qualified in the study of literature while being totally ignorant of the changes which modern logic and linguistics have brought to our sense of language, is an arrogant absurdity. To write yet another impressionistic or polemically-motivated treatise on the virtues of Henry James's prose or the wit of Donne, without grappling with the linguistic facts of the case, seems a largely private academic game. Yet half a century after the Moscow and Prague investigations into language and poetics it is, among Eng. Lit. faculties, still the common rule. The reasons are not far to seek. Modern linguistics exacts a good deal of mental effort. It requires some modest degree of acquaintance with formal logic. It asks of those who think about language seriously that they recognize the relevant neighbourhood of that other great idiom of human conjecture which is mathematics (a recognition that has given to certain XXth century writers such as Valéry, Broch, Borges and Raymond Queneau their distinctive magic). Dons are not always inclined to refurbish their dwindling stock of obsolete perceptions. But if literary studies are to have a future other than modish, if they are to emerge from an ambience of trivia and personal recrimination such as obtained in theology at the close of the last century, critical but honest collaboration with linguistics must occur. I do not accept Jakobson's claim that it is "the right and duty of linguistics to direct the investigation of verbal art in all its compass and extent"—*direct* being the overstatement, and literature being far too manifold a phenomenon for the exhaustive control of any linguistics as yet conceivable. But I subscribe fully to the conviction that the student of poetics and that of linguistics must work closely together if we are to gain further insight into the most decisive and complex of human acts—which is speech, the use and transmission of the *Logos*.

That insight is native to the poet, and it is in poems that make of language itself their theme that we draw nearest the centre. Let me, therefore, conclude with two texts: in the one, language is experienced as harbinger of death, in the other there is affirmed the mystery of its unquenchable vitality.

A private recitation of a sixteen-line poem on Stalin caused Osip Mandelstam's arrest on May 30th 1934 and led, later, to deportation and death. I cite Robert Lowell's free adaptation:

We live. We are not sure our land is under us.
Ten feet away, no one hears us.

But wherever there's even a half-conversation,
We remember the Kremlin's mountaineer.

His thick fingers are fat as worms,
His words reliable as ten-pound weights.

His boot tops shine,
his cockroach mustache is laughing.

About him, the great, his thin-necked, drained advisers.
He plays with them. He is happy with half-men around him.

They make touching and funny animal sounds.
He alone talks Russian.

One after another, his sentences hit like horseshoes! He
pounds them out. He always hits the nail, the balls.

After each death, he is like a Georgian tribesman,
putting a raspberry in his mouth.

It would be fatuous to attempt an exhaustive reading of this poem, particularly as I am unable to do so in Russian. Here language is acting at the utmost level of concentration, allusive range and tonality. Everything matters: every sound, every pause, the unequal lengths of lines. All I want to draw attention to is the way in which

Mandelstam's poem, or, if you will, sustained epigram—for there are touches in it that resemble the art of Martial—images and enacts a notion of language as being itself murderous. Such are the enforced silences of Stalinist terror, that no one hears a man's cry for help or intimation of love ten feet away. Only half-conversation is possible, the ashen whispering of the damned and of those soon to be shadows. In a fantastically powerful conceit, Mandelstam defines linguistically Stalin's lunatic omnipotence: he alone talks Russian, the rest of the vast land is silent or makes "funny animal sounds". In the final dictatorship, only one man can use the instruments of speech. He does so to castrate and kill, each word a ten-pound weight. And after language has killed, Stalin pops in his mouth the blood-red and musky flesh of the raspberry. This is a poem about the limits of language, about the decline of men into abject, comic animality when speech is denied them. But being itself so eminent an act of language, Mandelstam's fable defines the suicidal privilege and necessary job of the poet in the communities of the inhuman.

Because it must savage that in man which is most humane, namely the gift of language, barbarism has often sought out the poet. The eleventh book of Ovid's *Metamorphoses* (and Mandelstam, like Ovid, wrote a *Tristia*) tells of the slaying and dismemberment of Orpheus. Arthur Golding's version of 1565-7 is, of course, the one Shakespeare knew. It tells how "heady ryot out of frame all reason now did dash, / And frantik outrage reigned." Of how the crazed maenads

ran uppon the prophet who among them singing stands.
They flockt about him like as when a sort of birds have found
An Owle a day tymes in a tod: and hem him in full round,
As when a Stag by hungrye hownds is in a morning found,
The which forestall him round about and pull him to the
           ground . . .
And (wicked wights) they murthred him, who never till that
           howre
Did utter woordes in vaine, nor sing without effectuall powre.
And through that mouth of his (oh lord) which even the stones
           had heard,
And unto which the witlesse beastes had often given regard,
His ghost then breathing intoo aire, departed . . .

All nature mourns the death of the poet, the death of the singer who made the forest fall silent. The nymphs descend the mourning rivers "in boats with sable sayle". But *mirum*!—wonder:

> dum labitur amne,
> flebile nescio quid queritur lyra, flebile lingua
> murmurat exanimis, respondent flebile ripae.

> His head and harp both cam
> To *Hebrus* and (a wondrous thing) as downe the streame they
> swam,
> His Harp did yeeld a moorning sound: his liveless toong did
> make
> A certeine lamentable noyse as though it still yit spake,
> And bothe the banks in moorning wyse made answer too the
> same.

In death, his body rent, the poet sings still.

Let this be the metaphor— as is Orpheus' descent into Hades—of the singular power of language to bring and to overcome death. In Mandelstam's poem, words are the literal killers of the poet. In Ovid's narration of Orpheus, language is seen to endure, like a live flame, in the mouth of the dead singer. It is the business of the student of literature and of the linguist to listen closely, to explore, so far as he may, the wonder of creation which is speech. Reader, critic, linguist are answerable to the poet— in the full meaning of that word which contains both response and responsibility. There lies our common bond, and the fascinating job ahead.

NOTES

1 See, for example, P. F. Strawson's explanation of a formal semantic theory of meaning, and the subsequent discussion of its merits versus those of a communication intention theory. Lecture 5. (Ed.)

FURTHER READING

ERLICH, V.: *Russian Formalism.*
FOWLER, R. (Ed.): *Essays on Style and Language.*
HYMES, D. (Ed.): *Language in Culture and Society* (New York, 1964).
JAKOBSON, R.: "Retrospect" in *Selected Writings (1).*
LEVIN, S. R.: *Linguistic Structures in Poetry.*
SEBEOK, T. (Ed.): *Style in Language.*
SPITZER, L.: *Linguistics and Literary History.*
VACHEK, J.: *The Linguistic School of Prague.*

7

Language and anthropology

EDMUND LEACH

Provost of King's College, Cambridge

VERBAL AND NON-VERBAL COMMUNICATION

I have not had the advantage of attending the earlier lectures, but I have read the printed synopses and I notice that my piece has been strategically placed so as to provide a sort of bridge between the two halves of the series.

By and large all my predecessors have been using the word *language* in the straightforward sense of spoken language. I appreciate that last week Dr Steiner was talking about literature, that is, of the written word, but no one, so far as I can judge, has yet raised the question of just what is the connection between "speaking" and "writing". After all, speech in itself is behaviour of a very special kind . . . verbal behaviour; writing as such is not— it is just one of a great many kinds of activity which we perform with our hands. Yet once we have learnt the rules of the game we have no difficulty about feeling that the non-verbal activity of writing is a direct representation (a metaphorical transformation) of the verbal activity of speaking. This, when you come to think of it, is very surprising, and it raises the much more general question of the relation between language—in either of these specifically human forms— and the non-verbal sign codes which are used in the communication systems of non-human animals which will be the theme of the Russells in their first lecture after the Christmas vacation.

So let me start off by making the obvious point that we are animals as well as human beings. We can communicate with one another by non-verbal as well as by verbal means. We have a variety of different senses . . . we can pick up messages not only by listening but also by seeing, smelling, touching and feeling. Admittedly, hearing and sight tend to dominate our conscious awareness, but in fact we are all the time apprehending what is going on by using all our senses simultaneously.

STRUCTURE IN SENSE RESPONSES

Much earlier on, the point was made that, in a purely mechanical sense, a verbal utterance is simply a pattern of sound superimposed upon breath. This idea of pattern is all-important. It is patterning which distinguishes meaningful speech, or for that matter music, from mere noise, and it is patterning (or structure) which makes it possible to translate or transcribe a speech utterance from one form into another. The relation between the pattern of the shapes of the typewritten letters on this paper in front of me, and the shapes of the sound waves which I am imposing on my breath as I make these remarks is extremely complicated, but it is certainly a discoverable systematic relationship, otherwise it would be quite impossible for the sound and the written line to be recognized as having "the same" meaning. Similarly the reason that the eye can not only make sense of what it sees but that we can also feel our way around a room even in the dark, is that we all have a very deep-rooted capacity for decoding, transcribing and integrating coded patterns which reach our consciousness through different senses. Our capacity for understanding the speech sounds which we *hear* is directly tied in with a capacity to understand patterns which we *see*, or patterns which we *feel*.

Up to a point these sense responses are a part of our animal nature. Some signals will produce quite involuntary automatic responses: if you inadvertently pick up a hot cinder you will have let go again long before you realize what has happened. Quite a number of our ordinary day to day gestures and interpersonal behaviours are little more than signal-response mechanisms of this same basic *animal* kind. The Russells will no doubt be explaining to you just how complicated such mechanical chains of interaction between two individual animals may be, and they will, I am sure, make the point that such triggered responses can be learned as habits and are not just matters of instinct.

SIGNALS AND LANGUAGE

All of us have learned mechanical habits of this kind. We have learnt them as individuals, but since habit formation is the product of upbringing, all those who have the same social background (that is to say all those who have the same *culture*) tend to have much the same habits.

For example, if you have been brought up as a middle-class Englishman and I walk up to you, hold out my hand and say "how-do-you-do", the odds are that you will respond by doing exactly the same, quite without thinking, but if you were a Chinese you would just give me a blank stare. But I feel sure that the Russells will also make the point that such signal-response behaviours—even when they include bits of verbal behaviour of the "how-do-you-do" kind—are not instances of *true language*.[1]

True language is certainly a habit of a sort, but it is a habit with very special qualities. With true language, once we have learned the grammatical and phonological rules such as those which were discussed earlier by Professor Lyons and Professor Henderson, each individual is capable of making an indefinitely large number of brand-new utterances. And for the most part this is what we actually do. When we talk we use words and short phrases which we have often used before, but we are constantly stringing them together into new combinations and permutations ... and the surprising thing is that these new combinations convey meaning. Ordinary animal communication systems may be complicated, but they are highly repetitive—or at any rate if there are non-repetitive modes of signalling among animals (such as dolphins) we cannot easily recognize them as such or understand what they mean[2]—but with our fellow human beings it is different. Provided that you and I can speak "the same language" I can make an utterance which has never been made before in the whole history of the world, and you will still understand what I am saying. The question I want you to consider is how far this remarkable peculiarity extends into other areas of human communication behaviour besides that of spoken language. I have already cited examples which show that there is no straightforward distinction between verbal and non-verbal communication ... writing a letter is a non-verbal kind of behaviour, but it conveys information by verbal means; saying "how-do-you-do" is verbal behaviour, but it conveys information as if it were a triggered response of a non-verbal kind. Moreover, the meaning of verbal utterances is always situational and often depends directly on information which is being conveyed through other senses besides the ears ... If I say "Oh, what a lovely smell", you won't know what I am talking about unless you too can use your nose or your eyes to decide whether I am talking about a cup of coffee or a bunch of roses.

The converse is equally true. Every culturally defined situation conveys information to those who participate in it, but the non-verbal part of the information is usually incomplete unless it is elaborated by means of words. This poses the very general question of how much of our ordinary day to day behaviour can be thought of as a "transformation" of speech in much the same sense as a written text is a transformation of speech. Up to a point the analogies are quite obvious: if, for example, you just consider the arrangement of this room, the way the people in it are distributed, the way they are dressed, the way they are behaving—with me yattering away at one end and you keeping quiet, and with you looking at me—or falling asleep—instead of conversing with your neighbour sitting beside you, and so on—it should be immediately obvious that all these details, both in isolation and in combination, are "saying" a whole heap of things both about the situation as a whole and about the relations between the individual participants. We are all aware of what is being "said" in this way even though we have not thought about it. Each of us has assimilated this body of information at some sort of semi-conscious level.

Of course, you can describe the facts in other ways. If you like, you can use a game analogy rather than a language analogy, but it adds up to much the same thing. By coming into this room in order to attend this lecture you have all tacitly agreed to accept the conventions which apply . . . you recognize that a social game is to be played according to patterned rules, and you are prepared to play according to those rules. The rules do not have to be spelled out in detail . . . you have already picked them up as part of your general culture, sub-consciously, just as you have picked up the rules of phonology and syntax which govern English in the course of learning how to speak.

Let me develop this point because it contains the very kernel of what I am trying to say. I am arguing that the patterned conventions of culture which make it possible for human beings to live together in society have the specifically human quality that they are structured "like" human language.

It is very difficult to imagine the evolutionary steps by which human beings first became adapted to having a capacity for speech, but it is a faculty which must have developed very slowly over an immensely long period of time.[3] Although the individual child is not born with a knowledge of any particular language, it is born with an aptitude for acquiring language. And in a very similar way we all seem to be born with an inbuilt capacity for learning non-verbal codes of communication. And the non-verbal codes are strikingly similar to the verbal ones. For example, when we communicate with one another by means of visual signals rather than by speech, our gestures have the voluntary conventional quality which characterizes language proper. Only very seldom do they take the form of automatic signal-response mechanisms of the kind which predominate among non-human animals.

This is hardly surprising. The evolution of the human voice which entails the imposition of coded patterns on the breath must have gone on simultaneously with the development of the equally remarkable capacity which allows us to decode speech sounds when we hear them. It seems plain that both these faculties must be interconnected at some deeper level and indeed it is highly probable that we have some sort of general coding-decoding capability which can be tied in to any of our senses. The fact that deaf-mutes can be taught to speak by the guidance of a sense of touch illustrates what I mean.

Now if this is so, it would explain the ease with which human beings habitually attach coded meanings to all sorts of details of their cultural behaviour.

Perhaps I am labouring the obvious. We all know quite well from personal experience that the structure of human language and the structure of human culture are in some sense homologous, since we know that we can convey messages of a very similar sort through alternative channels—either by speaking or by performing an action, such as writing or gesturing. The problem I am asking you to think about is: How does this come about? When we transform spoken language into non-verbal forms or vice versa, what do we actually do?

CONVERSATION AS A GAME

Let me go back to the analogy of the game and think in particular of two-person games like chess and draughts, both of which, as you know, are played on the same kind of chequer board of 64 squares. The players make moves alternately—as they do in a conversation—and again as in a conversation, each move is a response to the other player's last move. In other words, making a move serves to convey information to the other player. The other player then responds not in a narrowly defined mechanical way but by assessing the overall situation in the light of the rules of the game.

Notice the difference here between draughts and chess. With draughts, the rules are very simple and the alternatives open to either player at any particular stage in the game are very limited. When one player makes a move he can often exactly predict how his opponent must react. The behaviour of the two players then comes very close to a trigger-response mechanism of the shake-hands-how-do-you-do variety.

But chess is quite different. The rules are much more complicated; at most stages in the game each player can adopt a wide range of alternative strategies. He must still take account of the overall situation and of his opponent's last move, but when he makes his own move he cannot predict what his opponent will do next. In this case the players are responding to one another in much the same way as in an ordinary conversation.

There is also another characteristic of chess which is very relevant if we are trying to establish an analogy with linguistics. For a good player a game consists of at least three sections: "an opening", "a middle game" and an "end game". There are a large number of possible openings and none of them is rigidly fixed; even the most conventional and long established "gambit" is subject to innovation from time to time. According to what opening is chosen the general overall pattern of the game is very roughly predictable from the start—e.g. whether the game will be fast or slow, full of slaughter or wrapped in intricate manoeuvre, yet even so each section of the game—the beginning, the middle, and the end—generates its own momentum and is at no point the fully automatic consequence of what has come before or what must necessarily come after. The point I am trying to make is simply this: although the tree diagrams which bespatter the pages of the transformational grammarians of the Chomsky school are not 100% convertible into descriptions of the strategies of a game of chess, there are very significant similarities between the two types of pattern.[4]

*   *   *

This contrast between a game of draughts and a game of chess exemplifies two different parts of my argument: firstly it illustrates the distinction between signal-response behaviour, which is predominantly characteristic of animals, and grammatically structured behaviour, which is predominantly characteristic of human beings in culturally defined situations. Secondly it brings out what is really special about grammatically structured behaviour. . . .

In draughts, there is just one kind of piece and at any time only two possibilities apply to any particular piece: firstly it can either move or not move; secondly, if it can move, it can move half left or half right. Signal-response animal behaviour is usually restricted in comparable ways. But in chess there are seven different kinds of piece (King, Queen, Pawn, Castle, Knight, Black Bishop, White Bishop) and different rule possibilities apply to each kind. Furthermore, the moves that are open to any particular piece depend not only on what kind of piece it is but on the distribution of all the other pieces on the board. This ordinarily provides an almost uncomputable range of alternative possibilities; most human custom is open-ended in the same sort of way. Indeed it is the unpredictable flexibility of the details of human behaviour which, more than anything else, differentiates man from other animals. And it is particularly in this respect that chess is also analogous to ordinary language, for here again a limited set of rules of grammar, when applied to a particular context, allows the speaker to say an infinite variety of different things and still be understood; he can be understood not so much because of the words he uses as because of the way they are arranged, in groups and ordered relationships. It is not sufficient just to utter words one after another; meaningful speech has to conform to an overall pattern, it must conform to the "rules of the game".

*　　*　　*

In the same way when we feel (either consciously or unconsciously) that we "understand" what is going on around us in the context of everyday life it is because we are interpreting the behaviour of our neighbours by making the assumption that the overall pattern of what they are doing conforms to "the rules of the game". You can tolerate what I am saying because, however pointless it may seem to be, you can predict with considerable confidence that in about forty minutes time you will have a chance to get up and go away.

The rules of the game in this latter case are cultural conventions (or customs) which we are likely to describe as fashions (when we are talking about dress), style (when we are talking about art or architecture), "basic principles of morality" (when we are talking about social and political organization). I concede that it is an hypothesis rather than a proven fact that these cultural rules are all structured "like" the rules of phonology and grammar which govern the production of speech. But my argument is that, since both true language and fully flexible cultural behaviour are unique peculiarities of human beings, it is rather likely that we carry out both kinds of activity in much the same way.

Anyway, for those who make this kind of assumption,—and they include myself—the prime task of the sociologist is to spell out what the rules are in their most fundamental form and to discover how they work.

Obviously this is a very complicated matter and the most that I can possibly do in a lecture of this sort is to give you some very rough illustrations.

LINEAR AND NON-LINEAR COMMUNICATION CODES

The most obvious characteristic of ordinary speech is that it is sequential—the words come from our mouths one after another. When we transcribe speech into writing we represent this sequence in time by linear relations in space. Nearly all modes of ordinary writing do this—ancient Egyptian hieroglyphs, Chinese ideograms, Arabic script, Roman script, and so on. But by stressing the linear aspects of speech in this way ordinary writing draws our attention away from other factors. The meaning of an utterance is not wholly contained in the sequence of the words or in the sequence of the grammatical components of the utterance; as a rule, the pace at which the words are uttered, the way they are stressed, the tone of the voice and so on all give added meaning. When we listen to speech we are not just decoding a single melodic line of sound, we are responding to a complicated harmony of several different kinds of signal all reaching the ear at the same time. When speech is written down in print most of the harmony is left out, but the reader is able to feed it back again because he "knows the language".

There are several relevant points that I would like to make here. First of all, it is not the case that *all* forms of writing are linear and melodic. Outside the context of books and newspapers there are all sorts of occasions when we use writing and diagrams in non-linear ways.

The most familiar example is that of a map, and there are many different kinds of map. If you decide to take your car to the South of France you will probably plan your journey in two ways. You will first buy a road map which represents the world as a flat land reduced to a rectangle of paper according to various standardized conventions, but you may also ask the A.A. to provide you with an itinerary. This will come in the form of a list of place names arranged vertically on one side of the page running from top to bottom, with a linear representation of the route running from bottom to top on the other.

Most of us are able, without too much difficulty, to translate any one of these three kinds of road guide into either of the other two and then to relate all three to the actual journey through space and time. But if you try to work out in detail just how you manage to do this you will see that it is a complex process. In order to understand the A.A.'s instructions in relation to the map you first have to accept a whole set of ad hoc transcription rules which are quite as elaborate as those which allow you to interpret linear writing as if it were sequential speech, or to transpose a written text in French into spoken English. And believe me, these rules are very elaborate even though quite young children can master them with ease. What I want you to recognize here is that the operations of "translation" and "transcription" are regularly applied to many other fields of human activity besides that of speech. In all kinds of contexts we can read meanings into one set of cultural products and then reinterpret those meanings by projecting them into another set of cultural products.

My second point is that linear transcriptions of information such as those which we encounter on the printed page of a newspaper are very inefficient. When we first learn to write, it is brought home to us that language is sequential and therefore we are liable to suppose that all other message bearing systems ought also to be sequential. But this is not so and provided we do not restrict ourselves in this way we can (and do) make much more effective use of the information space that is available by using patterned arrangements of other kinds.

In mathematics, for example, matrix algebra is ordinarily written out in little square diagrams which make the page look like a game of noughts and crosses. In this case, whatever is stated in the matrix rectangle could also be written out at much greater length in linear form but, since the sequential order of the operations doesn't matter, the linearity in this case would be redundant.

A more familiar case, which combines both linear and non-linear elements, is that of written music. Music like speech is heard as a sequence of patterned sounds, and on the written page we again represent the melodic sequence *in time* as a linear arrangement *in space*. But in order to represent harmony, in which several different sounds are heard simultaneously, we superimpose a vertical score on the left-to-right linear melody. These particular examples are drawn from our own culture but my general point is that reading and writing should not be regarded as a special kind of trick peculiar to highly sophisticated people who own typewriters and fountain pens. Diagrammatic, non-linear non-verbal writing can serve as a condensed store of information in just the same way as does the page of a book, and it is not necessary to be literate in order to understand diagrams. Many primitive peoples—the Australian Aborigines for example—who are completely "illiterate" in the ordinary sense of that term habitually annotate their story-telling with very complicated non-linear diagrams.[5] The fact that European observers can learn to understand these diagrams without too much difficulty demonstrates that they are coded in a quite systematic way.

Evidence of this kind suggests very strongly that all our different human forms of writing and patterned symbolic representation share with language itself certain basic coding procedures which are not just a peculiarity of particular languages or particular cultures but are human universals.

THE CODING OF NON-VERBAL CUSTOM

Perhaps all this is obvious, but if you have come with me so far then you must come the rest of the way. If you concede that coded description of visual diagrams is likely to have much the same relation to human thought as does the coded patterning of speech or the coded patterning of a written text, then you must also agree that when speech utterances are "represented" by dramatic forms or by dancing or by ceremonial of any kind, it must be the case that we can "understand" what the drama is about because it shares a common structure with the speech form of which it is a transcription.[6] But if this shared structure exists, how on earth do we set about finding out what it is? What is the language code of non-verbal human custom?

Anthropologists who have puzzled about this problem have so far borrowed two major ideas from the linguists. First of all, they find relevance in Jakobson's notion of "distinctive features linked with binary oppositions".[7] I don't know how far that sort of jargon rings any bells. Roughly speaking, Jakobson's point is simply this. When we decode a segment of speech-sound so as to give it meaning, the discriminations which we unconsciously distinguish are such contrasts as those between a vowel and a consonant, between a voiced consonant such as *b* and an unvoiced consonant such as *p*, between high frequency noise such as *i* and low frequency noise such as *u*. At this sort of level all the thousands of human languages which now exist operate in very much the same way.

Secondly, the anthropologists are becoming increasingly interested in what modern linguists of the school of Chomsky have got to say about the nature of grammar. The particular Chomskyan point that seems relevant is this: When we make a speech utterance we order the sounds in a particular sequence. In order to do this, we have to apply "rules of the game" as in my Game of Chess example. Evidently, the rules of the game—the rules of grammar and phonology—do not specify exactly what I must say in order to convey a particular meaning, for in most cases I can say the same thing in several different ways. For example:

"I am bored to tears with this lecture" means just the same as
"This lecture bores me to tears",

but although the words can be arranged in a number of different ways and still make sense the permissible sequences are very far from random. Thus you can't say

"Me tears this bores lecture to"

and claim that you are still talking English.

The Chomskyan problem is how to specify a set of rules which will enable the speaker to distinguish between sense and non-sense.[8] In practice, the linguists have become rather adept at spelling out rules which apply to particular languages such as English and French. What is much less clear is whether there are also deep-level rules which apply to all human languages everywhere. Clearly if we could discover such rules, we should be reaching deep down into the structure of human thought itself.

Anthropologists, like linguists, are faced with a "Chomskyan problem" of this sort. Our non-verbal customs are not rigidly determined as they would be if they were controlled by a simple signal-response mechanism. In almost every situation each individual has a wide range of choices. But some combinations of possible behaviour are felt to be "right", others are felt to be "wrong" or even "absurd". How do we know which is which? And if we manage to spell out the rules for one particular culture, is there also some deeper level at which we can specify rules which are applicable to all cultures? Are there moral universals? And if there are how can we explain them?

Anthropologists have always been interested in trying to discover the determinants of custom, but this linguistic way of looking at the facts is a new development; as a style of investigation it is particularly associated with the name of Claude Lévi-Strauss, and tonight I can do no more than give some tentative hints of the direction in which it may be going.

The point has already been made that speech is a communication system superimposed on an essential biological process, that of breathing.[9] Much of Lévi-Strauss' work is concerned with communication systems superimposed on two other essential biological processes, that of eating and that of sexual intercourse.

It seems that in all human societies the activities surrounding food and sex are a prime focus of cultural interest and symbolic elaboration. These symbolic activities have two fields of special emphasis. Firstly, like language proper, they serve to establish communication between individuals—the sharing of food and drink or the arranging of a marriage is everywhere a most positive assertion of friendship—and secondly, they function as determinants of social time and social position. Let us disregard the second aspect of the matter and concentrate our attention on the question of communication.

Suppose for the sake of argument that categories of food and categories of sexuality constitute elements of a language or languages analogous to the phonemes, distinctive features, words, phrases etc. with which the linguists play their grammatical games—these would be languages in which, to take two particular examples, the contrast between raw and cooked or between virginity and motherhood would play a comparable role to the contrast between voiced and unvoiced consonants in English phonology. What sort of categories would we have to consider in order to decode such a language?

MORAL RULES AND GRAMMATICAL RULES

In the case of sexuality the opposition between "maleness" and "femaleness" is clearly of a radical kind just as in speech formation the opposition between "vowel" and "consonant" is radical, for without these oppositions our enquiry would have no subject matter, but other distinctive features are probably a good deal less standardized than they are in normal spoken languages. For example the incest code which creates a polar opposition between the categories "sister" and "wife" is not a human universal. Certainly every code of sexual behaviour is based on an elaborate set of category distinctions and within these categories there are detailed distinctions between what is "right" and what is "wrong" but such codes vary enormously, not only between one culture and another but also within a single culture according to the context of situation. Moreover the distinction "right"/"wrong" may vary in intensity,—there are forms of possible behaviour which practically never occur and others which occur very frequently even though everyone concerned will agree that they should not. The linguistic parallels are very close: there are all sorts of possible word combinations which are most unlikely to be uttered (simply because the grammatical rules of the language say that they would be quite meaningless), on the other hand there are many things which we say regularly but which we all agree should not be said, at any rate "in polite society". Significantly many of these things which are sayable but should not be said have a manifest sexual connotation.

If we were to pursue these parallels systematically so as to think about the sets of sexual conventions which prevail within any one culture (or even cross culturally) as if they were parts of a linguistic code then the object of our enquiry would be to discover the simplest set of implicit rules which would fully account for what men do. We know that at an explicit level sexual behaviour is supposed to be governed by formally expressed rules of morality, but do the two frames of discourse—the implicit and the explicit fit together? To find out we should need to investigate the following questions.

First we should have to consider, in the abstract, a matrix of all possible patterns of sexual activity—auto-erotic, homosexual, heterosexual, marital, non-marital, dyadic, multi-lateral and so on. And for each form or combinations of forms we would need to consider what instances are socially tolerated and in what contexts.

We should then need to design a set of rules which would discriminate exhaustively between what is acceptable and what is not in such a way as to allow for everything that is actually observed in the ethnographic evidence. Finally we should need to see how far this logically derived set of "grammatical rules" corresponds or does not correspond to the moral principles which are formally expressed by the people under discussion. As I have said, the overall objective would be to try to account for the discrepancy between the rules of the grammar and the rules of the moral system.

* * *

Unfortunately I cannot give you any example of how this might work out in practice because I don't think that anyone has yet attempted the job. Very recently Professor Burling of the University of Michigan has attempted a rather similar exercise with regard to the residence customs of the Garo of Assam but this only gets us part of the way.[10]

The reason that nothing much of this kind has yet been accomplished is that most anthropologists who have dabbled in these matters hitherto have failed to consider the total range of possibilities (as the linguistic model suggests we should) and have operated instead within the framework of their own culturally defined prejudices. They have tended to assume, for example, that because homosexual relations are intrinsically abnormal they can be left out of any general theoretical discussion, or they have assumed that rules which prohibit marriage (rules of exogamy) are always indistinguishable from rules which prohibit heterosexual relations between near kin (rules of incest) because that is how the rules happen to operate in the Western European cultures to which most of the anthropologists themselves belong.

One aspect of this particular problem is that anthropologists have, generally speaking, discussed questions relating to incest and exogamy and marriage preference in an intellectual box all by themselves while treating sexual misdemeanours of the kinds which, in English, we class as adultery, fornication, homosexuality, bestiality and the like as belonging to quite a different field of enquiry. The linguistic analogy implies that we should consider all such factors together as elements of a single set of distinctive features and syntactic rules. In linguistics, a satisfactory grammar must not only specify the rules which generate all permissible meaningful utterances, it must also include rules which discriminate against utterances which are meaningless or unacceptable. A satisfactory anthropological "grammar" of sexual custom (or of any other class of custom) would need to be equally all embracing. It is a nice idea but it is a job for the future.

THE GRAMMAR OF FOOD

The analysis of the grammar of food behaviour is rather more advanced. In the case of food, significance attaches not only to the details of who eats with whom but also to the nature of the food itself, how it is prepared, the circumstances and sequence in which it is eaten, and so on. What is "right" in one situation is "wrong" in another. When we invite our friends to share a formal meal, we are seldom content just to eat any food which happens to be available. Matters must be arranged with formality; seating arrangements are a matter of detailed protocol; the dishes are separately cooked in special ways; the order of their appearance is formal and predictable. Notice that, in this context, a "good" cook is one who can exercise imaginative originality while still conforming to a strictly defined code of rules. This would also be an appropriate definition of a "good" chess player. And it may be that this is what we really mean by "goodness" in general. The distinction which Chomsky makes between "competence" and "performance" may yet turn out to have implications for general morality. But to get back to the grammar and phonology of food. We eat some food raw, some roast, some smoked, some when it is going rotten. The attitudes involved are quite arbitrary—a Stilton cheese crawling with maggots is a delicacy, a piece of beef in the same condition is inedible. Pork is inedible to an orthodox Jew but edible to an orthodox Christian. Dog is inedible to either the Jew or the Christian if he happens also to be an Englishman, but might be perfectly edible to the Christian if he happened to be a Cantonese! And so on. The limiting case here is that of cannibalism. As you all know, there have been various historical societies which have considered that it was proper, even a duty, to eat the flesh of human beings, usually a slain enemy or a dead kinsman, practices which arouse in ourselves feelings of the utmost loathing.

But our values here are quite strikingly inconsistent. If you were required knowingly to drink a glass of human blood taken from a dead man, most of you would promptly be sick. But why? Incorporating the blood of another is not in itself objectionable. In an emergency you would be quite ready to submit to a blood transfusion. It is the eating and drinking that matters. Yet even though you would resent being asked to drink real human blood, many of you will quite cheerfully sip sacramental wine in church and declare that it *is* human blood!

Powerful and illogical reactions such as these, which discriminate in an arbitrary way between good food and bad food, are not rational but they correspond closely to the reactions which we exhibit towards right and wrong forms of speech[11] and towards right and wrong forms of sexual behaviour. For a European to drink human blood in a secular context would be the equivalent of uttering a peculiarly offensive blasphemy or committing a highly publicized act of incest.

As between one society and another the conventions of sexual behaviour, of eating behaviour, and of speech behaviour may vary enormously but just as our own customs seem to make coherent sense to ourselves because they are part of a "language" which we understand, so also the eccentricities of other people's customs make sense in their own proper context. But can we go further than that? Is there a general grammar of human attitudes to food which is common to all human cultures everywhere. Some of Lévi-Strauss's more recent work suggests that there might be. It is an intriguing idea. But for most people so far it is still very much a matter of "might be", a possibility rather than an established fact.

CODE SWITCHING

I fully appreciate that for those of you who are not themselves anthropologists (and perhaps even for some who are) this kind of code switching between propriety in speech, propriety in food choice, and propriety in sexual choice may seem completely unjustified and yet why not? Speech behaviour, eating behaviour, sexual behaviour are all patterned by custom; may it not be that the principles of patterning are very similar in each case? Just as the distinctive features of phonology seem to derive from a small number of basic binary oppositions, so also the symbolism of food seems to be constructed out of such elementary oppositions as *raw* versus *cooked* and *boiled* versus *rotten*, while correspondingly the symbolic values associated with marriage customs are constructed out of such simple pairs as male versus female, sister versus wife. Furthermore there seem to be some almost universal cross-references between these last two frames of discourse and that of language proper.

For example, it is notoriously difficult to devise a form of words which will serve as a universally satisfactory definition of the institution which in English we call marriage, but at a behavioural level the problem seems less difficult. Ceremonials comparable to our wedding, which mark the legitimate beginning of a state of conjugal union, are to be found everywhere, and one of the markers of such ceremonials is that they always contain an element of food ritual. We ourselves treat this aspect of the matter very lightly but, even so, one of the ritual essentials of our custom is that the bride and bridegroom should jointly cut and eat their wedding cake. Elsewhere it may be a matter of eating from the same dish, drinking from the same cup, eating of the same sacrifice . . . but a marriage ceremonial which did not at some stage require the bride and bridegroom to exhibit their newly established sexual relationship by a demonstration of commensality would be most unusual. Anthropologists have long been aware that the deep-rooted equations between orality and sexuality which were postulated by early psycho-analytic theory receive strong support from the evidence of ethnography . . . what is now being proposed is that these basic patterns tie in closely with those which emerge from the study of general linguistics.

THE ORCHESTRATION OF COMMUNICATION

It is time that I wound up. I have been arguing mainly from analogy. Let me emphasize again what these analogies are:

I have already made the point that there is, at the present time, a great deal of interest among linguists in how it comes about that grammatical rules only partly determine the sequential order of the elements of a verbal expression and that even when he obeys the rules the speaker still has a wide area of choice in the details of what he says. A similar problem is of great interest to anthropologists. How much is determined by the rules, how much is optional? If you were to attend a series of English weddings in fairly quick succession it is unlikely that any two would be at all alike *in detail*, yet at a rather gross level they will all be, quite clearly, ceremonials of the same type. How then can we distinguish between the basic grammatical principles—the rules of the game which allow us to say that these performances are all "proceedings of the same type"— and the subsidiary contingent rules which allow for individual variation? I do not know the answer, but it seems highly likely that the investigations of linguists in the field of generative and transformational grammars will provide very profitable analogies for the anthropologist whose concern is with the transformational rules which govern custom. And of course what goes for weddings goes for any other kind of institutionalized sequence of events which you care to mention.

But the analogy should not be pressed too far. Earlier on I made the point that although a spoken utterance, when considered in isolation, is primarily a sequential phenomenon which on that account may conveniently be represented by linear writing, this linear aspect of speech must be contrasted with the multidimensional aspect of musical harmony. In his more recent writings Lévi-Strauss has argued with some force that if we are searching for an analogy for the structural patterning of non-verbal custom we should probably take music rather than speech as our model. Any customary activity is, like both speech and music, a process in time—it has a beginning, a middle and an end. But in the case of custom, at any particular moment in the proceedings, a great many very different things are usually all happening at once. The linear melodic theme which provides "the main plot" may really be only a minor part of the whole story. To see what is going on we need to study the orchestration.

* * *

None of which is at all satisfactory. All that I have really been saying is that what is now happening in the field of general linguistics is providing very great stimulus to the anthropologists, but that if ever we manage to come anywhere near to establishing a general grammar of customary behaviour the resulting rules are going to look like those of a very multi-dimensional game of chess. It's good fun, but whether the exercise is likely to be profitable is still open to doubt.

NOTES

1   Lecture 8, p. 167 (Ed.)
2   See Claire and W. M. S. Russell's discussion of dolphin signals, and the possibilities of language, Lecture 8, pp. 176–8 (Ed.)
3   Cf. the Russells' theory of the origin of language, Lecture 8, pp. 184–7 (Ed.)
4   Those who are interested in the utility and limitations of this kind of analogy may find it useful to refer to J. R. Pierce: *Symbols, Signals and Noise* (London, 1962), pp. 112–23 noting that Pierce's oversimplified sketch of Chomsky's ideas (p. 113) fits fairly well with my own oversimplified description of how to play a game of chess! The sceptics however will find support in C. F. Hockett: *The State of the Art* (The Hague, 1968), pp. 49–50; 85–7.
5   N. D. Munn: "Visual Categories: An Approach to the Study of Representational Systems", *American Anthropologist* Vol. 68 (1966), pp. 936–50.
6   Cf. Colin Cherry's warning: "The choice of signs for expression can reveal or conceal truth". Lecture 13, p. 272. However, he also points out that forms expressing systems of thought require rules, p. 276 (Ed.)
7   See Eugénie Henderson's summary, Lecture 2, pp. 46–9 (Ed.)
8   See John Lyons' outline and discussion of surface and deep structure rules. Lecture 3. (Ed.)
9   R. H. Robins, Lecture 1, p. 17 (Ed.)
10 Robbins Burling: "Linguistic and Ethnographic Description", *American Anthropologist* Vol. 71 (1969), pp. 817–27.
11 See Randolph Quirk's discussion of "Attitudes to Usage", Lecture 14, pp. 303–6 (Ed.)

FURTHER READING

GUMPERZ, J. J. and HYMES, D. (Eds.): *The Ethnography of Communication, American Anthropologist Special Publication* (December 1964).

HOIJER, H. (Ed.): *Language in Culture* (Chicago, 1954).

HYMES, D. (Ed.): *Language in Culture and Society*, a reader in Linguistics and Anthropology (New York, 1964).

LEACH, E.: *Lévi-Strauss* (London, 1970).

LÉVI-STRAUSS, C.: *The Savage Mind* (London, 1962).

LÉVI-STRAUSS, C.: *Structural Anthropology* (London, 1968).

ROMNEY, A. K. and D'ANDRADE, R. G.: *Transcultural Studies in Cognition, American Anthropologist Special Publication* (June 1964).

WHORF, B. L.: *Language, thought and reality* (Cambridge, Massachusetts, 1956).

8

Language and animal signals

CLAIRE RUSSELL
W. M. S. RUSSELL

University of Reading

The idea that animals have their own language or languages is an old one. Folklore teems with examples, and the subject is allotted several pages in Stith Thompson's enormous *Motif-Index of Folk Literature*. Methods of learning animal languages vary widely. You can do it by wearing a magic ring, like King Solomon, or by taking a cocktail of dragon's blood, like Siegfried. But there are much simpler ways, such as having your ears cleaned out, or carrying churchyard mould in your hat. Several people have published dictionaries of animal languages. The Abbé Guillaume-Hyacinthe Bougeant, a Jesuit Professor, published a glossary for several bird and mammal species in 1739, and got into serious trouble with his superiors. The French aristocrat Dupont de Nemours is famous for founding in America a firm that is one of the biggest in the world today (partly thanks to developing and making nylon). He had other interests, and in 1807 he compiled Crow-French and Nightingale-French dictionaries. In recent times, an English-Ape and Ape-English dictionary has been produced by a former assistant director of Washington Zoo called Schwidetsky. The chimpanzee word for "food", according to Schwidetsky, is *ngahk*; it is related to the German word for "nutcracking", which is *knacken*.

LANGUAGE AND SIGNAL CODES

We need not really worry unduly about the linguistic relations of German and Chimpanzee. But the idea that some animals may be capable of language is far from ridiculous. As we shall see, it is a matter of serious scientific study in the later 20th century. At first sight, indeed, there seems to be a lot in common between human spoken language and the calls used by a great variety of animals. A human language can be broken down into units of sound called *phonemes*,[1] which include consonants, vowels and certain double consonants and double vowels such as *ch*/[tʃ] and *ou*[au] (as in *house*). In terms of patterns of sound waves of different frequencies, a given phoneme is by no means always identical. Thus the *p* sounds in the words *pin*, *spin* and *nip* are somewhat different from each other in physical properties. But an English-speaker will recognize all of them as the *p* phoneme. English has between 35 and 45 of these phonemes, according to whether certain double vowels are counted as one or two units each. Italian has 27 phonemes, which must be a satisfactory number from the musical point of view, since Italian sounds so good when it is sung. The different human languages vary widely in number of phonemes, from 11 to 67. Any of us can make far more different sounds than this, and hence can learn other languages; but we rely on the basic number of phonemes when speaking our own language. Now animal call systems can similarly be broken down into basic signal units or calls, and the numbers of such units for different species of mammals and even birds fall roughly into the same range as do the numbers of phonemes of human languages, as is clear from the Table.

Animal Species	Number of Identified Basic Vocal Signals
Birds	
Chaffinch	12
Domestic chicken	20
European finch	20
White-throated warbler	25
Lower Mammals	
Coati	7
Brown lemur	7
Tree-shrew	8
Domestic and wild cow	8
Prairie dog	10
Pig	23
Fox	36
Dolphins	
Amazon freshwater dolphin, pulsed sounds (e.g. "squawk")	7
Pilot whale, whistles	7
Pacific bottlenose dolphin, whistles	16

Animal Species	Number of Identified Basic Vocal Signals
Pacific common dolphin, whistles	19
Atlantic bottlenose dolphin, whistles	17
Atlantic bottlenose dolphin, pulsed sounds	11
Monkeys and Apes	
Gray langur	10
Night monkey	10
Patas monkey	11
Cynocephalus baboons	15
Gibbon	15
Rhesus monkey	17
Howler monkey	20
Gorilla	23
Chimpanzee	25
Squirrel monkey	26
Vervet monkey	36
Japanese monkey	37
Human Languages	11–67

On this basis alone, we might be tempted to regard human languages and animal call systems as quite comparable. But the number of vocal units is not everything, and we need not suppose that Japanese monkeys, with 37 units, must be more sophisticated than human speakers of Hawaian, who make do with 13. About 2300 years ago, Aristotle put his finger on the crucial point. "The articulated signs of human language", he declared, "are not like the expression of emotions of children or animals. Animal noises cannot be combined to form syllables." It is the principle of combination that makes all the difference.

Aristotle was, however, being rather dogmatic. If we are seriously to consider whether any animals have languages, we must begin by considering some properties of languages and automatic signal codes. To begin with, human spoken language is generally conveyed by sound; and, as we've just seen, many animal signals are also calls. But this is not an essential feature of either language or animal signals. There are several different types of true sign or gesture language, evolved for communication between the deaf and dumb and between monks of religious orders forbidden to talk. These sign or gesture languages are perceived through the eyes instead of the ears. Animal signal codes too are often predominantly gestures or postures to be seen by the recipient. In teaching severely handicapped children such as Helen Keller, use has been made of communication by touch, and touch signals are also widely used by animals. Human language is not normally conveyed by smell or taste, though it could conceivably be coded in this way, but elaborate chemical signals are quite common among animals and simpler ones are involved in the human perfume industry. So the use of a particular physical medium or sense is not a crucial feature of language.

Another distinction we can make also cuts across the distinction between true language and automatic signal codes. Both can convey messages about two different kinds of things, which we can sum up as *emotion* and *economics*. We can talk about how we feel about somebody else; we can also talk about natural surroundings, things, techniques and technical aspects of our life in society. In the same way an animal's signals may convey, for instance, a readiness to groom another animal's coat (emotion) or the presence of food or danger (economics). This is an important distinction, but it is no help in deciding what is or is not true language.

The use of symbols or symbolization used to be regarded as unique to human language. This is now known to be nonsense. Symbolization simply means that a set of things or events can be translated into a set of signals, with one signal for each, and that the individual who receives the signals can translate them back into the things symbolized. There is no doubt at all that animals can symbolize in this sense, both as signallers and receivers, as we shall see most clearly in the case of honeybees. A more interesting contrast is that between two kinds of symbols, *representative* and *arbitrary*. A representative symbol has something structurally in common with the thing symbolized. When a herring gull lifts his wrist joints as if about to unfold his wings, and holds his head up straight with beak pointing downwards, this actually *looks like* the beginning of a fighting attack, in which the gull would raise his wings to beat his opponent, and raise his head to peck downwards from above. The raising of the wrist joints and the position of the head are examples of *intention movements*; they symbolize attack, and act as a threat: a gull so threatened will often retreat. On the other hand, an arbitrary symbol bears no particular formal resemblance to the thing it symbolizes. Herring gulls in a conflict between the urges to attack and flee may resolve their problem by doing a third, irrelevant thing derived from some other behaviour context—a *displacement activity*, as it is called. They may, for instance, pluck at the grass as if gathering material for a nest. This does not look at all like a real attack, but it also comes to symbolize attack, and acts as a threat which may cause another gull to retreat. Niko Tinbergen has shown that intention movements and displacement activities are the basic units of signal codes in many animal species: animals thus use both representative and arbitrary symbols.

Human language relies heavily on arbitrary symbols. The sound of the word *sun*, for instance, has nothing structurally in common with the sun itself. It is true that we sometimes use representational symbols in language. In spoken language, words that symbolize sounds often resemble the sounds themselves: words such as *thunder* and *hiss* really represent what they symbolize. In American Sign Language, used by the deaf in North America, many signs are arbitrary, but the symbol for *flower* is touching the two nostrils in turn with the tip of the tapered hand, which clearly suggests smelling a flower. Representational effects of a subtler kind are important in poetry, as Pope observed in his *Essay on Criticism*.

> 'Tis not enough no harshness gives offence,
> The sound must seem an Echo to the sense:
> Soft is the strain when Zephyr gently blows,
> And the smooth stream in smoother numbers flows;
> But when loud surges lash the sounding shore,
> The hoarse, rough verse should like the torrent roar.

But, on the whole, the lavish use of arbitrary symbols is a great advantage. Only by arbitrary symbols can we represent such complicated or abstract conceptions as *Institute*, *Contemporary* or *Arts*. We can see this well in the special case of written language, which advanced from simple picture signs as representational symbols to arbitrary symbols for the sound units of spoken language, and hence for the things which are symbolized in turn by the patterns of sound units making up words.

In the long run, too, arbitrary symbols lend themselves most readily to the formation of many combinations and recombinations. And here we do come to a crucial feature of true language. The signal units of many animals can be put together in many different combinations. Thus the calls and facial expressions of monkeys consist of units which can be combined in many ways. For instance, rhesus monkeys, observed at Whipsnade Zoo by Vernon Reynolds, had a number of different signal units for threat, such as bobbing the head up and down, raising the eyebrows, drooping the eyelids, opening the mouth without showing the teeth, and making a low-pitched noise described as *hough*. A number of different combinations of these units could be observed, according to the intensity of aggression expressed.[2] Even the threat postures of gulls can show a number of different combinations of units signalling various intensities of the urges to attack and flee, as Niko Tinbergen and his colleagues have shown.

But these animal signal combinations are both governed and limited by the close relation here between emotion and its expression in vocal and postural and facial symbols. Each signal is tied to a particular emotional state, and signal combinations reflect only combinations of emotions. Some combinations, for instance of units expressing extreme fear with units expressing extreme sexual desire, are simply impossible. Now any symbol units of true language can be uttered in any emotional state. Hence many new combinations become possible, and emotional rules of combination are replaced by logical ones, which we call grammar and syntax. In this way it becomes possible to form at any time totally new combinations of symbols, which the speaker may never have used before, and even combinations which no member of his language-group has ever used before. Human languages vary in their vocabularies or terms of reference, but they all have this potential flexibility. During World War II, when young East Africans were being trained for the Bantu Rifles, a problem arose because there were no words for "red" or "green" in the local language.[3] The problem was easily solved by using the phrases *colour of blood* and *colour of leaves*. By similar means, totally new situations can be described, or totally new possibilities envisaged. This power of producing new combinations is crucial to true language.

R. J. Pumphrey has noted another advantage of detaching symbols from the direct expression of immediate emotion. An alarm call indicating the presence of a lion is given only when the calling animal is feeling the special fear associated with seeing or hearing or smelling a lion. The word *lion*, on the other hand, can be used when no lions are about. "Whereas an emotive lion is necessarily in the present, an intelligible lion could be discussed in the future or in the past; and so tradition and forward planning about lions became possible."

True language,[4] therefore, involves the free combination of symbols limited only by logical rules of grammar and syntax, which themselves express *relations between* symbols and hence symbolize *relations between* things and individuals and events. In addition, true language must involve true communication. Compulsive utterance of signals in the absence of other individuals is not true communication. And signalling which produces automatic effects on other individuals is mere interaction. In true communication the signaller transmits information which enables the recipient to behave more freely, to have a greater range of choice and decision; so whereas interaction reduces, communication increases the variability of the recipient's behaviour. No doubt the combination of all these qualities is necessary before we can speak of true language, as opposed to an automatic code of signals.

AN ANIMAL WITHOUT TRUE LANGUAGE

Equipped with these general ideas, we can consider more exactly whether any animals have true languages. To begin with, it is worth glancing at the signal code of an animal which certainly cannot talk, namely the human infant[5]—the word *infant* is simply the Latin root meaning "speechless". Infants have, in fact, a very simple signalling system with at most 8 sound units. These are said to correspond to phonemes, 5 vowels and 3 consonants, but they are certainly not used as elements to be combined in a language. Four kinds of infant cries have been studied in 351 infants in Sweden and Finland, by means of sound spectrographs, which display on a sort of graph called a sonagram the amount of energy produced at different sound frequencies over the time-course of a cry. Birth cries were produced only at birth. Pain cries were produced when the baby was vaccinated. Hunger cries were produced about 4 hours 20 minutes after a feed. Pleasure cries were produced when the infant, after being fed and changed, was lying comfortably in bed or in the mother's or nurse's arms. The sonagrams showed that each kind of cry varied considerably but always differed in definite ways from the other 3 kinds of cry. Each cry was uttered only in its appropriate situation, so there was no question of combining them to produce, say, a sentence like *I was hungry, now I am comfortable*, still less to describe something unusual and new. All this, perhaps, is a bit obvious. But it shows rather clearly what we mean by a simple signal code as opposed to a true language. Adults have to interpret the signals much as they try to interpret the signals of a cat or a dog.

High-fidelity tape recordings of 6 of each of the 4 kinds of cries were played to 483 adults under 50, including 349 women, and these people were asked to identify the cries as birth, pain, hunger or pleasure cries. They were far from perfectly accurate in their interpretations. Pleasure cries were easiest to recognize, with 85% correct interpretations; then came hunger cries, 68%; pain cries, 63%; and birth cries, which most people hear very rarely, with only 48% correct interpretations. Experience naturally helps in such matters. Children's nurses were better at recognizing pain and hunger cries than mothers who had only had one child each; and, not surprisingly, the top score for recognizing birth cries was obtained by midwives.

If the signals of babies are so relatively difficult to interpret, it will be clear that it takes much work and skill to understand animal signals. The great decoders of animal signal codes, such as Karl von Frisch, Konrad Lorenz and Niko Tinbergen, have had to use as much ingenuity as those of Cretan Linear B or the script of the Mayas. If we are to consider whether any animals have true languages, we shall naturally focus our attention on the most promising candidates, whose signalling is enormously more elaborate than that of human babies. These animals fall into three groups, which we shall consider in turn, beginning with the extraordinary code of the honeybees. It is simplest to describe this as a language; whether it deserves to be called a true language will appear when we have seen what it does.

THE DANCE OF THE HONEYBEE

In 1788, Pastor Ernst Spitzner reported a surprising fact. When a honeybee finds a good supply of honey, she returns to the hive and there performs a curious circular dance. Spitzner put out some honey, brought 2 bees to it, watched them dance on their return to the hive, and saw that many of their fellow-bees came to the honey-place. He concluded that the returning bees had somehow told their colleagues about the honey. It was a beautiful observation and a true inference, but Spitzner went no further, and it was left to Karl von Frisch, in our own age, to interpret the language of the honeybees. How he made his discoveries can be read in his books. Here we will simply summarize some of what he and Martin Lindauer and their colleagues discovered, beginning with the language of the Carniolan honeybee.[6]

When a honeybee of this race discovers a new source of honey within about 10 m. of the hive, she returns to the hive and regurgitates drops of honey which are eagerly drunk by other bees. Then she begins to dance round in a circle; first she goes one way round, then she reverses and goes the other way round, then another reverse, and so on. This is called the *round dance*. Other bees follow her about, holding their antennae against her abdomen. After dancing, she "refuels" by taking a drop or two of honey back from some other bee, and flies back to the food source, which in natural conditions is a flower or group of flowers. The other bees who followed the dance do not fly after her. They fly out in all directions. But, fairly soon, a lot of them find the new food source. They do so because they have smelt the scent of the flower that clung to the dancer's body, and so look for the right kind of flower. In one experiment, bees informed by a dancer found the right flowers in a section of the Munich Botanical Garden where 700 different plant species were blooming at once. The round dance, therefore, tells the other bees to go out and search the near neighbourhood of the hive; the scent on the dancer's body tells them what flowers to look for.

But honeybees can forage for food at far greater distances than 10 m. They have been known to fly more than 13 km. in search of honey. A honeybee is only about 13 mm. long, so 13 km. for a bee is the equivalent of about 1000 miles for a human being—not a bad commuting trip. But of course, even at much smaller distances, a round dance would not be much use. If the discoverer of new food told her colleagues to go out and search in all directions for several km., she might just as well save her energy. They would never find the flowers. So when a Carniolan honeybee finds food at a considerable distance from the hive, say between 100 m. and 10 km., she returns to the hive, offers the honey she has found, and then performs a different kind of number, called a *tail-wagging dance*, which is somewhat reminiscent of the Charleston or Black Bottom. She dances along in a straight line for a certain distance, wagging her tail for all she is worth and buzzing away by means of slight vibrations of the muscles that flap her wings in flight. It is as if she was, so to speak, flying on the spot. At the end of this *waggling run*, she stops buzzing and wagging her tail, circles round to one side back to where she started, does another waggling run, circles round to the opposite side, does a third waggling run, circles to the first side, and so on. A number of other bees follow her around, showing special interest in the waggling runs. Bees cannot hear sounds in air, but they can feel the buzzing vibrations through the surface on which the dance is done. Like the round dance, the tail-wagging dance tells the bees who follow it that there is food available, and what flowers to look for, from the smell. But it tells them much more than this. It tells them exactly how far away the flowers are, and in exactly what direction. And so, even at distances of km., the bees who study the dance can fly with precision to the spot indicated and find the honey-bearing flowers.

The distance to the food is conveyed by the tempo of the dance. A quickstep tempo means a relatively nearby food source, a slow foxtrot tempo a more distant one. To be exact, as the distance increases so does the duration of each waggling run. A single waggling run may be inaccurate, but Von Frisch and his colleagues have shown that the bees who follow the dance study several waggling runs and calculate the average duration, which they then translate into distance by a mathematical rule.

The tail-wagging dance is sometimes done on a horizontal surface just outside the hive. When this happens, the dancer indicates the direction of the food by aiming her waggling run in exactly this direction. She can only do this if she can see the sun (or the polarized light of the blue sky, which indicates the position of the sun to bees, though not to us). So actually she is taking up a position in which she sees the sun at the same angle as during her flight to the honey source. The waggling run makes the same angle with the sun as her outward flight did.

But the dance is normally performed in the dark inside the hive, on the *vertical* surface of the comb. Here the angle between the flight path and the sun is translated into the angle between the waggling run and the vertical direction straight upwards. Thus if the flight path was, say, 30° to the right of the sun's position, the waggling run will be 30° to the right of the vertical. This symbolism is remarkable enough, but the dancing bee's achievements go even further. If on the flight there is a sidewind, the bee corrects for the tendency to drift sideways by flying with her body at an oblique angle to the flight path. So the angle at which she sees the sun is not the same as the angle between sun and flight path. Nevertheless, in the dance, she makes the necessary correction, and tells the other bees the true angle between sun and flight path. More remarkable still, if she has reached her goal (and returned from it) by an L-shaped detour, she uses the angles and lengths of the 2 segments of the flight to calculate the true direction of the goal by straight-line flight, and this is the direction she conveys in her dance, although she has never flown this direct route herself. One critic objected to the idea of a bee calculating, and proposed instead "a kind of 'mixture' of the neuronal learning effects during the segments". As Von Frisch observes, this is "a statement that simply clothes the phenomena in other words".

As for the bees who are following the dance, they are working literally in the dark and can only use touch to find out the angle of the dancer's waggling run with the vertical. They translate this back into a visual angle with the sun, fly off in this direction (allowing for any bending *they* have to do to oppose a sidewind) for the distance signalled by the waggling run tempo, and look for flowers of the scent they smelled on the dancer. Many experiments by Von Frisch and his colleagues show that they duly find the food.

On 14 August 1946, Von Frisch returned from a trip in the mountains to his field base. His daughters told him they had set up a new station with sugar-water for the bees in his experimental hive, but they would not tell him where it was. He must ask the bees! Von Frisch did ask the bees (by observing their dances), and he found the feeding station. On 22 September 1951, while doing some experiments, Von Frisch noticed lively dancing going on in a hive. He decoded the dances, entered the spot indicated on a map, and found it was a place (600 m. away) where a local dealer kept his bees. An assistant went over and found the dealer had just spun down honey from some combs, and then put them out in the sun for his own bees to gather back the remaining traces of honey. The assistant told the dealer Von Frisch's bees were stealing this honey and had told Von Frisch where it was. The dealer told the assistant he had to be joking, and never did believe this story, which, however, is perfectly true.

Even all this does not exhaust the symbolism of the honeybee dances. They can also vary in liveliness and total duration. They are livelier and longer the sweeter the food, the easier it is gathered, the better the weather. When honey is short in the hive, any returning bee will be eagerly badgered for honey drops, and this stimulates her to longer and livelier dances; when there is plenty of honey in the hive, the returning bee will have to search hard for customers, and this makes for shorter and less lively dances. If, of two food sources, one is richer, fewer customers are left for bees returning from the other, so even the relative attractions of different sources are represented. All this makes for flexibility and economy of labour and a readiness to exploit a variety of flowers as each ripens. The dances do not compel a reaction from every bee that the dancer meets; as Von Frisch nicely puts it, there is a most subtle regulation of "supply and demand on the flower market".

So far we have described the language of the Carniolan race of the honeybee. Other races have different dialects. German, North African, Caucasian, Italian and Egyptian honeybees[7] all begin to indicate distance and direction at much shorter distances than the Carniolan race. Italian honeybees, for instance, start indicating these data by a modified tail-wagging dance at about 10 m., as opposed to about 85 m. in the Carniolan bees. All the races indicate distance by dance tempo, but on different scales. Thus Italian honeybees dance slower than Carniolan ones for any distance of the food source. When a colony was made up of Italian and Carniolan bees, misunderstandings arose. When Italian bees danced, Carniolan ones flew too far; when Carniolan bees danced, Italian ones did not fly far enough. Each race was using their own scale to interpret the other's dances. Bees of different species, living in India and Ceylon, the Indian honeybee, dwarf honeybee and giant honeybee,[8] show similar but more extreme differences in tempo scales. The dwarf honeybee dances in the open on top of its comb, which is unprotected from the weather, and thus on a horizontal surface; unlike all the other honeybees, she cannot translate the angle with the sun into the angle with the vertical.

Wonderful as the bee language is in its precise and elaborate symbolism, there are many indications that it is really a matter of automatic signalling and not a true language after all. One experiment will perhaps make this clear. We have mentioned that the Italian bee uses a modified tail-wagging dance at 10 m. At smaller distances, this bee uses round dances in the usual way. On one occasion Von Frisch and his colleagues put a hive of these bees on the concrete foundation of a radio tower, and brought 10 bees a distance of 50 m. straight *up* the inside of the tower to a station with rich sugar water. The 10 bees flew down to the hive and danced "most vigorously" for 4 hours. But the honeybee languages contain no symbols for "up" or "down". All the dancers could do was to perform round dances (indicating that the food source was not far away *horizontally*). Consequently their colleagues all set out and scoured round the neighbourhood of the hive at ground level. Not one of them found her way up to the feeding station high up in the tower right over the hive. In Von Frisch's words, the dancers "sent their hivemates astray—their ability to communicate broke down when faced with the unaccustomed task". Thus the bee language, unlike human languages (such as the East African one we mentioned) cannot generate new combinations of symbols to describe a completely unusual event. We are bound to conclude it is not a true language. Studies of other insects suggest origins for both the round and the tail-wagging dances in automatic circling and wagging movements performed by flies and moths, respectively, without any communicative function. The moths even wag their bodies more the further they have just flown. Even the marvellous translation of sun angle into vertical angle can be seen to have developed from a widespread automatic tendency of insects to translate responses to light into responses to gravity in darkness. This arises from the simple fact that an insect can generally move upwards either by going towards the light or, of course, by going against gravity. What the honeybees have evolved from these elements is marvellous indeed, but it is not a true language.[9]

THE VOICE OF THE DOLPHIN

For our next candidates, we can choose animals much more like ourselves—individualistic mammals: the whales, dolphins and porpoises, notably dolphins and above all the best studied and so far the most remarkable species, the Atlantic bottlenose dolphin.[10] Dolphins are, so to speak, the monkeys of the sea: they have evolved many similar aspects of behaviour. Both groups of animals show prolonged and intense parental care for their young, and with this go very long-term relationships between mother and offspring. Amicable relations between 3 generations—grandmother, mother and daughter—have been seen among chimpanzees and in bottle-nose dolphins. Male Japanese monkeys and bottlenose dolphins "baby-sit" for the females when these are otherwise occupied; on one occasion, a bottle-fed baby dolphin, suffering from wind due to a badly composed formula, had his buoyancy relations upset and could not stay upright: he was cured in a rough but effective way by an adult male, who gave him a bang on the belly to empty out the wind. In both groups, mothers become so attached to their babies that they cannot be parted from them even after the baby has died of some illness. A rhesus monkey mother will carry a dead infant around till it is completely decomposed, and the same is observed in dolphin mothers, for instance one observed at sea "supporting the partially decomposed head of a dolphin young with its own head"; it "withdrew support only long enough to surface and breathe, then returned to its burden". Live dolphin infants are normally held at the surface after birth to enable them to take their first breath—for of course dolphins are mammals and need to surface regularly for air.

The prolonged parental care gives young dolphins, like young monkeys, the opportunity for a great deal of play and exploration. They make up a great variety of games. For instance, in captivity in a tank, one young dolphin will put an object over an intake jet and let it go, allowing the current of water to whirl it up towards the surface, where another youngster catches it, and immediately returns it to the jet while the first player goes up to catch it in his turn. Even as adults, dolphins, like monkeys, are highly exploratory animals.

The powerful parental urge is also extended, in both groups, to a care for the welfare and survival of other adults. In the wild, adult monkeys will remove thorns and clean wounds for each other, and a band of monkeys will rush into danger to rescue one of their number who has fallen down a well or been captured by human beings. In the open sea, adult dolphins and also many species of large whales will stand by a wounded comrade; 19th-century whalers knew this well, and would regularly wound a whale without killing it so that they could easily kill his comrades, who would not leave while he was alive; the procedure was risky, because sometimes the comrades managed to release the first victim or even attacked the whale-boats. Dolphins have extended to sick or injured adults the practice of holding the patient's head above water to let him breathe, just as they do with babies. When dynamite is exploded at sea near a school of dolphins, they will all leave the area at once. But on one occasion one dolphin was stunned by the explosion. Two comrades at once came and held the victim's head out of water; when they had to surface to breathe themselves, two others relieved them; the whole school stayed around till the stunned dolphin recovered completely, whereupon all left at once.

In captivity, under crowding stress, monkeys and dolphins can be as cruel as human beings under such pressures. Monkeys will cruelly wound and kill each other, including females and young. Dolphin adult males and females have been observed to bite juveniles and bash them against the tank wall, and one adult male bottlenose dolphin bit and bashed a small female so viciously, drawing much blood, that she had to be separated from him to save her life. But even in captivity, the care for others in distress can also be seen. J. C. Lilly found that sick dolphins often recover without treatment provided they are left with other dolphins, who support them at the surface. He found that dolphins will instantly help sick or stunned *strangers*, even of different species. On one memorable occasion, reported by D. H. Brown, a female Pacific Common Dolphin[11] was giving birth to a stillborn baby, whose fin stuck in the birth canal. Two females of *other* species acted as midwives. One of them[12] pulled out the foetus, and helped the mother to hold the stillborn baby at the surface (in vain, unfortunately). The other female[13] pulled out the afterbirth. On another occasion, Lilly reports that two bottlenose dolphins, male and female, supported a conscious adult female with a back injury at the surface for 48 hours till she recovered. They worked out 10 different methods of keeping her head out of water, the simplest being to hold her tail on the bottom in such a way that she was pushed upright. During this and similar occasions, Lilly has noted prolonged and complicated exchange of calls between the patient and his or her helpers, and it is hard to resist the suggestion that they may be exchanging requests and information in true language, or even discussing what to do.

The dolphin brain resembles the human brain in being very large and having its cerebral cortex (surface layer) very wrinkled, and in certain other respects.[14] But some say the cortex is so wrinkled only for mechanical reasons, because it is very thin, and that in fine structure of layering it is simpler and cruder, and has a lower density of nerve cells, than that of a rabbit. So if we seek for evidence from the dolphin brain about the dolphin's capabilities, we are back where we started. The behaviour observations, however, are so suggestive that in the past two decades people have been seriously studying the calls of the dolphins to find out whether they are a true language.

Dolphins are extremely vocal animals. As Gregory Bateson has put it, "adaptation to life in the ocean has stripped the whales of facial expression". Their heads and bodies are naked, rigid and streamlined, and anyway visibility under water is probably usually not good enough to recognize subtle facial expressions or bodily postures. So nearly all their signalling is by sound. It seems likely from records of their calls that they produce discrete vocal signal units in more elaborate sequences or combinations than any other animals, though this leaves open the question whether the rules of combination are emotional or truly logical, with grammar and syntax.

Dolphin calls are of three kinds. They produce sequences of clicks. These are probably used mainly for echolocation ("sound radar") but to some extent for signalling also—among sperm whales, where click sequences are the only calls, they are almost certainly used for signalling. The two other kinds of dolphin calls are pulsed sounds (such as squawks and mews) and whistles, and both these are certainly signals. The pulsed sounds are easily recognized as different-sounding unit calls. The analysis of the whistles can be done by exactly the methods used to analyse certain human languages.

A number of human languages, in North America, East Asia, and Africa south of the Sahara, are said to be *tonal*.[15] That is, much of the meaning of the words is carried by the relative *pitch* at which they are uttered. There are a varying number of pitch levels or *registers*, higher or lower. The voice goes up or down so that syllables are *relatively* higher or lower, and it is the difference or contrast and not the absolute pitch that matters; hence women and boys can talk on average at a higher pitch than men without misunderstandings. Tone may be so important that a language can be almost completely intelligible without hearing vowels and consonants at all. Hence many African tribes construct drums with the same number of registers (pitch levels) as their languages, and can transmit long conversations over long distances by drumming. The distinguishable units of tone languages are often *glides*, in which the voice goes up, down, up and down, down and up, starting and ending at different levels, changing pitch faster or slower, and so on. These units can be represented on paper as *contours*, in which a line goes up and down to represent rising and falling pitch; a contour in the shape of the letter V, for instance, would mean that the voice gets lower and then suddenly rises again in pitch by the same amount; and all other variations can be represented in this sort of way. A similar method was used for writing down music in Georgia in the 8th to 11th centuries A.D.

Some peoples speaking tonal languages have also evolved actual whistling languages which they use in addition. Whistling languages have been studied on Gomera Island in the Canaries, in the village of Aas in the French Pyrenees, and among the Mazatecos, Zapotecos and Tlapanecos of Mexico. Among the Mexican peoples, only the men whistle. It is considered bad form to raise the male voice, so the men began to communicate over the mountain trails by whistling. Women do not normally whistle, but they understand the language and can demonstrate it (with a certain embarrassment). G. M. Cowan heard a young man whistle to a girl for several minutes. It was far more detailed than a wolf whistle, and she understood every word he whistled—finally she answered him back furiously in ordinary words. These whistling languages can also be represented as sets of contours.

John J. Dreher and René-Guy Busnel have tried to study dolphin whistling as if it were a human tonal or whistled language (respectively). The idea is to represent each different whistle unit by a contour, and then try to decipher whole sequences of contours as if one were deciphering sequences of hieroglyphs from some ancient script, or, for that matter, the Georgian medieval musical contour notation, which actually has been deciphered from Georgian musical documents preserved in the monasteries of Mount Athos and Mount Sinai. Such decoding methods depend on analysing the frequency of different units and how they combine together. In addition, of course, since this is a living language, or at least a living signalling system, the occurrence of each different sound unit and each combination can be related first to what is happening to the signalling dolphin, and second to what other dolphins do in response. Both whistles and pulsed sounds have been studied in this way in Atlantic bottlenose dolphins, and Dreher has also played different whistle units back to dolphins and obtained different complicated responses in the form of actions and long sequences of calls. So far a number of units have been related to simple emotional situations, such as the distress call, a whistle of falling pitch, and the sex yelp of the male. But these are quite on a par with the simple automatic signal codes of many animals. Little progress has yet been made in deciphering long sequences of calls. J. C. Lilly, and later T. G. Lang and H. A. P. Smith, have recorded long exchanges of calls between pairs of dolphins who could not see each other. But many animals will exchange vocal signals, and there is no certain evidence that these are real conversations, though there is some indication that a dolphin can distinguish the naturally changing calls of another dolphin from repeated playback of a standard dolphin call recording.

It was against this background of uncertainty that Jarvis Bastian, in 1966, reported on a highly imaginative experiment. Two Atlantic bottlenose dolphins, a male and a female, were kept in a large tank and trained to work together in pressing paddles to be rewarded by an automat which disgorged fish when the proper paddles were pressed. At a certain stage in the complicated sequence of training procedures, the tank was divided by an opaque partition, with the male on one side and the female on the other. The arrangement was then as follows. Both the male and the female were warned by lamps being switched on that the game was ready to begin. Then another lamp was switched on to give *either* a continuous *or* a flashing light. In the former case, the right-hand paddle must be pressed, in the latter case the left-hand paddle. Now the female could see this signal lamp, but the male *could not see either the lamp or her.* Both dolphins got fish if, and only if, the *male first* pressed the correct paddle on his side of the tank, and *then the female* pressed the correct paddle on her side, there being a pair of paddles for each of them. So the male had to press the correct paddle without seeing the lamp that signalled which paddle to press.[16] On the face of it, he could only do this if *the female told him, by her calls, which paddle to press, when she saw whether the lamp was flashing or steady.* Nevertheless, over many thousands of runs, the male pressed the correct paddle and the dolphins succeeded in earning their reward on more than 90% of the tests. Analysis of the female's calls indicated that she made different pulsed sounds when her lamp was flashing and steady, responding sooner, longer and at faster pulse rate to the steady light; it is quite possible the male, hearing her, could tell the difference between the two kinds of call. The dolphins' success was only prevented if *either* the female was not rewarded with fish (as happened accidentally in two test series through a defect of her automat), *or* her signal light was hidden from her as well as from the male, *or* the barrier between male and female was made sound-proof. It seems certain from this amazing experiment that *in some sense* the female was telling the male whether the light was flashing or steady, so that he could press the correct paddle in response.

Was this true language? The dolphins were surely presented with a most unusual and novel situation and problem, and, unlike the honeybees, they solved it. Were they using a new combination of symbols to deal with this problem in communication? In 1966, the answer was uncertain. But alas! in 1969 Bastian published further findings. It now seemed all too clear that true language was not involved after all. Apparently the female went on giving her different calls in response to flashing and steady light when the barrier was taken down, the male could see the light himself, and the calls were quite superfluous. And she went on doing it after this even after the male had been taken out of the tank before her very eyes and she was "talking" all by herself. This and other detailed evidence made it extremely likely that the female had become conditioned to giving different calls in response to the different light signals, because this *worked* in getting her fish, without realizing that it worked by telling the male what to do; and that the male had become conditioned to pressing different paddles in response to the two different calls of the female, because this also *worked* for him, without realizing why she gave these calls. This is pretty remarkable in itself, and the male did make a very quick transfer from using visual clues (when he could see the signal lamp) to using sound clues (when he could only hear the female's calls); people have said in the past that this easy juggling between the senses was necessary for human language and not present in animals. But, after all, we cannot speak of true language where both signalling and reaction were conditioned and compulsive and not a true communication between individuals. So the dolphins, so far, like the bees, cannot be said to have a true language. There have been other indications that these enigmatic animals may not be quite so bright as they sometimes appear. One female bottlenose dolphin had a 5-foot leopard shark[17] in a tank with her. She apparently mistook it for a baby dolphin, and held its head repeatedly above water. Dolphins breathe in air, but sharks are fishes and breathe in water, and within a day the wretched shark had suffocated and died. So far this could have been the intelligent use for killing a shark of a technique evolved for saving baby dolphins. But the dolphin really was making a mistake, it seems, for she carried the dead shark about for 8 days as if it were a dead infant, fed little as if in mourning, and would not let divers take the carcass away till it was decomposed. It seems inescapable that this particular dolphin was not very bright, unless she was as short-sighted as Mr McGoo.[18]

THE MONKEY'S PAW

After honeybees and dolphins, it is natural to turn back to what have always seemed the most hopeful candidates for true animal language, the monkeys and apes (for convenience, we refer to both as *monkeys*). Though, as we have seen, monkeys have much in common with dolphins, they differ from them strikingly in at least one respect. They have agile bodies and mobile faces. Most species have considerable repertoires of calls, and some species living in dense forest rely heavily on these. But many species live partly on the ground and/or in relatively open country, where visibility is good; and these include the species we know most about. Among these monkeys, visual signals, made by gesture, posture and facial expression, are far more important than vocal signals made by calls. Thus in the rhesus monkey[19] colony studied by Vernon Reynolds at Whipsnade Zoo, 73 signal units could be distinguished. Of these 63 were visual signals, and only 10 were calls. In another rhesus community, Stuart A. Altmann recorded a total of 5504 signalling events. Only 5·1% of these social signals involved calls (with or without accompanying gestures), and only 3% consisted of calls alone. Comparable counts have not been made for chimpanzees, among whom the richness and sensitivity of facial expression are considerably greater than among rhesus monkeys.

Unlike the honeybee code, which concerns itself entirely with information about economics—whereabouts of food, weather conditions, state of the hive's food reserves, and so on—monkey signalling is mainly concerned with emotional states and events and interpersonal relationships. Thus 36 vocal units have been distinguished in vervet monkeys[20] by Thomas T. Struhsaker, working in the Amboseli Reserve of Kenya. Only 7 of these refer to events in the natural surroundings (sighting, approach or sudden movement of various kinds of predatory animals); 3 are not really signals (coughing, sneezing, vomiting); the other 26 all refer to different social situations (such as a subordinate monkey appeasing a dominant one nearby, a female protesting she is not in the mood for sex, or several monkeys warning of the approach of a "foreign" group of the same species).

In Struhsaker's study of the vervet monkeys, he found that the calls occurred in at least 21 different situations, and produced at least 22 different responses in the monkeys who heard them. As with the dolphins, studies of the situations evoking different signals and their effects on other individuals have been made in many monkey species, in this case for visual as well as vocal signals. One result of great interest has been the finding that different communities of the *same species* may have different signal codes. This is a special case of the fact that different communities of the same monkey species differ in many aspects of their behaviour, including diet, way of getting food, and even mating taboos. Thus among Japanese monkeys[21] one community scratches up edible roots, another invades rice-fields, others do neither. It appears that young monkeys acquire the customs of their band by imitation and because some of their actions are encouraged, others discouraged, by mothers and leaders. Occasionally a new habit is adopted by a young monkey and accepted by his or her mother, and gradually spreads through the kinship group in the mother's line, and eventually to the whole band (except some of the older monkeys who, like old dogs, will not learn new tricks), being afterwards transmitted to subsequent generations. This has happened, for instance, in a band on Kōshima Island, with the practices of washing sweet potatoes before eating them and separating wheat grains (supplied by human observers) from the sand on which they have fallen by washing out a handful of grain and sand in water. In this way each band has its own *culture*, and this includes its own signal units.[22] The Kōshima monkeys have acquired a completely new gesture for asking for food. A rhesus monkey community in Regent's Park Zoo used regularly to smack their lips as a friendly gesture and to execute a kind of press-up by bending and stretching their arms as a form of threat; neither gesture was ever seen in the rhesus community at Whipsnade.

Monkey signal codes have been much more studied than those of dolphins, and we know enough about them to be quite sure that they are simply automatic codes of signals which, as we saw earlier, are combined only according to emotional and not according to logical rules. Monkeys certainly have not evolved true languages. But so many combinations are at least possible, and monkey behaviour is so variable and exploratory, that several scientists have tried seriously to teach a *human* language to chimpanzees, the most variable and exploratory of them all. It has long been known that chimpanzees can respond separately to as many as 60 different human words. But then even a seal can do so to 35 words, and an elephant to 20. The real test is whether chimpanzees can be taught to use human words themselves, and to combine them, in appropriate ways. A very intensive attempt to teach a chimpanzee to talk was made some years ago by a married couple, both scientists, K. J. and Cathy Hayes. They adopted a baby chimp called Viki, and brought her up in their house exactly as if she were a human child, but using in addition the most sophisticated methods of teaching available. The result was disappointing. After 6 years of great effort and ingenuity, Viki had learned to utter only 4 sounds resembling English words. From this and other studies, it looked as if chimpanzees cannot be taught a human language.

So matters stood until June 1966, when another scientist couple, R. A. and Beatrice T. Gardner, began work at the University of Nevada with a female chimpanzee between 8 and 14 months old, whom they named Washoe after the county where the University is situated. Benefiting from the Hayes' experience, the Gardners had had an imaginative new idea. We have seen that most monkeys rely more on visual than on vocal signals. Even the actual vocal apparatus of chimpanzees is very different from man's. So instead of trying to teach *spoken* English, the Gardners decided to teach Washoe American Sign Language, as used by the deaf in North America, in which English words or concepts are represented by signs made with the hands; some of these symbols are representational, others are arbitrary, and all can be combined according to principles of English grammar and syntax. The Gardners and their colleagues brought up Washoe in shifts so that she never lacked for affectionate human company. They played all sorts of games with her and seem to have given her a very good time. All the time they were chattering among themselves in Sign Language, for it is known that simply being exposed to adults talking helps human children to learn to talk. They encouraged Washoe to imitate them, prompted her to get a sign right by repeating it themselves or by placing her hands in the right position, introduced plenty of toys and other objects to increase her vocabulary, encouraged her to "babble" with her hands, as a child does with his voice, and rewarded her for correct usage by tickling her, which she greatly enjoyed.

The results of all this were as follows. After 22 months of teaching, Washoe could use 34 words correctly in the appropriate circumstances. (She was only counted as knowing a word if three observers independently saw her use it correctly and without prompting). Whenever Washoe learned a new word, she very soon and quite spontaneously transferred it from a particular object, such as the key of a cupboard, to a whole class of objects, such as all keys. She would spontaneously call the humans' attention to objects by making the correct signs. She used the sign for "dog" when she saw a picture of a dog or even heard a dog bark without seeing it; evidently, like the dolphins, she had the capacity, previously supposed to be unique to man, of transposing patterns from one sense to another.

All this is remarkable, but Washoe did more. Without any prompting and apparently quite spontaneously, as soon as she had about 10 signs in her repertoire, Washoe began to *invent combinations* of signs and use them in a perfectly appropriate way. Among combinations which she invented are:—*open food drink*, for opening the refrigerator; *go sweet*, for being carried to a raspberry bush; *open flower*, to be let through the gate to a flower garden; and *listen eat*, at the sound of an alarm clock signalling meal-time. Just before the Gardners published their first results (in August 1969), Washoe had learned the pronouns *I-me* and *you*, "so that combinations that resemble short sentences have begun to appear". It only remains to add that Washoe's learning was accelerating—she had learned 4 signs in the first 7 months, 9 in the next, and 21 in the last 7 months.

Since Washoe unmistakably combines and recombines signs to describe objects and situations new to her in perfectly appropriate ways, this wonderful experiment seems to have established beyond doubt that a chimpanzee is capable of learning true language. True, at 3 years of age, she only has 34 words; at the equivalent age in terms of development, namely 5 years old, the average human child has a vocabulary of hundreds of words and makes sentences averaging 4·6 words in length. Sheer numerical differences of this kind may be important for the potentialities of human language. But the Gardners' achievement remains epoch-making. An animal has been taught to use true language, to communicate with human teachers.

THE ORIGIN OF LANGUAGE

So far, however, we have no evidence of any animals spontaneously evolving true language without anybody to teach them. Man *did*. How, and when, did this happen? What are the origins of human language? Our study of animal signals may help in some ways towards answering these questions.

How old is human language? Obviously it is at least as old as writing. The art of writing evolved rapidly in ancient Iraq between 3500 and 2900 B.C. A series of tablets from Erech, Jamdat Nasr, Ur and Fara tell the story of a transition from pictured objects and numbers to true writing with conventional signs for the syllables of the spoken language. But of course, even the first stage pre-supposes language itself, which must therefore be older than 3500 B.C. Much earlier than this, some time between 9000 and 6500 B.C., there lived at Ishango, on the shores of Lake Edward in the Congo, a people, apparently Negro, of great technological achievement for their time. The excellent bone harpoons they manufactured were exported as far as the Upper Nile and almost to the coast of West Africa. A bone tool-handle found at Ishango is marked with 3 series of notches grouped together in sets. One series has 11, 13, 17 and 19 notches—the 4 prime numbers between 10 and 20. Another has groups suggesting multiplication—3 and 6, 4 and 8, 10 and 5 and 5. The third series has 11 (10 + 1), 21 (20 + 1), 19 (20 − 1) and 9 (10 − 1), suggesting a decimal system. If these people really had a number system, they certainly must have talked, and we can put the age of language back to at latest 6500 B.C.

Now let us go back to the other end of man's story. Man-like beings who made and kept stone tools seem to have been at Olduvai Gorge in Tanzania 1,750,000 years ago, to judge from potassium dating. Now human language is connected with another peculiarity of man: his brain functions in an asymmetrical way. Language is controlled by the left side of the brain in 97% of human adults.[23] The asymmetry also appears in the fact that most people are right-handed, whereas in monkeys right- and left-handedness appear to be about equally common. E. H. Lenneberg has suggested, for complicated reasons, that there is a *necessary* connection between the two things, language and an asymmetrical brain. Washoe has, perhaps, proved him wrong in one way; but the idea may still be relevant for the *initial spontaneous evolution* of language, as opposed to the capacity to learn it. It is said that the earliest human stone tools show evidence of a predominance of right-handed tool-makers; so if Lenneberg is right, man had the potentiality of developing language from his earliest beginnings.

But did he develop it at once? For nearly all of his 1,750,000 years, man continued to make simple hand-axes and flake tools. All these crude stone implements look virtually alike to those of us who are not experts in prehistoric archaeology; there is scarcely any obvious difference between hand-axes hundreds of thousands of years apart. Then, suddenly, in the last Ice Age, about 100,000 years ago, there was a breakthrough: people began to manufacture more and more elaborate stone and bone tools in greater and greater diversity. To us, the conclusion has seemed inescapable that this efflorescence was made possible by the emergence of true language.

We reached this conclusion a few years ago, and have since found we are not the first to reach it. In 1951, in his Inaugural Lecture as Derby Professor of Zoology in the University of Liverpool, R. J. Pumphrey presented just this hypothesis. Throughout those hundreds of thousands of years, he wrote, "the hand-axe and flake cultures show an extraordinary conservatism of type and an improvement in the technique of manufacture so gradual as to make the intervention of what we should call 'reason' unlikely in the extreme. . . . And then in the last Ice Age the picture changes . . . with dramatic suddenness." Pumphrey had already stressed the relationship between true language and planning for the future ("forward planning about lions"). He noted that in the last Ice Age a wide range of stone tools began to be designed and made *to make other tools* by boring, scraping, cutting and polishing bone and antler, "clear evidence of an objective reached through a planned and orderly succession of *different* operations". And so, he suggested, "characteristically human speech" appeared about 100,000 years ago in the last Ice Age.

A similar idea had apparently suggested itself independently to the Australian archaeologist V. Gordon Childe. In an article published in 1953, he too noted the enormous acceleration of technical progress in the last Ice Age, and concluded that this "apparent change in tempo might reasonably be attributed to the increasing use of a more flexible system of symbols with which to 'operate in the head' as a substitute for physical trial-and-error processes".

Suppose that true language did originate in or just before the last Ice Age: we have still to consider what stimulated this momentous development. Now we have seen that monkey bands are regulated by automatic codes of signals, and that these signal codes *vary* between bands of the same species. This creates no new problems of communication, for when monkey bands meet they do not normally mix, interacting only by a set of common threat signals, simpler than those used within the band. When bands of howler monkeys meet, for instance, each band sets up a howl, and the louder band must be the larger; the smaller and less noisy band discreetly withdraws. Human beings originally moved about in similar small groups, and there was probably comparatively little contact between these groups. While still living under these conditions, they developed the manufacture of durable tools. They could very well manage to continue to function thus, tools and all, on the basis of automatic monkey-like codes of signals. Chimpanzees are known to shape sticks and straws to size, for fighting leopards and for luring termites out of their nests, respectively.

But about 300,000–400,000 years ago, man achieved control of fire, gathered on lavafields or from lightning brush fires and carefully kept burning, and some time between then and the last Ice Age he discovered how to *light* fires himself. These tremendous advances gave him a new control over his environment, notably in defence against predators and protection from the cold; the world human population increased considerably, and spread out over the continents, invading temperate and even colder regions for the first time. Now there were many more small groups, and more likelihood of their meeting frequently. Moreover, tools at last began to become gradually more elaborate and diversified from group to group. With this frequent contact between groups, and this incentive to borrow and copy each other's tools, a new development began. The old automatic signal codes would not work *between* groups (compare the Carniolan and Italian honeybees). The automatic noises and gestures that had formerly sufficed would eventually have to be replaced by *words*—overriding and controlling automatic moods— intelligible and intelligent between groups with different cultures. In this way man was stimulated to break the link between signal and automatic mood, and begin the logical combination of signals, or true language. Claire Russell has shown that a connection between the dawn of language and contact between culturally different groups can be detected in myths from several parts of the world. Gordon Childe has summarized the considerable evidence for trade and technical influence, and hence for communication, between culturally different groups great distances apart in the last Ice Age. So we may plausibly suppose that increasing contact between culturally separate groups was the stimulus for the evolution of true language. Even today, intercultural relations can stimulate new combinations of words—as in the case cited earlier of East African recruits and the phrases *colour of blood* and *colour of leaves*.

It remains to ask, why vocal rather than sign language, especially since chimpanzees and other advanced monkeys are, as we have seen, so geared to visual signals? Now we have also seen that where visibility is poor, calls predominate, as in dolphins or monkeys of dense forest. Martin Moynihan studied a Central American monkey active at night—the night monkey.[24] Though this species has only 10 calls, it has even fewer visual signals, and uses the calls far more. Now human eyes are not much use at night, and one of the results of man's control of fire was a new ability to continue his activities after sundown. Kenneth Oakley has suggested that "the lighting aspect of fire was probably almost as important as its heating aspect in extending man's range northwards". But visibility is *far from perfect* on a dark night around a flickering fire, and we may suppose that, as man became active at night, the value of vocal signals would greatly increase. So, we may conjecture, when true language appeared, it was conveyed by voice and not by gesture, until the deaf and their teachers, and certain monks, evolved sign languages to translate existing spoken ones.

THE FUTURE OF LANGUAGE

Finally, let us return to our contrast of economic and emotional information. We have seen that monkey signalling is heavily biased towards emotion. With the coming of true language in man, the balance tipped towards economics. For purposes of handling tools, techniques, science, our natural surroundings, language has come a long way since the last Ice Age, and made possible the achievement of many marvels, from bone harpoons to moon-walks. But for

purposes of communicative mood, for conveying subtle and sophisticated aspects of emotion and human relationship, language was,
and still is, only developed to a rudimentary degree. We continue
to convey emotion by crude, often unconscious, automatic signal
codes, carried by "calls"—our *tone of voice* when speaking—or by
the posture changes, gestures and facial expressions with which we
are interacting all the time—as you can easily see by turning off the
sound on your television set during an interview, discussion or
documentary. These signals vary from group to group, transmitted
as a crude and automatic culture in the monkey way, while true
language is transmitting its creative culture of accumulated knowledge. The gesture we call beckoning means a summons in Britain,
a dismissal in Italy, a deadly insult in Malawi—such variation is an
obvious source of cross-purposes. In an isolated Scandinavian village, a scientist noticed that everyone bowed to a certain white-
washed wall. They did not know why—they did not even know
they were doing it till he asked. He removed the whitewash, and
found a religious ikon, *centuries* old. How is such a pattern transmitted? We once saw, on documentary film, a Japanese mother in
traditional dress with her baby on her back, bowing to a Shinto
shrine. As she bowed, she put her hand behind her own head and
pushed the baby's head down.

Language itself is involved in this automatic signalling, through
tone of voice and also accent, which differs from group to group like
other patterns, and forms the basis for crude stress behaviour of a
highly automatic kind. At worst, it directs violence: the ancient
Israelites are said to have massacred, on one occasion, all who could
not pronounce the word *shibboleth*; the medieval Sicilians, rising
against the French, killed all who could not pronounce the word
ciceri. At mildest, such signal differences may affect cultural cross-
mating, as neatly indicated in the Ira Gershwin lyric—"You say
potartoes and I say potaytoes, You say tomartoes and I say
tomaytoes, Potartoes, potaytoes, Tomartoes, tomaytoes, Let's call
the whole thing off."

Our very talking may be as compulsive and conditioned as that
of Bastian's female dolphin: humans, too, are liable to talk when
alone, and often when two apparently converse, neither is listening
to the other or really concerned whether the other listens to them.
We may also be conditioned by words—and conditioning is the
reduction of variability of behaviour, whereas learning is the increase

of variability. Russian scientists have "trained" human individuals to blink in reaction to spoken sentences. The sentences worked as a conditioning signal even if the word order was reversed, just as the song of a robin has been recorded, reversed and played back (by the French scientists Bremond and Busnel) to another robin, who reacted exactly as to the usual song. Language is here debased to the level of a crude signalling system. And all these many indications of deficiency and degradation of language appear far more when we discuss emotion than when we discuss technical matters.[25] Indeed language has so far been of little help in relieving the sense of emotional isolation from which humans have always suffered. "What are the sorrows of other men to us" wrote Daniel Defoe, "and what their joy? . . . Our passions are all exercised in retirement; we love, we hate, we covet, we enjoy, all in privacy and solitude. All that we communicate of those things to any other is but for their assistance in the pursuit of our desires; the end is at home . . . it is for ourselves we enjoy, and for ourselves we suffer."

Mankind, then, has achieved technical wonders by means of his true language such as no animal could begin to achieve. It is now time—and high time, for we live in an age of emotional turmoil under the stress of population pressure—for man to begin to achieve wonders of emotional relationship and social harmony. Perhaps, to emancipate signals from immediate emotional impulse, the stimulus of discussing technical matters was necessary. But now we may hope to use the subtlety and power of language for true *communication* about our emotions. Art, and above all poetry, has been man's chief effort so far in this direction, and it is fitting that this series of lectures is launched by the Institute of Contemporary Arts. It is fitting, too, to end our story with a poem (by Claire Russell) about language.

> Words, like pebbles galore
> At the mouth of the sea,
> Litter the shore
> Of society.
> Worn into every shape and size
> Their hard reality defies
> The sea's speechless agitated tongue
> That lives and cries
> Upon the wind, unsung.

I wonder what these words are for
That I pick up along the shore;
I wander restlessly to seek
For pebbles of reality,
I wander restlessly along the shore to speak
Against the stormy agitated feelings of society.
But the storm defies
The pebbly scientific tongue
And a voice that dies
Upon the wind, unsung.

Pebbly words galore
Litter the shore,
While speechless feelings seek
To speak;
And a voice that lives and cries
With an agitated tongue
Echoes a voice that ever lives and dies,
As waves upon the wind, a far off magic legend that is sung.

NOTES

1 A more detailed account of phonemes is given by Eugénie Henderson, Lecture 2, pp. 40–4 (Ed.)

2 V. Reynolds: Dissertation (University of London, 1961).

3 For discussion of language and colour recognition, see R. H. Robins, Lecture 1, p. 31 and Stephen Ullmann, Lecture 4, pp. 83–4 (Ed.).

4 See also Edmund Leach, Lecture 7, pp. 140–1 (Ed.)

5 See also M. M. Lewis, Lecture 9. (Ed.)

6 *Apis mellifera carnica.*

7 *A. m. mellifera, intermissa, caucasica, ligustica* and *fasciata,* respectively.

8 *A. indica, florea, dorsata.*

9 The honeybee signal code introduces us to yet another distinction. The signalling of distance by waggling run duration, and the signalling of angle of flight path with sun by angle of waggling run with vertical, are both examples of *continuous*

signalling. Distance and direction vary continuously, and so do the signals for them. In human languages, signalling is normally done by separate or *discrete* signal *units*, such as phonemes, combined in various ways. As we have seen, many animal signal codes are also based on combinations of discrete units, and the whole science of animal behaviour study is based on the description and observation of such units of social behaviour. Signal units may be arbitrary or representational, as we have seen in the case of human words (*sun* and *hiss*, respectively). Continuous signals could in theory be arbitrary—for instance, bees could signal a flight angle of 40° by a dance angle of 10°, an angle of 60° by 11°, 80° by 9°, and so on. But, as Stuart A. Altmann has pointed out, in such a system any slight error in signalling would lead to serious mistakes, so continuous signalling must in practice be representational, as it is in honeybees, with a real formal relationship between signals and events.

10 *Tursiops truncatus.*
11 *Delphinus bairdi.*
12 *Lagenorhynchus* species.
13 *Pseudorca* species.
14 Nearly all of the dolphin cerebral cortex, like that of man, is made up of the most recently evolved kind of structures (neocortex); but this may only be because the older structures are related to the sense of smell, which is much reduced in these sea animals. It is also said that large areas of the dolphin cortex, as of the human cortex, are not directly concerned with control of muscular activity.
15 See also Eugénie Henderson, Lecture 2, pp. 43–4 (Ed.)
16 Very elaborate control experiments ensured that the male could not be guided by noises from the lamps or even by echolocation to find which paddle the female was nearest to, for putting the paddles far apart or side by side made no difference to the results.
17 *Triakis semifasciatum.*
18 But before dismissing dolphin capabilities altogether, we must make one reservation. As Dreher and Evans have pointed out, not all the work being done on dolphins is being published: much of it is enveloped in military secrecy. Already in 1963, L. Harrison Matthews, then Director of the London Zoo, remarked that "some people are proposing to prostitute their

biological work on the Cetacea and involve the animals in human international strife by training them as underwater watch-dogs to guard naval installations from frogmen, or to act as unmanned submarines. Intelligent as the animals may be, they are, unfortunately, not sufficiently intelligent to refuse cooperation and treat their trainers to some of those characteristic underwater noises which, if produced in the air, would be regarded as gestures of contempt".

19   *Macaca mulatta.*
20   *Cercopithecus aethiops.*
21   *Macaca fuscata.*
22   "Symbols are derived out of experience and history—i.e. out of institutions". Colin Cherry, Lecture 13, p. 284 (Ed.)
23   See Oliver Zangwill, Lecture 10. (Ed.)
24   *Aotus trivirgatus.*
25   Colin Cherry, however, warns us that the choice of signs may conceal the truth in "technical matters" also. Lecture 13, pp. 272–7 (Ed.)

FURTHER READING

1. Babies

IRWIN, O. C.: *Infant Speech, Scientific American Reprint* 417 (San Francisco, 1949).

WASZ-HÖCKERT, O.; LIND, J.; VUORENKOSKI, V.; PARTANEN, T.; VALANNÉ, E.: *The Infant Cry* (London, 1968), with 45 rpm record.

2. Bees

VON FRISCH, K.: *The Dance Language and Orientation of Bees,* translated by L. E. Chadwick (London, 1967).

3. Whales, Dolphins and Porpoises

ANDERSEN, H. T. (Ed.): *The Biology of Marine Mammals* (New York and London, 1969).

BUSNEL, R. H. G. (Ed.): *Animal Sonar Systems: Biology and Bionics,* Vol. 2 (Jouy-en-Josas, France, 1966).

NORRIS, K. S. (Ed.): *Whales, Dolphins and Porpoises* (Berkeley and Los Angeles, 1966).

TAVOLGA, W. N. (Ed.): *Marine Bio-Acoustics* (Oxford, London and New York, 1964).

4. Monkeys and Apes

ALTMANN, S. A. (Ed.): *Social Communication among Primates* (Chicago and London, 1967).

DEVORE, I. (Ed.): *Primate Behavior* (New York and London, 1965).

GARDNER, R. A. and GARDNER, B. T.: "Teaching Sign Language to a Chimpanzee", *Science* 165, pp. 664–72 (15th August, 1969).

MORRIS, D.: *The Naked Ape* (London, 1967).

MOYNIHAN, M.: *Some Behaviour Patterns of Platyrrhine Monkeys*. 1. *The Night Monkey* (Aotus trivirgatus) (Washington, 1964).

RUSSELL, C. and RUSSELL, W. M. S.: *Violence, Monkeys and Man* (London, 1968).

SOUTHWICK, C. J. (Ed.): *Primate Social Behaviour* (Princeton and London, 1963).

5. Language and Animal Signals: General

CORNWALL, I. V.: *The World of Ancient Man* (London, 1964).

COUNT, E. W.: "An Essay on Phasia: on the Phylogenesis of Man's Speech Function", *Homo* 19, pp. 170–227 (1969).

GERARD, R. W.; KLUCKHOHN, C. and RAPOPORT, A.: "Biological and Cultural Evolution: Some Analogies and Explorations", *Behavioral Science 1*, pp. 6–34 (1956).

HASTINGS, H. (Ed.): *Abbé Bougeant: Amusement Philosophique sur le Language des Betes* (Geneva and Lille, 1954).

HEINZELIN, J de: "Ishango", *Scientific American Reprint* 613 (San Francisco, 1962).

HOCKETT, C. D.: "The Origin of Speech", *Scientific American Reprint* 603 (San Francisco, 1960).

KALMUS, H.: "Ethnic Differences in Sensory Perception", *Journal of Biosocial Science* Supplement 1, pp. 81–90 (1969).

LENNEBERG, E. H.: *Biological Foundations of Language* (New York and London, 1967).

MÉTRAUX, G. S. and CROUZET, F.: *The Evolution of Science* (London, 1963).

OAKLEY, K.: "Fire as Palaeolithic Tool and Weapon", *Proceeding of the Prehistoric Society* 21, pp. 36–48 (1955).

PIKE, K. L.: *Tone Languages* (Ann Arbor, 1948).

PUMPHREY, R. J.: *The Origin of Language* (Liverpool, 1951).

RUSSELL, C.: *Forbidden Fruit* (Stockholm, in press).

RUSSELL, C. and RUSSELL, W. M. S.: *Human Behaviour: a New Approach* (London, 1961).

RUSSELL, W. M. S.: "Animals, Robots and Man; Signals and Shibboleths", *The Listener* 68, pp. 169–70, 207–8, 213 (2nd and 9th August, 1962).

RUSSELL, W. M. S.: *Man, Nature and History* (London, 1967).

SMITH, F. and MILLER, G. A. (Ed.): *The Genesis of Language* (Cambridge, Mass., and London, 1966).

THOMPSON, S.: *Motif-Index of Folk-Literature* Volume 1 (Helsinki, 1932).

TINBERGEN, N.: *The Herring Gull's World* (London, 1953).

TINBERGEN, N.: *Social Behaviour in Animals* (London, 1953).

WOOLLEY, Sir Leonard: *The Beginnings of Civilization* (London, 1963).

9

The linguistic development of children

M. M. LEWIS

University of Nottingham

THE ROOTS OF LANGUAGE

What are we talking about this evening? This: ... the infant, mewling and puking in his nurse's arms. I don't know about puking; what I can say is that there is nothing more important for a child than his mewling. His crying is the beginning of his language. On his very first day, as soon as he cries and his mother comes to him, we have the basic pattern of language between people—one person utters sounds and another responds.

It is on his first day also that a child often shows that he is already aware of sounds. Recent investigations have demonstrated, as early as this, an "auditory orienting reflex"—a movement of the child's head towards the source of a sound.[1] Within a couple of weeks this has usually become more specific: the child responds more readily and more regularly to a high-pitched human voice than to any other auditory stimulus.[2] And of course the most frequent high-pitched human voice is his mother's.

During these early days a child not only cries; he coos. When he is hungry or uncomfortable he cries; when he is content and comfortable he coos.[3]

The next new thing to come from the child—different from his crying and his cooing—is his babbling. Often as early as his sixth week he will be heard uttering strings of sounds, repeating them with a rhythm and intonation, apparently for the pleasure of making them; playing with sounds.[4]

He cries or coos or babbles; to each of these his mother is likely to respond in a specific way. He cries and she attempts to alleviate his discomfort; he coos and she comes and smiles and perhaps pets him; he babbles and she may well encourage him by joining in, imitating him in fun, so that in turn he imitates her.

The simple pattern of interchange is enlarged as the child begins to respond to speech in its situation. These are the rudiments of comprehension; how far back in his history they begin it is impossible to say. His earliest response to *Baby, Milk!* may be to his mother's voice as an auditory stimulus specific to him as a human infant. From this there will be a transition to the time when he responds to the phonemic form of *milk* in the situation in which he hears it, the context of circumstances, even when he can see neither the speaker nor the milk.

While these are the rudiments of meaning in what a child hears, there are also rudiments of meaning in what he utters. From the beginning, his crying and his cooing have each of them its own context of situation in the child himself—discomfort, distress when he cries, contentment when he coos. This, of course, is not to say that at the beginning he himself is aware of the connection between his crying and discomfort, or his cooing and contentment. But we who are with him have to recognize, from a very early moment, the rudimentary semantic content of his crying or his cooing. His babbling has another place in his development: he plays, practises, experiments.[5]

ADVANCE IN EARLY CHILDHOOD

The speed of linguistic development is phenomenal. By the end of the third year most children have a working command of a good many of the phonemic and syntactical structures of the mother tongue and of their use and comprehension in communication. Five years later this has normally extended to the whole range of the structures of the language; what has yet to come is an increase in the size and scope of vocabulary and in the complexity of syntax; above all, in the development of the complex relationships between the structural and the semantic systems of the language.[6]

All this has been seen by mothers and others from time immemorial; seen, but rarely observed. Not the least remarkable thing about children's linguistic development is that we know so little about it. Today we have barely reached the centenary of the first systematic studies. One of the pioneers is Darwin, who made a record of his son as early as 1840, though he refrained from publishing it until 1877.[7]

During the greater part of the present century, while there has been a stream of sporadic attempts at description and interpretation, gaps have remained unfilled. But now, suddenly, in the last few years, there has burst upon us an explosion of concern, thought and observation. This is one of the major products of modern psycholinguistics, from which the name of Noam Chomsky is now inseparable.

Chomsky has been hailed as the herald of revolution in the study of language, as the Einstein of modern psycholinguistics. Here we ask what he has to say to us about the development of language in children.

HALF-A-CENTURY OF STUDY

Chomsky offers hypotheses which have injected fresh vigour into observation and experiment by a variety of workers. What is new in these hypotheses is best seen in the perspective of the ideas current before he arrived.

We go back to the beginning of the century, to the pioneers, William and Clara Stern, whose book *Die Kindersprache* first appeared in 1908. They take as the fundamental explanation of linguistic development the principle of "convergence": the interaction between what comes from the child—the drive in him to use language (Sprachdrang)—and what comes to him from his linguistic environment.[8] This would no doubt seem to many even today irrefutable if innocuous. But it soon proved to be altogether too broad a formulation to satisfy the growing demand in psychology for precision; least palatable was the somewhat mystical hypothesis of an inborn "drive".

During the following half-century the main line of thought about linguistic development took a different course. In the U.S.A., under the influence of studies of the processes of learning; in the U.S.S.R., under the influence of Pavlov, in both, the balance of "convergence" shifted to a heavier emphasis on the outside forces acting upon the child. In the U.S.A. the development of language was seen by many as the reinforcement of a child's responses to others. There was a solid movement of thought in this direction, among philosophers, sociologists and linguists no less than among psychologists. Of these we may name Skinner as one of the latest as well as one of the most thoroughgoing exponents of the function of reinforcement in linguistic development.[9]

The parallel with work in the U.S.S.R. on conditioning is too obvious to need more than a mention. The genesis of language was one of the main preoccupations of Pavlov because of its far-reaching relationships with every aspect of human behaviour.

Pavlov envisaged language as the "second signal system", established by the conditioning of primary conditioned reflexes.[10] The fertility of this concept of linguistic development is attested by the quantity and quality of the work carried out under its influence by such men as Vigotsky and Luria.

THE CHOMSKY REVOLUTION

Reinforcement or conditioning; these were as strongly entrenched explanatory concepts as any in the history of psychology. But in 1957, five decades after *Die Kindersprache*, there appeared a treatise with an innocent title-page: *Syntactic Structures*, by N. Chomsky. Apparently addressed to professional linguists, it dealt with problems which might be regarded as of limited interest even to them: the syntactic structures of a language could be shown to be logically "generated in accordance with the rules, the grammar of the language".[11]

If this was new in linguistics, it was not obviously a revolution in psycholinguistics. But although Chomsky was careful to point out that his description of the generation of structures must not be taken as an account of actual genesis, its implications for the understanding of linguistic development soon appeared. The cat among the pigeons was seen to have sharp claws.

The pigeons were Skinner's. In a series of elegant experiments he had demonstrated that by selecting some more or less random movements of a pigeon and reinforcing a succession of these by appropriate "rewards", a complex pattern of behaviour could be set up. The behaviour of the pigeon was determined by what we did to him.

When Skinner applied the same principles to verbal behaviour in his book of that name, his treatment seemed to many to be vitiated by a serious limitation: the suggestion that a child's linguistic development is mainly determined by what we do to him. Chomsky was roused to a ferocious polemic, reminiscent of the cut-and-thrust of seventeenth-century philosophers' battles. In a slashing review he set about clawing Skinner's book into shreds, not without some glee.[12] Not merely by negative strictures, but by positive refutations Chomsky expounded his ideas on language and linguistic development. As subsequently elaborated by him and his colleagues, they are revolutionary to this degree, that they have given a new direction to thought about language and a new stimulus to the examination of the linguistic development of children.

BACK TO THE PAST

Like many another revolutionary, Chomsky takes a step backward in order to take two forward. There was already in the U.S.A. something of an uneasy movement back to the past. It is startling to find a modern psychologist of the calibre of J. McV. Hunt "revisiting" McDougall for his insistence on primary drives as factors in development; still more, recalling one Montessori for her recognition of children's initiative and creativeness.[13]

Chomsky takes a wider sweep, back to a golden age, long before the philosophy of language was polluted by Behaviorism and S-R learning theory. He invokes a line of honourable ancestry for his ideas: Descartes and Leibniz and the seventeenth-century thinkers about language, Goethe and von Humboldt in the following century.[14] He turns to them for support as he expounds his hypotheses. From the logical genesis of language by generative processes he goes on to suggest implications for the linguistic development of children, still denying that he can offer a factual account of what actually happens.

CHOMSKY ON LINGUISTIC DEVELOPMENT

Chomsky's exposition consists of six main statements:

There is an innate predisposition to achieve the mastery of language

The structures of a language are generated from primary deep structures

The linguistic development of children is a process of maturation

In the process of development the child is essentially creative

Imitation is a subsidiary factor in the acquisition of a language

Analogy is a complex factor in this development.

We look at these in turn.

The most fundamental and at the same time the most controversial of Chomsky's hypotheses is that we are born with a disposition to acquire language. This he regards as peculiar to man; or, in

7*

Lenneberg's terms, it is "species-specific".[15] In Chomsky's terms, children are born with a potential knowledge of grammar. Nonsense? But as Chomsky uses them, "knowledge" and "grammar" are pickwickian terms. By knowledge he means what he also calls "competence" in language, to be sharply distinguished from "performance".[16] And the meaning of "grammar" he extends to include the whole system of rules covering the relationships of the phonemic, syntactic and semantic components of a language. Chomsky is maintaining that we are born with an aptitude to acquire these rules, and that as linguistic development goes on there is "a grammar which each individual has somehow and in some form internalized".[17]

Thus "competence" is the grasp, more or less conscious, of the rules of a language; "performance" actual linguistic behaviour which will be—more or less—in accordance with these rules. By the systematic study of children's performance we can infer the nature and degree of their competence.

One of Chomsky's chief grounds for postulating innate competence is the speed with which a child attains the mastery of the complex system of skills that constitute a language, "on the basis of a fairly restricted amount of evidence".[18] In passing, it may be pointed out that Chomsky is underestimating the richness of a child's linguistic experience. A child with normal hearing, born into a society of speakers, is surrounded by language from the moment of his birth. In his first three years, say his first one thousand days, he must hear some millions of words.

Is there anything new in Chomsky's insistence on the innate bases of language? This: while it has always been recognized that there are innate roots of *speech*, Chomsky postulates an innate competence in *language*. Indeed, as Lenneberg has shown, language may develop in the absence of speech, even comprehension of spoken language in the absence of articulation.[19] To say that there is an innate basis of competence means that it is natural for a child growing up in a linguistic society to become linguistic.

The second main idea of Chomsky's is that competence develops out of basic innate deep structures, through a succession of transformations. The genesis of a language for a child, as Chomsky sees it, is this:

Deep structures . . . kernel sentences . . . infantile structures . . . structures of the mother tongue.

Deep structures are the hypothetical capacities inferred from a child's overt language later. It is not surprising therefore if different readers of Chomsky's exposition do not agree in their ideas of deep structures.[20]

Chomsky would seem to suggest that while deep structures are dispositions to acquire language, they are not themselves linguistic. They are pre-linguistic; cognitive, but in forms that lend themselves to language. Chomsky concurs with Descartes' description of them as "a simple reflection of the form of thought"; and with von Humboldt's conclusion "that the force that generates language is indistinguishable from that which generates thought".[21]

To test our interpretation of Chomsky we may attempt an example of a basic deep structure and its subsequent progressive transformations into a structure of English. The argument would run on something like the following lines.

We may reasonably suppose that when an infant, even in his earliest days, sees the movement of a bird across the sky, his perception is already different from that of a dog, however intelligent. While the dog, we may suppose, has a single integral perception of the bird in flight, the child is born with more advanced cognitive capacities. His perception, we would assume, soon has the rudiments of two components—the bird and its movement. He begins to see the *bird* . . . flying, and the *flying* . . . as performed by the bird. If all this is highly hypothetical, it is what is implied by saying that a child, by contrast with a dog, begins with deep structures which will lend themselves to language.

As a child acquires words, he may begin to use them to symbolize his perception. *Bird!* he announces—more probably, *Birdie!*—later perhaps, *Bird flying!* This is a kernel sentence; so too was *Bird!* earlier; it has long been recognized that many of a child's single early words are semantically sentences. From a kernel sentence there is a transformation or a series of transformations to a structure of current English: *The bird is flying.* A French child, beginning with same basic deep structure, ends up with *l'oiseau qui vole*—not with the English schoolboy's *l'oiseau est volant.*

Chomsky's third main idea is that the linguistic development of a child is a process of *maturation*, not the imposition upon him of the forms of the mother tongue by authority from above, through conditioning, reinforcement or any other means.

This is a very important tenet in Chomsky's system and he and his colleagues have taken a great deal of trouble to demonstrate the validity of this principle of development. For support, Chomsky again goes back to von Humboldt, citing him to the effect that language grows by the maturation of relatively fixed capacities under appropriate external conditions.[22] Among Chomsky's colleagues a principal exponent of this view is Lenneberg, who adduces evidence to show that, like progress in walking, talking develops by the unrolling of tendencies already present in the child. Environment may, of course, be more or less favourable—but it is a condition, not the source, of linguistic development.[23]

The last three of Chomsky's general hypotheses expound a most important implication of the first three: that a child is creative in his linguistic development.

For Chomsky this is indeed an indispensable concept for the understanding of all human behaviour. He brings in the support of Descartes for the doctrine that "a fully adequate psychology of man requires the postulation of a 'creative principle'." This has become so intrinsic in Chomsky's view of language that one of his exponents, McNeill, heads a paper with a title that is surely meant to be provocative: "The Creation of Language by Children".[24] This sets itself to counter the line of thought which so long had seen the development of language as a process of social influence upon the child, whether by reinforcement or conditioning or example.

What then immediately becomes unavoidable is the crucial question of the function of imitation. Nothing could be more obvious than that the linguistic differences between English and French children must be due to imitation. Chomsky asks, How far due to imitation? And he brings forward two lines of argument to show that imitation is much less important than would appear at first sight: first, the nature of imitation itself as a psychological process; and secondly the relation between imitation and other factors in linguistic development.

Imitation Chomsky points out, is not only a means by which we learn; imitation itself has to be learnt. Lenneberg enjoins us to remember "that imitation implies the learning of analytic tools, namely grammatical and phonemic rules".[25] Imitation in language thus goes far beyond mere mimicry; the child is active in that he forms for himself systems of rules and applies them. When a child has encountered a particular usage of language, his imitation consists of similar usages in similar circumstances.

More than this: the rôle of imitation, though powerful, is limited. How else can we explain some of the mistakes children make? *I taked*; *I eated*. These, and so many others, can only be due to a process that we must call reasoning by analogy, even though in saying this we realize that a good deal of the time the "reasoning" is unconscious.

The more closely we observe children the clearer does it become that in their linguistic development both imitation and analogy are at work. It is found, for instance, that some children, at a time when they are saying *I breaked*, are also saying *I broke*.[26] It is worth noticing that each of these owes something to imitation, something to analogy. *Breaked* is by analogy with such a form as *walked*, which directly or indirectly comes from imitation. *Broke* is imitated, but then used, analogically, in a new situation.

Chomsky is so anxious to stress the function of creation that he maintains that even "analogy" may be misleading; that it would be truer to say that the child behaves as though he were reasoning by analogy when in fact he is acting creatively in a new situation.[27]

Throughout Chomsky's exposition there runs this thought: to say that a child acquires language is misleading if it is taken to mean that he gathers and enlarges a stock of structures which he learns to understand and utter. It is rather that the child extends his competence over the rules of the language as he generates structures in accordance with these rules.

LANGUAGE IS CREATION

Chomsky's six hypotheses are likely to have important influences on our knowledge of children's linguistic development. As hypotheses some are open to direct verification, others not.

The first—the innate basis of competence—can be tested only indirectly, by inference from the observed facts of children's development. The second hypothesis—the generation of the structures of a language—lends itself somewhat more readily to verification, but only through careful and even subtle experiment and controlled observation.

The hypothesis of maturation as the process of development is rather better supported by available data, particularly of the kind presented by Lenneberg; and it gains some additional force from its agreement with Piaget's principle of the biological adaptation of the child to his society.

The last three hypotheses of Chomsky's are of a different kind. The creativeness of the child and the functions of imitation and analogy in his linguistic development—these are descriptive of actual "performance", so that their validity rests on the systematic observation of children, supplemented where possible by experiment. Both observation and experiment have been given a powerful impetus by the discussions of Chomsky and his colleagues; and it is to the work in the field that we look for the closure of the gaps in our knowledge of the linguistic development of children. We may hazard the prediction that more will be found to depend on a child's linguistic environment than Chomsky seems inclined to allow.

In the meantime let us record a new outlook on the nature of language itself. There is a new creed. Its major tenets have nowhere been stated so clearly as by Miller who, among the disciples of Chomsky, may rank as the apostle of common sense. In an admonitory epistle to the psychologists he announces a revelation: "Language is exceedingly complicated". And he makes his confession of faith: "I now believe that mind is something more than an Anglo-Saxon four-letter word; human minds exist".[28]

NOTES

1 R. H. Walters and R. D. Parke: "The Role of the Distance Receptors in the Development of Social Responsiveness", in L. P. Lipsitt and C. S. Spiker: *Advances in Child Development and Behaviour* (1965), p. 75.

2 *Ibid*, p. 65.

3 M. M. Lewis: *Language, Thought and Personality in Infancy and Childhood* (1963), pp. 16–19.

4 *Ibid*, p. 20.

5 *Ibid*, pp. 20–22.

6 M. C. Templin: *Certain Language Skills in Children* (1957), p. 141.

7 C. Darwin: "The Biography of an Infant", *Mind*, II (1877).

8 C. and W. Stern: *Die Kindersprache* (1908), p. 123.

9   B. F. Skinner: *Verbal Behaviour* (1957).
10 I. P. Pavlov: *Conditioned Reflexes*, trans. G. V. Anrep (1927).
11 N. Chomsky: *Syntactic Structures* (1957). See John Lyons, Lecture 3. (Ed.)
12 N. Chomsky: Review of Skinner's "Verbal Behaviour", *Language*, 35 (1959).
13 J. McV. Hunt: "The Importance of Pre-verbal Experience", in M. Deutsch *et al*: *Social Class, Race and Psychological Development* (1968).
14 N. Chomsky: *Cartesian Linguistics* (1966).
15 E. H. Lenneberg: *Biological Foundations of Language* (1967), p. 296.
16 See also Basil Bernstein, Lecture 11, p. 229 (Ed.)
17 N. Chomsky: "Methodological Preliminaries", in L. A. Jakobovitz and M. S. Miron: *Readings in the Psychology of Language* (1967), p. 89.
    N. Chomsky: "The Formal Nature of Language", in E. H. Lenneberg: *Biological Foundations of Language* (1967), p. 408.
    N. Chomsky: Review of Skinner's "Verbal Behaviour", *Language*, 35 (1959), p. 170.
18 N. Chomsky: "The Formal Nature of Language", in E. H. Lenneberg: *Biological Foundations of Language* (1967), p. 437.
19 E. H. Lenneberg: "Speech as a Motor Skill", *Child Development Monograph* (1964), p. 127.
20 John Lyons, for example, Lecture 3, p. 70 regards deep structure as linguistic abstractions. (Ed.)
21 F. Smith and G. A. Miller: *The Genesis of Language* (1966), p. 6.
    N. Chomsky: *Cartesian Linguistics* (1966), pp. 30 and 35
22 N. Chomsky: *Cartesian Linguistics* (1966), p. 64.
23 E. H. Lenneberg: *Biological Foundations of Language* (1967), pp. 136, 142.
24 N. Chomsky: *Cartesian Linguistics* (1966), p. 6.
    D. McNeill: "The Creation of Language by Children", in J. Lyons and R. J. Wales: *Psycholinguistic Papers* (1966).
25 E. H. Lenneberg: "Speech as a Motor Skill", *Child Development Monograph* (1964), p. 122.
26 S. M. Ervin: "Imitation and Structural Change in Children's Language", in E. H. Lenneberg: *Biological Foundations of Language* (1964), p. 179.
27 N. Chomsky: *Cartesian Linguistics* (1966), p. 12.

28 G. A. Miller: "Some Preliminaries to Psycholinguistics" in R. C. Oldfield and J. C. Marshall: *Language* (1968), p. 212.
G. A. Miller: "Some Psychological Studies of Grammar" in L. A. Jakobovitz and M. S. Miron: *Readings in the Psychology of Language* (1967), p. 217.

FURTHER READING

CHOMSKY, N.: *Cartesian Linguistics* (London, 1966).
LENNEBERG, E. H.: *Biological Foundations of Language* (New York, 1967).
LENNEBERG, E. H.: *New Directions in the Study of Language* (Massachusetts Institute of Technology, 1964).
LEWIS, M. M.: *Language, Thought and Personality in Infancy and Childhood* (London, 1963).
OLDFIELD, R. C. and MARSHALL, J. C.: *Language* (London, 1968).

IO

The neurology of language

OLIVER L. ZANGWILL

The Psychological Laboratory, Cambridge

INTRODUCTION

Although I am not a neurologist, I must confess to a deep fascination with the neurology of language. The source of this goes back to the last War when I had the good fortune to work as a research psychologist in Professor Norman Dott's Brain Injuries Unit at Edinburgh. Here my job was to assess as objectively as possible the effects on psychological capacity of injuries to the brain and to do what I could to help with the re-education and resettlement of the patients. The latter—most of whom were ex-servicemen—included many with what neurologists call *aphasia*—that is to say, loss or defect of speech due to damage of particular parts of the brain. I therefore became familiar not only with the wide variety of language disorders that may result from brain injury but also with the great difficulty they present from the standpoint of effective rehabilitation. It is only too apparent that fuller understanding of the neurological basis of language is essential if we are to place our methods of remedial education on a truly scientific foundation.

CEREBRAL DOMINANCE

The general plan of the central nervous system is essentially the same in man and the subhuman primates. Why, then, have not at all events the higher apes evolved something resembling human language? The reason cannot lie in lack of intelligence as apes, in particular chimpanzees, are often capable of solving problems well outside the capacity of an intellectually defective child who is none the less able to acquire the rudiments of speech. In part, the difficulty appears to be one of gaining voluntary control over vocalization. Some years ago, Keith and Cathy Hayes succeeded in teaching a young chimpanzee a few words but she never became truly able to use them in a volitional way. This does not, however, imply that the chimpanzee is necessarily incapable of acquiring some degree of symbolic communication. Quite recently, R. A. and B. T. Gardner have succeeded in teaching an engaging young female chimpanzee called "Washoe" a considerable number of signs from the official American Sign Language.[1] Indeed, by the age of 21 months Washoe had learnt eighteen signs which she used freely and spontaneously, and for the most part accurately. Sometimes, she combined two signs without specific training, i.e. those for "please" and "hurry", indicating that she possessed the rudiments of syntax. Washoe was also able to use, without special training, a given sign in a context other than that in which it had been originally acquired, e.g. the sign for "open" learned in reference to a door was spontaneously used in reference to a box. This indicates a very real capacity for generalization. While these studies are still incomplete, the results so far obtained make it abundantly clear that the ape is capable of acquiring and using a specialized gestural system of communication.

In spite of the great interest of the Gardners' work, it would be unwise to under-estimate the width of the gap between ape and man, at all events with regard to language.[2] Under natural conditions, apes do not appear to have evolved gestural communication systems of any real sophistication or to possess anything that can possibly be called a language. It would therefore seem that there must be some special property of the human nervous system that predisposes man to acquire speech and to use it in communication with his fellows. Have we any clue as to what this property might be?

I venture to suggest, very tentatively, that this property may lie in a certain asymmetry in the function of the two halves—or *hemispheres*—of the human brain. Although aphasia has been known to doctors virtually since the dawn of medicine, it was only about a hundred years ago that its exclusive connection with injury to one side of the brain—usually the left but occasionally the right—became established. Paul Broca, a pioneer in the study of aphasia, was not only in large part responsible for establishing this correlation but also offered a plausible explanation of its cause. In his view, one half of the brain is innately predisposed to mature more rapidly than its fellow and thereby to gain a certain preeminence in the development of psychological function. As the great British neurologist, John Hughlings Jackson, put it, the left hemisphere "takes the lead" in the growth of dexterity and in acquisition of language, which have been traditionally regarded as closely linked. In the left-handed individual, Broca supposed, the position is reversed and the right hemisphere "takes the lead". This might however also occur in a naturally right-handed individual who had suffered extensive damage to the left hemisphere in infancy prior to the onset of speech.

Table 1

AUTHORS	Left Hemisphere				Right Hemisphere			
	Rt. Handers		Lt. Handers		Rt. Handers		Lt. Handers	
	Cases	Aphasic	Cases	Aphasic	Caess	Aphasic	Cases	Aphasic
CONRAD (1949)	338	175	19	10	249	11	18	7
BINGLEY (1958)	101	68	4	2	99	1	10	3
PENFIELD and ROBERTS (1959)	157	115	18	13	196	1	15	1
RUSSELL and ESPIR (1961)	288	186	24	9	221	3	24	4
HECAEN and AJURIAGUERRA (1963)	163	81	37	22	130	0	22	11
	1047	625	102	56	895	16	89	26
		59·7%		54·9%		1·8%		29·2%

Although everyone today accepts the evidence for a difference between the two hemispheres in the control of speech—or *cerebral dominance* as it is generally known—its relation to handedness has proved rather more complicated than the early neurologists supposed. While it remains perfectly true that aphasia from right hemisphere lesion in right-handed individuals is exceedingly rare, aphasia from left hemisphere lesions in left-handed individuals and in those with mixed hand preferences is relatively common. I have recently looked into the evidence about handedness, side of brain lesion and incidence of aphasia in over 2000 patients who had sustained damage exclusively limited to either the left or the right side of the brain, and the findings are given in Table 1. It will be seen from this that 59·7% of right-handed and 54·9% of left-handed patients developed aphasia after lesions of the left hemisphere. This difference is not however statistically significant, i.e. it could have occurred purely by chance. On the other hand, the differential incidence of aphasia associated with lesions of the right hemisphere —1·8% of the right-handed and 29·2% of the left-handed patients— is highly significant. Although the position is far from clear, it is at least plain that some connection exists between hand-preference and the cerebral control of language.

These findings gain support from the results of some very interesting experimental studies carried out by Dr Brenda Milner and her colleagues at the Montreal Neurological Institute. Their technique involves injecting a barbiturate drug into the carotid artery, which has the effect of temporarily arresting function of the hemisphere of the brain on the same side as that of the injection. If injection is on the same side as the dominant hemisphere, transient aphasia results; if, however, it is on the opposite side, no disturbance of language occurs. (True, a few patients develop aphasia after injection on either side, which might suggest that in these rare cases speech is subserved by both halves of the brain.) One must emphasize that this test is given only where it is absolutely essential to determine which side of the brain is dominant for purposes of essential neurosurgery.

Table 2

Handedness and Carotid-Amytal Speech Lateralization

Handedness	No. of Cases	Speech representation		
		Left	Bilateral	Right
Right	48	43 (90%)	0 (0%)	5 (10%)
Left or Ambidextrous				
Without early left brain damage	44	28 (64%)	7 (16%)	9 (20%)
With early left brain damage	27	6 (22%)	3 (11%)	18 (67%)

Dr Milner's main findings are shown in Table 2. From this it will be seen that, in the group of right-handed patients, 90% have left hemispheric dominance. In the group of patients who are either left-handed or ambidextrous, however, the position is rather different. Among those who had no history of early left-sided brain damage, 64% have left and 20% right hemisphere dominance, which agrees fairly closely with the clinical observations summarized in Table 1. On the other hand, among those who had sustained early left-sided brain damage, the proportion of right cerebral dominance is very much higher, thus confirming Broca's prediction that, in a naturally right-handed person, control of speech may be shifted to the right hemisphere in the event of early damage to the left. Although the limits of this "vicarious function" of the right half of the brain in speech are not known for certain, it is generally supposed that once speech has begun to appear it becomes increasingly difficult to transfer dominance from one hemisphere to the other. Indeed after the age of 6 or 7 years little transfer of this kind is to be anticipated.

These general findings might suggest that the key to the evolution of language in man is the existence of cerebral dominance, i.e. a differentiation in functions of the two hemispheres of the brain.[3] "Washoe" notwithstanding, such a difference does not appear to exist in any other known species of animal and may quite conceivably be linked with the evolution of unilateral hand-preferences and the growth of manipulative skill which, along with speech, is so vital a human characteristic.

LANGUAGE AND THE RIGHT HEMISPHERE

Man's possession of a dominant hemisphere does not necessarily mean that no part at all is played by its fellow in the activities of language. Indeed Hughlings Jackson long ago suggested that dominance is a graded characteristic, being most marked for propositional speech, which is essentially volitional, and least marked for the comprehension of speech, which at a day-to-day level at all events is achieved without obvious volitional effort, i.e. is essentially automatic. These views old as they are, have gained fresh prominence in the light of recent advances in brain surgery. In certain cases of severe and intractable epilepsy, a new operation has been devised to control seizures by dividing the anatomical connections (or commissures) between the two hemispheres of the brain and thereby depriving them of direct functional connection with one another. Quite incidentally, this state of affairs provides a unique opportunity to study the behaviour of each half of the brain operating more or less independently of the other. It should be stressed that this operation has so far been carried out only in one or two centres in the United States and must at present be regarded as essentially experimental.

As many people will know, each hemisphere of the brain is related principally to sensation and movement on the opposite side of the body. Normally, of course, both hemispheres work in synchrony but if they are anatomically disconnected from one another, motor control of the left limbs can be initiated only by the right hemisphere and of the right limbs by the left hemisphere. Further, the layout of the visual pathways is such that messages from the left half of each retina (the sensitive surface of the eye) travel to the left hemisphere and those from the right half of each retina to the right hemisphere. In what has become known as a "split-brain" patient therefore, an image falling on the left half of each retina (which would be given by an object on the individual's right-hand side) will travel to the left hemisphere and one falling on the right half of each retina (projected by an object on the individual's left-hand side) to the right hemisphere. In consequence if the eyes are kept perfectly still and a visual display (say a word or picture) flashed to the observer so that its image falls exclusively on the left half of each retina, and if the duration of the flash is too brief to allow movement of the eyes, the image received by the eyes will be transmitted exclusively to the left hemisphere. And similarly images projected onto the right half of each retina will be transmitted to the right hemisphere. Thus the possibility exists of delivering visual information to one hemisphere only and testing for its reception by signalling with the hand on the same side or—in the case of the left hemisphere only—by speech.

This technique has been developed by Dr Roger Sperry and his associates at the California Institute of Technology to study the rôle of the right cerebral hemisphere in relation to perception and language. Their experimental set up, which is very simple, is shown in Fig. 1. For example, a picture of an object, such as a hammer, is briefly exposed on the screen, the patient being asked to fix his eyes on the central asterisk. In the case of a "split-brain" patient, when

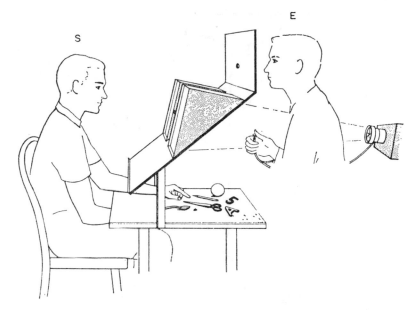

Fig. 1. Testing the split-brain patient: The slanting shield on the table prevents the subject (S) from seeing test objects on the table, his own hands or the examiner (E). It contains a ground glass viewing screen for back projection of slides enabling words or designs to be briefly exposed in either the left or the right visual fields, or in both simultaneously. The examiner flashes the slides only when the patient's gaze is seen to be properly centred on the central fixation point.

the hammer is shown to the left of the fixation point (as in Fig. 2), its image will be transmitted to the right hemisphere, and when it is shown to the right of the fixation point it will be transmitted to the left hemisphere. The patient is asked to select, with his left or right hand, an object that corresponds to the picture he has just seen, but without the use of vision. If the picture of the object has been transmitted to the left hemisphere, it can not only be named but matched with a real hammer but if it is transmitted to the right hemisphere, it cannot be named but can still be matched with a real hammer, but only when the left hand is used for this purpose. Hence the right hemisphere can recognize the object but cannot evoke its name.

Very similar results are obtained if a name is substituted for a picture. A name flashed to the left hemisphere can be read aloud or

Fig. 2. What the split-brain patient sees: If the patient is fixating the central asterisk, the image of the hammer is projected onto the right side of the retina of each eye and the information conveyed exclusively to his right cerebral hemisphere. While he can select a hammer from among other hidden objects using his left (though NOT his right) hand, he can neither name it nor describe to others what he has seen.

matched to the corresponding object explored with the right hand. On the other hand, a name flashed to the right hemisphere cannot be read aloud but can likewise be matched to the corresponding object explored with the left hand. Hence the right hemisphere can "read" the name silently but cannot translate it into oral speech. At the same time, it is important to bear in mind that the reading capacity of the right hemisphere is distinctly limited: it does not appear to comprehend commands or to possess more than a rudimentary comprehension of syntax.

In the understanding of spoken speech, however, the right hemisphere does somewhat better. For example, if the patient is given a description of an object and then shown a series of pictures (in his left visual field) he can press a key (with the left hand) when a picture is shown that matches the description. Thus if the description is "used to tell the time", he can instantly select the picture of a watch, when it is shown to him. Hence the right hemisphere does appear to possess a measure of comprehension of speech, along with at all events short-term verbal memory.

Although much more work remains to be done, these findings lend substance to Hughlings Jackson's views. Clearly, the more automatic use of language, as shown in reading or comprehension, is to some extent vested in both hemispheres, whereas expressive speech is predominantly, if not wholly, controlled by the left hemisphere alone. What is even more striking, perhaps, is that the two hemispheres can, in these exceptional circumstances, work entirely independently of one another and that the right hemisphere can never communicate its experiences through language. Nor can the information received simultaneously by the two hemispheres be integrated. This is shown by the following example: if the two words "HE" and "ART" be simultaneously flashed to the subject, one on each side of the fixation point (Fig. 3), the subject can write HE with his left hand and simultaneously ART with his right hand. He can also, if requested, read the word ART aloud. But under no

HE ✴ART

Fig. 3. The split word: If HE is flashed to the right hemisphere and ART to the left hemisphere, the patient can read aloud only the word ART though he can copy both words, one with each hand. He cannot put together the two words to produce the single word HEART.

circumstances can he combine them to form the single word HEART, i.e. to put together the information received from the two separated hemispheres. There is a sense, therefore, in which under these circumstances at least each hemisphere can sustain its own independence in mental life.

There is one other operation that can throw light upon the potentiality of the right hemisphere for language. In cases in which one hemisphere of the brain is grossly diseased, neurosurgeons sometimes undertake the operation of *hemispherectomy*, i.e. total excision of the diseased hemisphere. This is not uncommonly carried out nowadays in cases in which damage to one side of the brain has been sustained very early in life but is only rarely done when the damage is of recent origin—and then for the most part only in cases in which the damaged hemisphere is the right. There have, however, been a handful of cases in which total operative removal of the *left* (i.e. dominant) hemisphere has been undertaken in cases of progressive unilateral brain disease of recent origin which would otherwise rapidly prove fatal. One such patient, operated on by Dr C. W. Burkland, I was recently able to study by his courtesy and that of Dr Aaron Smith, who has published a detailed report. Their patient, aged 47 at the time of his operation, showed as one might expect severe sensory and motor deficit over the right half of his body as well as an almost total loss of expressive speech. None the less, he could say "yes" and "no" correctly, repeat a few words to request, and emit an occasional expletive or short phrase such as "Dammit, I can't!" Moreover, he could understand what he was told surprisingly well and carry out simple instructions without error. He could read some individual words though not sentences and his writing (with his left hand) was virtually restricted to printing his name or copying a few letters or words. It is however interesting to note that this extraordinary patient's intellectual capacity, as assessed on intelligence tests of a diagrammatic or non-verbal kind, still remained within the average range and his social judgment appeared to all intents and purposes to be intact. Although this patient may have relearned a little speech after his operation—it was eighteen months post-operatively that I saw him—it seems likely that he owed the greater part of such language function that he still possessed to his intact right hemisphere. Indeed he was capable of a degree of comprehension and a minimum of speech very early after his operation.

The findings in this case agree fairly closely with those reported in the "split-brain" patients, at all events in so far as the right hemisphere is concerned. Taken together they indicate that "dominance" is shown principally in the expressive aspect of language—though certain highly automatic utterances appear to be sustained by both sides of the brain. Comprehension can clearly be maintained to a considerable degree by the "non-dominant" hemisphere. Hence it must be assumed that whereas both hemispheres play some part in language it is the left hemisphere essentially which is responsible for expressive and in particular propositional speech.

THE SPEECH AREA

So far, we have considered only the respective parts played by the two hemispheres in relation to language and the problem of cerebral dominance. We must now ask whether language shows any evidence of localization *within* the hemispheres, i.e. whether it can be related to the activities of a particular region of the cerebral cortex. This is a controversial question. While, as we shall see, there is good evidence for the existence of a "speech area" in the dominant hemisphere, damage to which selectively impairs language, it cannot be said that the localization of a *lesion* giving rise to a disorder of language is the same thing as the localization of language itself. Indeed some people doubt whether any psychological function can be localized in the brain. None the less, if we can link lesions of particular regions of the brain with relatively circumscribed psychological disorders, we have at least taken the first step towards specifying the physical basis of mind.

In 1864, Broca presented his classical evidence that loss or defect of articulate speech is produced only by lesions involving the third frontal convolution of the left hemisphere. Broca's patients could utter few, if any, words but on the whole understood well what was said to them. That their disorder was not due simply to paralysis of the articulatory musculature was clearly shown by the fact that the patients were unable to express themselves any better in writing than in speech. Hence the disorder is often called *motor aphasia*, implying a defect in symbolic formulation and expression, i.e. the expression in language of thought or intention. It may vary in severity from virtually total speechlessness to relatively mild loss of fluency, hesitancy in evoking words and phrases and a certain simplification of grammar and syntax ("telegram style"). As many people who have had occasion to look after "stroke" patients will know, motor aphasia is commonly linked with paralysis of the right side of the body.

By and large, Broca's localization of motor aphasia has stood the test of time extremely well and there is general agreement that the area he designated (often called "Broca's area") does have a very important link with the voluntary control of expressive speech. At the same time, lesions involving any part of the brain in the general vicinity of the central fissure may produce a motor speech disorder. This is well shown in Fig. 4, which indicates the site of injury giving

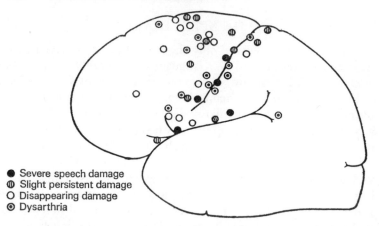

● Severe speech damage
⊕ Slight persistent damage
○ Disappearing damage
◉ Dysarthria

Fig. 4. The site of brain wounds causing Broca's aphasia: The severity and duration of the aphasia differ appreciably from case to case but bear no obvious relation to the site of injury. "Dysarthria" connotes defect in articulation without real defect in speech itself. It will be noted that the site of injury is in most cases anterior to the central fissure.

rise to motor aphasia in sixteen cases of penetrating left-hemisphere brain wounds studied by the German neurologist, K. Conrad. Whether the aphasia results directly from the injury or through some indirect effect on a more limited region of the brain, e.g. Broca's area, is conjectural.

Motor aphasia, though the best-known cerebral speech disorder, is by no means the only one. Exactly one hundred years ago, Carl Wernicke described a second form of aphasia in which the disability lies not so much in expressive speech—indeed the patients talk fluently, sometimes unduly so—but in their choice of appropriate words and in understanding fully what is said by others. Unlike motor aphasia, it is seldom accompanied by paralysis of the right side of the body though there is commonly a defect of sight in the right visual fields. This variety of speech disorder is known as *sensory aphasia* and is often associated with severe defect in reading and writing. In speech, reading and writing, the patient may substitute one word for another, e.g. producing "broth" instead of "brush" or "apple" instead of "orange", and occasionally producing words of no known meaning, such as "cosmey" or "jerry-knife". He is almost always unaware of his speech errors and even when they are called to his attention is seldom capable of correcting them. For this reason, it has often been supposed that his aural monitoring of his own speech output is at fault. In Wernicke's view, sensory aphasia is associated with lesions of the posterior part of the left temporal lobe, in particular the first temporal convolution.

Although not many people today believe that the understanding and monitoring of speech are controlled by a "centre" localized quite so precisely as Wernicke supposed, there seems no doubt that

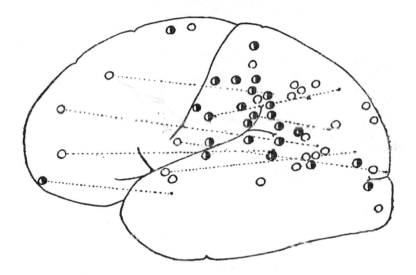

Fig. 5. The site of brain wounds causing Wernicke's aphasia: The site of injury in patients with predominantly receptive language defects is almost always posterior to the central fissure and involves principally the temporal and posterior parietal regions of the brain. The unfilled circles represent cases in which the most marked difficulty was in evoking names ("amnesic aphasia").

posterior temporal and tempro-parietal lesions give rise to defects of language of the kind he described. Indeed defects of understanding and the incidence of incorrect words (paraphasia) appear very closely linked with posterior temporal lesions and defects in reading and writing with tempro-parietal and posterior parietal lesions. Fig. 5 shows the incidence of sensory aphasia due to penetrating unilateral wounds of the brain in twenty-six of Conrad's cases, the great majority of which involve the posterior temporal or tempro-parietal regions. (A number of cases of "amnesic aphasia", in which the defect affects predominantly the capacity to recall and utilize object names, are also shown.)

We thus arrive at the concept of a "speech area", which is defined in a negative sense by Fig. 6, showing the sites of injury in Conrad's material of all patients with left-sided lesions who showed *no* disorder of speech. In a positive sense, the "speech area" has been

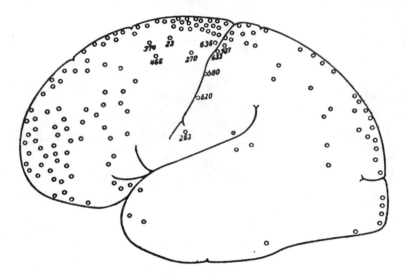

Fig. 6. The speech area: The site of injury in all non-aphasic cases with left-sided lesions. The few cases (numbered) who "ought" to have aphasia but did not are explained by exceptional circumstances, e.g. left-handedness.

mapped by Wilder Penfield, the distinguished brain surgeon, and his colleagues using methods of electrical stimulation in conscious patients. As will be readily appreciated, it is often essential in neurosurgical operations to establish precisely which parts of the cortex are essential to speech in order, so far as possible, to avoid damaging them. Now electrical stimulation within the "speech area" is likely to produce definite signs of interference with language, e.g. failure to name or misnaming an object. From the results of many such explorations of the brain cortex the area shown in Fig. 7 has been delimited. It corresponds reasonably well with maps of the speech area as established on the basis of clinico-pathological study.

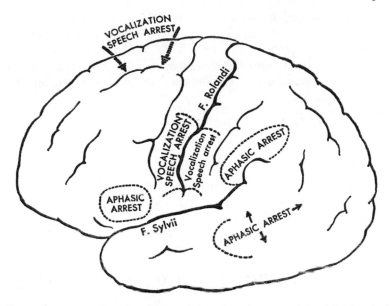

Fig. 7. Experimentally induced aphasia: The speech area as defined by electrical stimulation of the brain. Stimulation within this area produces interference with speech such as inability to name an object or naming it incorrectly.

CONCLUSION

While it is important to know what parts of the brain appear to be concerned with the mechanisms of speech, it cannot alas be said that this knowledge has, as yet, enabled us to understand at all clearly how these mechanisms actually work. All we really know with confidence is that the posterior parts of the speech area seem to be concerned with the understanding of speech and the formulation of thought—i.e. the embodiment of thought in proper syntactical and grammatical form and with correct choice and usage of words— whereas the more anterior parts appear to be concerned with the expression and communication of oral and written language. These processes appear too complex and too closely inter-related to warrant our ascribing them to "centres" with highly discrete and specialized functions, e.g. auditory or visual word-recognition, motor speech control, etc. as was the practice among neurologists fifty years ago. We have to think today rather in terms of the dynamic activities of a very large number of cerebral systems or sub-systems and fruitful

8

analyses may well be sought in the field of computer science. Although not all brain activity can be fruitfully explored on the basis of "computer models" there is no doubt that the neurologist has much to learn from the design of man-made communication systems in endeavouring to understand those bequeathed him by organic evolution.

NOTES

1 This experiment is described in some detail by Claire and W. M. S. Russell, Lecture 8, pp. 182–4 (Ed.)
2 See also Lecture 8, pp. 161–7 (Ed.)
3 See also Lecture 8, pp. 184–7 "The origins of language". (Ed.)

FURTHER READING

LORD BRAIN: *Speech Disorders* (London, Second Edition, 1965).

11

Language and socialization

BASIL B. BERNSTEIN

Institute of Education, London

I want first of all to make clear what I am not concerned with. Chomsky in "Syntactic Structures" neatly severs the study of the rule system of language from the study of the social rules which determine their contextual use. He does this by making a distinction between competence and performance.[1] Competence refers to the child's tacit understanding of the rule system, performance relates to the essentially social use to which the rule system is put. Competence refers to man abstracted from contextual constraints. Performance refers to man in the grip of the contextual constraints which determine his speech acts. Competence refers to the Ideal, performance refers to the Fall. In this sense Chomsky's notion of competence is Platonic. Competence has its source in the very biology of man. There is no difference between men in terms of their access to the linguistic rule system. Here Chomsky, like many other linguists before him, announces the communality of man, all men have equal access to the creative act which is language. On the other hand, performance is under the control of the social—performances are culturally specific acts, they refer to the choices which are made in specific speech encounters. Thus from one point of view, Chomsky indicates the tragedy of man, the potentiality of competence and the degeneration of performance (Hymes, 1966).

Clearly, much is to be gained in rigour and explanatory power through the severing of the relationship between the formal properties of the grammar and the meanings which are realized in its use. But if we are to study speech, *la parole*, we are inevitably involved in a study of a rather different rule system, we are involved in a study of rules, formal and informal, which regulate the options we take up in various contexts in which we find ourselves. This second rule system is the cultural system. This raises immediately the question of the relationship between the linguistic rule system and the cultural system. Clearly, specific linguistic rule systems are part of the cultural system, but it has been argued that the linguistic rule system in various ways shapes the cultural system. This very briefly is the view of those who hold a narrow form of the linguistic relativity hypothesis. I do not intend this evening to get involved in that particular quagmire. Instead, I shall take the view that the code which the linguist invents to explain the formal properties of the grammar is capable of generating any number of speech codes, and there is no reason for believing that any one language code is better than another in this respect. On this argument, language is a set of rules to which all speech codes must comply, but which speech codes are realized is a function of the culture acting through social relationships in specific contexts. Different speech forms or codes symbolize the form of the social relationship, regulate the nature of the speech encounters, and create for the speakers different orders of relevance and relation. The experience of the speakers is then transformed by what is made significant or relevant by the speech form This is a sociological argument because the speech form is taken as a consequence of the form of the social relation or put more generally, is a quality of a social structure. Let me qualify this immediately. Because the speech form is initially a function of a given social arrangement, it does not mean that the speech form does not in turn modify or even change that social structure which initally evolved the speech form. This formulation, indeed, invites the question—under what conditions does a given speech form free itself sufficiently from its embodiment in the social structure so that the system of meanings it realizes points to alternative realities, alternative arrangements in the affairs of men. Here we become concerned immediately with the antecedents and consequences of the boundary-maintaining principles of a culture or sub-culture. I am here suggesting a relationship between forms of boundary maintenance at the cultural level and forms of speech.

I am required to consider the relationship between language and socialization. It should be clear from these opening remarks that I am not concerned with language, but with speech, and concerned more specifically with the contextual constraints upon speech. Now what about socialization? I shall take the term to refer to the process whereby a child acquires a specific cultural identity, *and* to his responses to such an identity. Socialization refers to the process whereby the biological is transformed into a specific cultural being. It follows from this that the process of socialization is a complex process of control, whereby a particular moral, cognitive and affective awareness is evoked in the child and given a specific form and content. Socialization sensitizes the child to various orderings of society as these are made substantive in the various rôles he is expected to play. In a sense then socialization is a process for making people safe. The process acts selectively on the possibilities of man by creating through time a sense of the inevitability of a given social arrangement, and through limiting the areas of permitted change. The basic agencies of socialization in contemporary societies are the family, the peer group, school and work. It is through these agencies, and in particular through their relationship to each other, that the various orderings of society are made manifest.

Now it is quite clear that given this view of socialization it is necessary to limit the discussion. I shall limit our discussion to socialization within the family, but it should be obvious that the focusing and filtering of the child's experience within the family in a large measure is a microcosm of the macroscopic orderings of society. Our question now becomes what are the sociological factors which affect linguistic performances within the family critical to the process of socialization?

Without a shadow of doubt the most formative influence upon the procedures of socialization, from a sociological viewpoint, is social class. The class structure influences work and educational rôles and brings families into a special relationship with each other and deeply penetrates the structure of life experiences within the family. The class system has deeply marked the distribution of knowledge within society. It has given differential access to the sense that the world is permeable. It has sealed off communities from each other and has ranked these communities on a scale of invidious worth. We have three components, knowledge, possibility, invidious insulation. It would be a little naive to believe that differences in knowledge, differences in the sense of the possible, combined with invidious insulation, rooted in differential *material* well-being would not affect the forms of control and innovation in the socializing procedures of different social classes. I shall go on to argue that the deep structure of communication itself is affected, but not in any final or irrevocable way.

As an approach to my argument, let me glance at the social distribution of knowledge. We can see that the class system has affected the distribution of knowledge. Historically and now, only a tiny percentage of the population has been socialized into knowledge at the level of the meta-languages of control and innovation, whereas the mass of the population has been socialized into knowledge at the level of context-tied operations.

A tiny percentage of the population has been given access to the principles of intellectual change whereas the rest have been denied such access. This suggests that we might be able to distinguish between two orders of meaning. One we could call universalistic, the other particularistic. Universalistic meanings are those in which principles and operations are made linguistically explicit whereas particularistic orders of meaning are meanings in which principles and operation are relatively linguistically implicit. If orders of meaning are universalistic, then the meanings are less tied to a given context. The meta-languages of public forms of thought as these apply to objects and persons realize meanings of a universalistic type. Where meanings have this characteristic then individuals have access to the grounds of their experience and can change the grounds. Where orders of meaning are particularistic, where principles are linguistically implicit, then such meanings are less context-independent and *more* context-bound. That is tied to a local relationship and to a local social structure. Where the meaning system is particularistic, much of the meaning is embedded in the context and may be restricted to those who share a similar contextual history. Where meanings are universalistic, they are in principle available to all because the principles and operations have been made explicit and so public.

I shall argue that forms of socialization orient the child towards speech codes which control access to relatively context-tied or relatively context-independent meanings. Thus I shall argue that elaborated codes orient their users towards universalistic meanings, whereas restricted codes orient, sensitize, their users to particularistic meanings: that the linguistic realization of the two orders are different, and so are the social relationships which realize them. Elaborated codes are less tied to a given or local structure and thus contain the potentiality of change in principles. In the case of elaborated codes the speech is freed from its evoking social structure and takes on an autonomy. A university is a place organized around talk. Restricted codes are more tied to a local social structure and have a reduced potential for change in principles. Where codes are elaborated, the socialized has more access to the grounds of his own socialization, and so can enter into a reflexive relationship to the social order he has taken over. Where codes are restricted, the socialized has less access to the grounds of his socialization and thus reflexiveness may be limited in range. *One of the effects of the class system is to limit access to elaborated codes.*

I shall go on to suggest that restricted codes have their basis in condensed symbols whereas elaborated codes have their basis in articulated symbols. That restricted codes draw upon metaphor whereas elaborated codes draw upon rationality. That these codes constrain the contextual use of language in critical socializing contexts and in this way regulate the orders of relevance and relation which the socialized takes over. From this point of view, change in habitual speech codes involves changes in the means by which object and person relationships are realized.

I want first to start with the notions of elaborated and restricted speech variants. A variant can be considered as the contextual constraints upon grammatical-lexical choices.

Sapir, Malinowski, Firth, Vygotsky, Luria have all pointed out from different points of view that the closer the identifications of speakers the greater the range of shared interests, the more probable that the speech will take a specific form. The range of syntactic alternatives is likely to be reduced and the lexis to be drawn from a narrow range. Thus, the form of these social relations is acting selectively on the meanings to be verbally realized. In these relationships the intent of the other person can be taken for granted as the speech is played out against a back-drop of common assumptions, common history, common interests. As a result, there is less need to raise meanings to the level of explicitness or elaboration. There is a reduced need to make explicit through syntactic choices the logical structure of the communication. Further, if the speaker wishes to individualize his communication, he is likely to do this by varying the expressive associates of the speech. Under these conditions, the speech is likely to have a strong metaphoric element. In these situations the speaker may be more concerned with how something is said, and when it is said—silence takes on a variety of meanings. Often in these encounters the speech cannot be understood apart from the context and the context cannot be read by those who do not share the history of the relationships. Thus the form of the social relationship acts selectively on the meanings to be verbalized, which in turn affect the syntactic and lexical choices. The unspoken assumptions underlying the relationship are not available to those who are outside the relationship. For these are limited, and restricted to the speakers. The symbolic form of the communication is condensed yet the specific cultural history of the relationship is alive in its form. We can say that the rôles of the speakers are communalized rôles. Thus, we can make a relationship between restricted social relationships based upon communalized rôles and the verbal realization of their meaning. In the language of the earlier part of this talk, restricted social relationships based upon communalized rôles evoke particularistic, that is, context-tied meanings, realized through a restricted speech variant.

Imagine a husband and wife have just come out of the cinema and are talking about the film: "What do you think?" "It had a lot to say." "Yes, I thought so too—let's go to the Millers, there may be something going there." They arrive at the Millers, who ask about the film. An hour is spent in the complex, moral, political, aesthetic subtleties of the film and its place in the contemporary scene. Here we have an elaborated variant, the meanings now have to be made public to others who have not seen the film. The speech shows careful editing, at both the grammatical and lexical levels, it is no longer context-tied. The meanings are explicit, elaborated and individualized. Whilst expressive channels are clearly relevant, the burden of meaning inheres predominantly in the verbal channel. The experience of the listeners cannot be taken for granted. Thus each member of the group is on his own as he offers his interpretation. Elaborated variants of this kind involve the speakers in particular rôle relationships, and *if you cannot manage the rôle, you can't produce the appropriate speech*. For as the speaker proceeds to individualize his meanings, he is differentiated from others like a figure from its ground.

The rôles receive less support from each other. There is a measure of isolation. *Difference* lies at the basis of the social relationship, and is made verbally active, whereas in the other context it is *consensus*. The insides of the speaker have become psychologically active through the verbal aspect of the communication. Various defensive strategies may be used to decrease potential vulnerability of self and to increase the vulnerability of others. The verbal aspect of the communication becomes a vehicle for the transmission of individuated symbols. The "I" stands over the "We". Meanings which are discreet to the speaker must be offered so that they are intelligible to the listener. Communalized rôles have given way to individualized rôles, condensed symbols to articulated symbols. Elaborated speech variants of this type realize universalistic meanings in the sense that they are less context-tied. Thus individualized rôles are realized through elaborated speech variants which involve complex editing at the grammatical and lexical levels and which point to universalistic meanings.

Let me give another example. Consider the two following stories which Peter Hawkins, Assistant Research Officer in the Sociological Research Unit, University of London Institute of Education, constructed as a result of his analysis of the speech of middle-class and working-class five-year-old children. The children were given a series of four pictures which told a story and they were invited to tell the story. The first picture showed some boys playing football, in the second the ball goes through the window of a house, the third shows a woman looking out of the window and a man making an ominous gesture, and in the fourth the children are moving away.

Here are the two stories:

(1) Three boys are playing football and one boy kicks the ball and it goes through the window   the ball breaks the window and the boys are looking at it   and a man comes out and shouts at them   because they've broken the window   so they run away   and then that lady looks out of her window and she tells the boys off.

(2) They're playing football   and he kicks it and it goes through there   it breaks the window and they're looking at it   and he comes out   and shouts at them   because they've broken it   so they run away   and then she looks out   and she tells them off.

With the first story the reader does not have to have the four pictures which were used as the basis for the story, whereas in the case of the second story the reader would require the initial pictures in order to make sense of the story. The first story is free of the context which generated it, whereas the second story is much more closely tied to its context. As a result the meanings of the second story are implicit, whereas the meanings of the first story are explicit. It is not that the working-class children do not have in their passive vocabulary the vocabulary used by the middle-class children. Nor is it the case that the children differ in their tacit understanding of the linguistic rule system. Rather, what we have here are differences in the use of language arising out of a specific context. One child makes explicit the meanings which he is realizing through language for the person he is telling the story to, whereas the second child does not to the same extent. The first child takes very little for granted, whereas the second child takes a great deal for granted. Thus for the first child the task was seen as a context in which his meanings were required to be made explicit, whereas the task for the second child was not seen as a task which required such explication of meaning. It would not be difficult to imagine a context where the first child would produce speech rather like the second. What we are dealing with here are differences between the children in the way they realize in language use apparently the same context. We could say that the speech of the first child generated universalistic meanings in the sense that the meanings are freed from the context and so understandable by all. Whereas the speech of the second child generated particularistic meanings, in the sense that the meanings are closely tied to the context and would be only fully understood by others if they had access to the context which originally generated the speech.

It is again important to stress that the second child has access to a more differentiated noun phrase, but there is a restriction on its *use*. Geoffrey Turner, Linguist in the Sociological Research Unit, shows that working-class, five-year-old children in the same contexts examined by Hawkins, use fewer linguistic expressions of uncertainty when compared with the middle-class children. This does not mean that working-class children do *not* have access to such expressions, but that the eliciting speech context did not provoke them. Telling a story from pictures, talking about scenes on cards, *formally framed* contexts, do not encourage working-class children to consider the possibilities of alternate meanings and so there is a reduction in the linguistic expressions of uncertainty. Again, working-class children have access to a wide range of syntactic choices which involve the use of logical operators, "because", "but", "either", "or", "only". The constraints exist on the conditions for their *use*. Formally framed contexts used for eliciting context-independent, universalistic meanings may evoke in the working-class child, relative to the middle-class child, restricted speech variants, because the working-class child has difficulty in managing the rôle relationships which such contexts require. This problem is further complicated when such contexts carry meanings very much removed from the child's cultural experience. In the same way we can show that there are constraints upon the middle-class child's use of language. Turner found that when middle-class children were asked to rôle play in the picture story series, a higher percentage of these children, when compared with working-class children, initially refused. When the middle-class children were asked "What is the man saying", or linguistically equivalent questions, a relatively higher percentage said "I don't know". When this question was followed by the hypothetical question "What do you think the man might be saying?" they offered their interpretations. The working-class children rôle played without difficulty. It seems then that middle-class children at five need to have a very precise instruction to *hypothesize in that particular* context. This may be because they are more concerned here with getting their answers right or correct. When the children were invited to tell a story about some doll-like figures (a little boy, a little girl, a sailor and a dog) the working-class children's stories were freer, longer, more imaginative than the stories of the middle-class children. The latter children's stories were tighter, constrained within a strong narrative frame. It was as if these children were dominated by what they took to be the *form* of a narrative and the content was secondary. This is an example of the concern of the middle-class child with the structure of the contextual frame. It may be worthwhile to amplify this further. A number of studies have shown that when working-class black children are asked to associate to a series of words, their responses show considerable diversity, both from the meaning and form-class of the stimulus word. In the analysis offered in the text this may be because the children for the following reasons are less constrained. The form-class of the stimulus word may have reduced associative significance and so would less constrain the selection of potential words *or* phrases. With such a weakening of the grammatical frame a greater range of alternatives are possible candidates for selection. Further, the closely controlled middle-class linguistic socialization of the young child may point the child towards both the grammatical significance of the stimulus word and towards a tight logical ordering of semantic space. Middle-class children may well have access to deep interpretive rules which regulate their linguistic responses in certain formalized contexts. The consequences may limit their imagination through the tightness of the frame which these interpretive rules create. It may even be that with *five*-year-old children, the middle-class child will innovate *more* with the arrangements of objects (i.e. bricks) than in his linguistic usage. His linguistic usage is under close supervision by adults. He has more *autonomy* in his play.

To return to our previous discussion, we can say briefly that as we move from communalized to individualized rôles, so speech takes on an increasingly reflexive function. The unique selves of others become palpable through speech and enter into our own self, the grounds of our experience are made verbally explicit; the security of the condensed symbol is gone. It has been replaced by rationality. There is a change in the basis of our vulnerability.

So far, then, I have discussed certain types of speech variants and the rôle relationships which occasion them. I am now going to raise the generality of the discussion and focus upon the title of the paper. The socialization of the young in the family proceeds within a critical set of inter-related contexts. Analytically, we may distinguish four contexts.

1. The regulative context—these are authority relationships where the child is made aware of the rules of the moral order and their various backings.

2. The instructional context, where the child learns about the objective nature of objects and persons, and acquires skills of various kinds.

3. The imaginative or innovating context, where the child is encouraged to experiment and re-create his world on his own terms, and in his own way.

4. The interpersonal context, where the child is made aware of affective states—his own, and others.

I am suggesting that the critical orderings of a culture or sub-culture are made substantive—are made palpable—through the forms of its linguistic realizations of these four contexts—initially in the family and kin.

Now if the linguistic realization of these four contexts involves the predominant use of restricted speech variants, I shall postulate that the deep structure of the communication[2] is a restricted code having its basis in communalized rôles, realizing context bound meanings, i.e., particularistic meaning orders. Clearly the specific grammatical and lexical choices will vary from one context to another.

If the linguistic realization of these four contexts involves the predominant usage of elaborated speech variants, I shall postulate that the deep structure of the communication is an elaborated code having its basis in individualized rôles realizing context-free universalistic meanings.

In order to prevent misunderstanding an expansion of the text is here necessary. It is likely that where the code is restricted, the speech in the regulative context may well be limited to command and simple rule-announcing statements. The latter statements are not context-dependent in the sense previously given for they announce general rules. We need to supplement the context-independent (universalistic) and context-dependent (particularistic) criteria with criteria which refer to the extent to which the speech in the regulative context varies in terms of its *contextual specificity*. If the speech is context-specific then the socializer cuts his meanings to the *specific* attributes/intentions of the socialized, the specific characteristics of the problem, the specific requirements of the context. Thus the general rule may be transmitted with degrees of *contextual specificity*. When this occurs the rule is individualized (fitted to the local circumstances) in the process of its transmission. Thus with code elaboration we should expect:

1. Some developed grounds for the rule

2. Some qualification of it in the light of the particular issue

3. Considerable *specificity* in terms of the socialized, the context and the issue.

This does *not* mean that there would be an *absence* of command statements. It is also likely that with code elaboration the socialized would be *given* opportunities (rôle options) to question.

Bernstein and Cook (1965), Cook (1971) have developed a semantic coding grid which sets out with considerable delicacy a general category system which has been applied to a limited regulative context. Turner, G., linguist to the Sociological Research Unit, is attempting a linguistic realization of the same grid.

We can express the two sets of criteria diagrammatically. A limited application is given by Henderson (1970).

Realization of the Regulative Context

Universalistic

Specific————————————|————————Non-specific

Particularistic

It may be necessary to utilize the two sets of criteria for *all* four socializing contexts. Bernstein (1967 published 1970) suggested that code realization would vary with context.

If we look at the linguistic realization of the regulative context in greater detail we may be able to clear up another source of possible misunderstanding. In this context it is very likely that syntactic markers of the logical distribution of meaning will be extensively used.

"If you do that, then . . ."

"Either you . . . or . . ."

"You can do that but if . . ."

"You do that and you'll pay for it"

Thus it is very likely that young children may well in the *regulative* context have access to a range of syntactic markers which express the logical/hypothetical irrespective of code restriction or elaboration. However, where the code is restricted it is expected that there will be reduced specificity in the sense outlined earlier. Further, the speech in the control situation is likely to be well-organized in the sense that the sentences come as wholes. The child responds to the total *frame*. However, I would suggest that the informal *instructional* contexts within the family may well be limited in range and frequency. Thus the child, of course would have access to and so have *available*, the hypotheticals, conditionals, disjunctives, etc. but these might be rarely used in *instructional* contexts. In the same way, as we have suggested earlier, all children have access to linguistic expressions of uncertainty but they may differ in the context in which they receive and realize such expressions.

I must emphasize that because the code is restricted it does not mean that speakers will at no time use elaborated speech variants. Only that the use of such variants will be infrequent in the socialization of the child in his family.

Now, all children have access to restricted codes and their various systems of condensed meaning, because the rôles the code pre-supposes are universal. But there may well be selective access to elaborated codes because there is selective access to the rôle system which evokes its use. Society is likely to evaluate differently the experiences realized through these two codes. I cannot here go into details, but the different focusing of experience through a restricted code creates a major problem of educability only where the school produces discontinuity between its symbolic orders and those of the child. Our schools are not made for these children; why should the children respond? To ask the child to switch to an elaborated code which presupposes different rôle relationships and systems of meaning without a sensitive understanding of the required contexts must create for the child a bewildering and potentially damaging experience.

So far, then, I have sketched out a relationship between speech codes and socialization through the organization of rôles through which the culture is made psychologically active in persons. I have indicated that access to the rôles and thus to the codes is broadly related to social class. However, it is clearly the case that social class groups today are by no means homogeneous groups. Further, the division between elaborated and restricted codes is too simple. Finally, I have not indicated in any detail how these codes are evoked with families, and how the family types may shape their focus.

What I shall do now is to introduce a distinction between family type and its communication structure. These family types can be found empirically within each social class, although any one type may be rather more modal at any given historical period.

I shall distinguish between families according to the strength of their boundary-maintaining procedures. Let me first give some idea of what I mean by boundary-maintaining procedures. I shall first look at boundary maintenance as it is revealed in the symbolic ordering of space. Consider the lavatory. In one house, the room is pristine, bare and sharp, containing only the necessities for which the room is dedicated. In another there is a picture on the wall, in the third there are books, in the fourth all surfaces are covered with curious postcards. We have a continuum from a room celebrating the purity of categories to one celebrating the mixture of categories, from strong to weak boundary maintenance. Consider the kitchen. In one kitchen, shoes may not be placed on the table, nor the child's chamber pot—all objects and utensils have an assigned place. In another kitchen the boundaries separating the difference classes of objects are weak. The symbolic ordering of space can give us indications of the relative strength of boundary-maintaining procedures. Let us now look at the relationship between family members. Where boundary procedures are strong, the differentiation of members and the authority structure is based upon clear-cut, unambiguous definitions of the status of the member of the family. The boundaries between the statuses are strong, and the social identities of the members very much a function of their age, sex and age-relation status. As a shorthand, we can characterize the family as *positional*.

On the other hand, where boundary procedures are weak or flexible, the differentiation between members and the authority relationships are less on the basis of position, because here the status boundaries are blurred. Where boundary procedures are weak, the differentiation between members is based more upon *differences between persons*. In such families the relationships become more ego-centric and the unique attributes of family members more and more are made substantive in the communication structure. We will call these *person-centred* families. Such families do not reduce but increase the substantive expression of ambiguity and ambivalence. In person-centred families, the rôle system would be continuously evoking, accommodating and assimilating the different interests, attributes of its members. In such families, unlike positional families, the members would be making their rôles, rather than stepping into them. In a person-centred family, the child's developing self is differentiated by continuous adjustment to the verbally realized and elaborated intentions, qualifications and motives of others. The boundary between self and other is blurred. In positional families, the child takes over and responds to the formal pattern of obligation and privilege. It should be possible to see, without going into details, that the communication structure within these two types of family are somewhat differently focused. We might then expect that the reflexiveness induced by positional families is sensitized to the general attributes of persons, whereas the reflexiveness produced by person-centred families is more sensitive towards the particular aspects of persons. Think of the difference between Dartington Hall or Gordonstoun Public Schools in England, or the difference between West Point and a progressive school in the USA. Thus, in person-centred families, the insides of the members are made public through the communication structure, and thus more of the person has been invaded and subject to control. Speech in such families is a major medium of control. In positional families of course, speech is relevant but it symbolizes the boundaries given by the formal structure of the relationships. So far as the child is concerned, in positional families he attains a strong sense of social identity at the cost of autonomy; in person-centred families, the child attains a strong sense of autonomy but his social identity may be weak. Such ambiguity in the sense of identity, the lack of boundary, may move such children towards a radically closed value system.

If we now place these family types in the framework of the previous discussion, we can see that although the code may be elaborated, it may be differently focused according to the family type. Thus, we can have an elaborated code focusing upon persons or an elaborated code in a positional family may focus more upon objects. We can expect the same with a restricted code. Normally, with code restriction we should expect a positional family; however, if it showed signs of being person-centred, then we might expect the children to be in a situation of potential code switch.

Where the code is elaborated, and focused by a person-centred family, then these children may well develop acute identity problems, concerned with authenticity, of limiting responsibility—they may come to see language as phony, a system of counterfeit masking the absence of belief. They may move towards the restricted codes of the various peer group sub-cultures, or seek the condensed symbols of affective experience, or both.

One of the difficulties of this approach is to avoid implicit value judgements about the relative worth of speech systems and the cultures which they symbolize. Let it be said immediately that a restricted code gives access to a vast potential of meanings, of delicacy, subtlety and diversity of cultural forms, to a unique aesthetic whose basis in condensed symbols may influence the form of the imagining. Yet, in complex industrialized societies its differently focused experience may be disvalued, and humiliated within schools or seen, at best, to be irrelevant to the educational endeavour. For the schools are predicated upon elaborated code and its system of social relationships. Although an elaborated code does not entail any specific value system, the value system of the middle class penetrates the texture of the very learning context itself.

Elaborated codes give access to alternative realities yet they carry the potential of alienation of feeling from thought, of self from other, of private belief from rôle obligation.

In conclusion, I have tried to show how the class system acts upon the deep structure of communication in the process of socialization. I refined the crudity of this analysis by showing how speech codes may be differently focused through family types. I must point out that there is more to socialization than the forms of its linguistic realization.

Finally, it is conceivable that there are general aspects of the analysis which might provide a starting point for the consideration of symbolic orders other than languages.

NOTES

1 See also M. M. Lewis, Lecture 9, p. 202 (Ed.)
2 I.e. the underlying principles which regulate performances in the four critical socializing contexts.

FURTHER READING

BERNSTEIN, B.: "Education Cannot Compensate for Society", *New Society* No. 387 (February 1970).

BERNSTEIN, B.: "Family Role Systems, Socialisation and Communication", Manuscript, Sociological Research Unit, University of London Institute of Education (1962); also in Hymes, D. and Gumperz, J. J. (Eds.): "A Socio-Linguistic Approach to Socialisation", *Directions in Sociolinguistics* (New York, 1970).

BERNSTEIN, B. and COOK, J.: "Coding Manual for Social Control", Sociological Research Unit, University of London, Institute of Education (1965).

BERNSTEIN, B. and HENDERSON, D.: "Social Class Differences in the Relevance of Language to Socialisation", *Sociology*, Vol. 3, No. 1 (1969).

BRIGHT, N. (Ed.): *Sociolinguistics* (1966).

CARROLL, J. B. (Ed.): *Language, Thought and Reality: selected writings of Benjamin Lee Whorf* (New York, 1956).

CAZDEN, C. B.: "Sub-cultural Differences in Child Language: an inter-disciplinary review", *Merrill-Palmer Quarterly* 12 (1969).

CHOMSKY, N.: *Aspects of Linguistic Theory* (Cambridge, 1965).

COOK, J.: "An Enquiry into Patterns of Communication and Control Between Mothers and their Children in Different Social Classes", Ph.D. Thesis presented to the University of London (1971).

COULTHARD, M.: "A Discussion of Restricted and Elaborated Codes", *Educational Review* 22, No. 1 (1969).

DOUGLAS, M.: *Purity and Danger* (London, 1966).

DOUGLAS, M.: *Natural Symbols* (London, 1970).

FISHMAN, J. A.: "A Systematisation of the Whorfian Hypothesis", *Behavioural Science*, 5 (1960).

HALLIDAY, M. A. K.: "Relevant Models of Language", *Educational Review* 22, No. 1 (1969).

HAWKINS, P. R.: "Social Class, the Nominal Group and Reference", *Language and Speech*, 12, No. 2 (1969).

HENDERSON, D.: "Contextual Specificity, Discretion and Cognitive Socialisation: with Special Reference to Language", *Sociology*, Volume 4, Number 3 (September 1970).

HOIJER, H. (Ed.): "Language in Culture", *American Anthropological Association Memoir No.* 79 (1954, also published in Chicago).

HYMES, D.: "Models of the Interaction of Language and Social Setting", *Journal of Social Issues* 23 (1967).

HYMES, D. and GUMPERZ, J. J. (Eds.): *Directions in Sociolinguistics* (New York, 1970).

HYMES, D.: "On Communicative Competence", Research Planning Conference on Language Development among Disadvantaged Children, Ferkauf Graduate School, Yeshiva University (1966).

LABOV, W.: "Stages in the Acquisition of Standard English", Shuy, W. (Ed.): *Social Dialects and Language Learning*, Champaign, Illinois, National Council of Teachers of English (1965).

LABOV, W.: *The Social Stratification of English in New York City*, Washington, D.C., Centre for Applied Linguistics (1966).

MANDELBAUM, D. (Ed.): *Selected Writings of Edward Sapir* (California, 1949).

PARSONS, T. and SHILS, E. A. (Eds.): *Toward a General Theory of Action*, Harper Torchbooks TB1083N, Chapter 1, especially.

TURNER, G.: "Social Class and Linguistic Expressions of Uncertainty", *Language and Speech* (in press).

WILLIAMS, F. and NAREMORE, R. C.: "On the Functional Analysis of Social Class Differences in Modes of Speech", *Speech Monographs* Vol. XXXVI, No. 2 (1969).

12

Language and the teaching of English

FRANK PALMER

University of Reading

LINGUISTICS AND THE TEACHER

The teaching of English means so many different things to different people that it is difficult to know where to begin. We might be thinking about the teaching of English literature, teaching reading and writing, teaching composition, teaching immigrants or teaching English overseas. We might well be thinking primarily of none of these, for although linguistics may have something to offer in all these fields, the main interest of linguistics, in the sense in which I am a linguist, is in the description of language. I intend, therefore, to concentrate my attention largely upon the teaching of the facts of the English language as they are seen in terms of a linguistic analysis.

We have more linguistic knowledge of English than of any other language in the world. In recent times especially, there has been an increasing volume of published work, most of it originating in the United States of America. Very little of this has, unfortunately, yet reached those who are engaged in the actual teaching of the language. Leonard Bloomfield, who a few years ago would have been considered the "father" of American linguistics, commented in 1946: "The basic teaching of our schools, in reading and writing, in standard language and composition (and in their incredible courses on 'general language'), is dominated still by educationists who, knowing nothing about language, waste years of every child's time, and leave our community semi-literate."[1] This was even then an over-harsh judgment and few linguists today would wish to repeat such remarks, but the need for much more communication between those who concentrate on research into language and those who teach it is clear enough.

THE MANY RAMIFICATIONS OF ENGLISH TEACHING

Among the many possible ramifications of English teaching there is one very important distinction that has to be made at the start.

There is the world of difference between teaching English to native speakers of English and teaching English as a second or foreign language. Naturally the same people often find themselves at the same or at different times engaged in both exercises. Many who teach English overseas were once teachers of English here in England, and in recent times, when the teaching of immigrant children has become important, some teachers have the two tasks in the same place and at the same time. No doubt there are important points of contact between these two kinds of teaching, but they are different, and the man who thinks he can teach English in Nigeria, Turkey or Pakistan simply because he was an English teacher in an English school is to be firmly discouraged.

There is, of course, a real sense in which we cannot teach English at all to those who already speak it. Our native language is learnt, but it is hardly taught at all. We can no more teach our own school-children English than we can teach them to walk or run. They have acquired all these skills before they reach school age. At the age of five a normal child (and I include in the definition of normal the fact that the child has not suffered language deprivation) has almost complete mastery of the phonetics, phonology, grammar and semantics of his own language. I am here reminded of the suggestion that if anyone comments that a certain language is difficult (and the notion of "difficult" has official status since in some organizations the rewards are higher for learning difficult languages), the best reply is "Oh no, surely not. Why, even the little children can speak it."

Although, as I have suggested, the linguist's main attention must be upon the linguistic description of the language there are other areas of the English teaching that must in some degree be of interest to him. Let us look briefly at some of these.

To begin with the child has to be taught to read and write. He has, that is to say, to learn to use written symbols in the place of speech. This would seem to be a linguistic problem concerning the relation between sound and symbol or rather, perhaps, between speech and writing for the use of the terms "sound" and "symbol" begs too many questions. In this area linguists have contributed far less than they could. This is surprising, even deplorable, when one considers how busy they have been in the past decades providing orthographies for more exotic languages. Indeed the great interest in the phoneme stemmed largely from the wish to produce orthographies. One of the best-known books on the subject[2] had as its sub-title *A technique for reducing languages to writing*. There have, of course been occasional outbursts. Some years ago an American book entitled *Why Johnny can't read*[3] attacked the then popular "look and say" method of reading on the grounds that it ignored the obvious phonetic or phonemic features of English, and not only became a best seller but received favourable reviews in the linguistic journals. The main cause of linguists' comparative lack of interest in the teaching of reading and writing is, perhaps, related to their general lack of enthusiasm for spelling reform. This lack of enthusiasm, or in some cases outright hostility, stems largely from a clearer understanding of the relation between speech and writing (Is it really the function of the written language to "mirror" the spoken?) and from the knowledge that there are enormous practical problems associated with the vast variation of the spoken form and, more importantly, perhaps that our present orthography is not quite as ridiculous as it is sometimes portrayed. But I will return to this theme later.

A second aspect of the teaching of English concerns the teaching of the better use of the English language in both its written and its spoken form. This is the teaching of a skill and like the teaching of the skills of football or carpentry is largely a matter of imitation and practice. (Note here I am NOT suggesting that the learning of language is mere imitation and practice—I am referring to the development of the more advanced skills of oracy or literacy.) It is not to be expected that the linguist can have much to offer here. But there are two points to make. First it is important to realize that the spoken and written forms of the language are different—they are in some ways almost different languages and these differences can be brought out by careful linguistic investigation. Secondly, it is in this field that we often hear the silly accusation that linguists have no standard, that for them all language is equally good and that they, therefore, obstruct the training of the young in the use of their language. This criticism is, of course, like the ignorant accusation of immorality or amorality that is sometimes levelled at the anthropologist, the psychologist, the sociologist or the moral philosopher who dares to take an objective view of morality. In matters where people feel strongly—and there are few areas in which people feel more strongly than language—objectivity is a crime. There are, however, two points on which linguists have been critical of the teaching of English in this sense. First, they have shown that some of the rules of grammar have no real validity, but are little more than grammarians' inventions. Secondly, they have shown that many of the judgments about good or bad English are not linguistic judgments, but social ones. "Good" English is often no better on any kind of purely linguistic criterion, but is the English spoken by the "better" people. These two points have largely been accepted today, though sometimes I wonder if more than lip-service is paid to them in some places—and I speak as one who has had four children in grammar schools. There are, of course, judgments that one can and should make—about clarity, unambiguity, consistency and sheer aesthetic quality. But these have nothing to do with many of the traditional rules about good and bad.

Thirdly, there is the teaching of English literature. I do not wish to say much as language and literature has already been the subject of an earlier paper. One comment, however, is appropriate. No linguist should ever hope to explain the aesthetic values of literature by linguistic investigation any more than the values of great music can be explained simply by a careful examination of the score. But literature no less than everyday speech is language and as such is a proper subject for linguistic investigation, even if there are some who would regard the linguistic analysis of a poem as a kind of blasphemy.

We are left, finally, with the teaching of the language itself—teaching children who already speak and write English *about* the language. The aim here must surely be to make explicit what the pupil already knows implicitly. For it is a remarkable fact that the speakers of a language "know" all the rules of their language (including all the exceptions to the general rules) in the sense that they use them unhesitatingly, and can produce at will those sentences which conform and reject those which do not, without being in the slightest degree aware of what the rules actually are.

It is a matter of great surprise and regret to me that so little of this basic knowledge is ever available to our school children. The reason is, perhaps, two fold. First, teachers who have been students of literature are on the whole likely to be uninterested in the mechanics of language. It is natural enough that they should be unwilling to turn their attention to areas that seem to be more the domain of scientific investigation than of the arts. Secondly, the teaching of grammar especially has fallen into disrepute because so much of it, especially the exercise of parsing, seemed to be both boring and pointless. But this is an argument against the methods and the subject matter selected, not against grammar teaching as a whole. In the teaching of mathematics great changes have taken place, largely designed to do away with mechanical procedures whose purpose and justification were simply not understood, in favour of providing a clear understanding of what the subject is about. I see no reason to suppose that we cannot envisage a similar approach to the English language. But I must stress that I find it remarkable and deplorable that many teachers of English seem even to take a delight in the exclusion of any teaching about the language (in a linguistic sense) at all. Surely knowledge of one's language and of language in general is as important a part of a child's education as almost any other subject—even more important than most, since language is with him continually, and almost continuously. To exclude language study seems to me to be totally indefensible.

So far I have been speaking about teaching English to speakers of English. The teaching of English as a second or foreign language is a very different matter. Indeed the situation is almost totally reversed. The students now have to be taught English—they have to learn to speak it, to understand it, to write it and to read it from the very beginnings. Most of the areas of teaching of English that are so important for native English speaking children on the other hand are of lesser importance; indeed most of them are largely irrelevant to the basic need to teach the language.

There is here no problem of improving the students' English since to begin with they have no English to improve and it will be only at the highest level that there is a serious need to teach them how to express themselves more clearly and concisely. Nor sadly is English literature very relevant—however deplorable this statement may seem to the English scholar. Most of the students who learn English abroad have neither the need nor the wish to become fully acquainted with the great literature either of the past or of the present day. They are more interested in English as a tool of communication in a world in which English has become *the* international language. Naturally enough many of their teachers, whether they are themselves English or not, will have been trained in the study of English literature but their familiarity with it will be of little value when they are faced with the teaching of the skills of language. That is not to say, of course, that literature cannot be used as a means of teaching English; at the higher levels of education at least it is possible to make teaching more pleasurable by using interesting material, but it is, sadly, only for a tiny minority that literature can be an end in itself rather than a means to a quite different end.

There is one very important point about the teaching of English as a second or foreign language. Above all the students wish to learn to speak the language and to understand it when it is spoken. Sometimes, perhaps quite often, this may be a mistaken view since most of their real needs would be met by the ability to read and to write. They want to be able to write and receive letters, to read technical books, scientific works, catalogues, handbooks, etc., and perhaps even to publish in English. It is above all in science and commerce that English is so important. But nearly all students feel that this is not enough. They want to be able to talk to others in English, even to others who are not native speakers, and to travel to England or the United States. Above all, there is the radio. It is because of this that linguistics has seemed relevant to the teaching of English. For linguists have been very interested in the spoken language, even if not all would agree with Hockett[4] in making a distinction between language and writing—with the implication that the real language is the spoken one.

TRADITIONAL GRAMMAR

For both the English child and the student of English overseas the traditional approach has been through the grammar book. In particular J. C. Nesfield's grammar book[5] has sold thousands of copies at home and abroad, a huge percentage of them in the old British Empire, particularly India. But the traditional books are of limited value, mainly because they are not purely descriptive, not simply concerned, that is to say, with stating facts of the language as clearly and concisely as possible. Let us look briefly at some of their shortcomings.

First they have been far too interested in history and often confused historical statements with statements about the language as it is. This stems quite naturally from the great interest that was aroused in the nineteenth century in comparative philology—in the comparative and mainly historical study of the Indo-European languages, which stemmed from the discovery announced in 1789 by Sir William Jones that Sanskrit, Latin and Greek were all descended from a common ancestor. This study is in itself a fascinating and scholarly pursuit, but it is almost entirely irrelevant to our purpose. As you will know, the Swiss linguist, Ferdinand de Saussure, drew a clear line between synchronic and diachronic linguistics—between the study of language as it is at one period of time and the study of language at successive periods of time. Linguists have been interested chiefly, though not exclusively, in synchronic description.

What is important is that we should not confuse synchronic and diachronic statements, but such confusion abounds in the traditional approaches. It exists, for instance, in the kind of explanation given to the question "Why do we say that?" The usual reply would be in historical terms, yet all too often the student is not looking for the history of the linguistic item but for its place in the language structure. For instance why do we say *He ought to go* instead *He oughts to go* on the analogy of *He wants to go*? There is a simple historical explanation. *Ought* is the past tense of *owe* and like all past tense forms does not have an -*s* ending. But there is also a synchronic explanation that is much more illuminating. *Ought* is one of "modal" auxiliaries of which the others are *will, shall, can, may* and *must* (there are possibly two or even three others). These have several features in common. They are used like all auxiliaries in questions e.g. *Can I go?* and in negation e.g. *I can't go*. In particular they have no -*s* form. There is no more *He oughts to go* than *He wills go* or *He cans go*. This explanation is surely more useful, especially to the learner of English, and it is an explanation of a scientific kind—one that places a single item under a more general rule. The traditional grammars often, moreover, make statements that are true historically but not synchronically. It is not true that '*Ought* IS the past tense of *owe*" for the past tense of *owe* is *owed*. What is true is that *ought* WAS the past tense of *owe*—a fact of history. In a similar vein it is not true, as is suggested in the traditional grammars, that *dice* is the plural, of *die*, for there is no singular form *die* at all, at least not to refer to one of those little cubes with spots on them. Frankly, I do not know what is the singular of *dice*. Is it *dice* or do we usually avoid the problem by talking about *one of the dice*? Similarly it is almost certainly for historical reasons that grammarians insist on *whom* instead of *who* or more commonly the absence of any relative pronoun as in *The man I saw*. There is a much quoted passage from Shaw (*The village wooing*):

> *Z* If it doesnt matter who anyone marries
> then it doesnt matter who I marry and
> it doesn't matter who you marry.
> *A* Whom, not who.
> *Z* Oh, speak English: youre not on the
> telephone now.

In the area of meaning, appeals to history are even more common. The "real" meaning of a word will usually turn out to be a meaning it once had. The usual example here is *nice*. For however desirable it may be to dissuade our children from the excessive use of *nice*— "We went for a nice walk down a nice road one nice day and saw a nice house...", it is NOT true that *nice* means "fine" or "subtle". *Nice* means "nice". Certainly it once meant "fine" or "subtle", and this meaning still survives in the formalized forms *a nice point, a nice distinction*. But it also once meant "foolish"— closely related to Latin *nescius* from which it came, and it must have come earlier from forms meaning "not" and "cutting", which might suggest "blunt", almost the opposite of its alleged "real" meaning. But at what point in history do we look for such "real" meanings?

Secondly the traditional grammars are almost wholly interested in the written language with scant if any attention to speech. Yet there are many differences between spoken and written languages apart from the obvious fact that our orthography is, or appears to be, a very poor indication of the way we speak. There are more important features to note than that *ough* is pronounced in six different ways as in *cough, tough, bough, though, through* and *thorough*. There are all the facts of stress and intonation. Intonation, in particular, allows us to communicate a great deal that written language cannot. Consider for instance, the use of the fall–rise intonation line. If I say *She's very clever* with a fall or a rise, I shall be making a bald or a tentative statement about her intelligence. But if instead I use a fall–rise intonation you immediately know that I mean "She's very clever but...." Now this is as important a distinction as the question *Is she clever?* or the negative *She isn't clever*. But while negation and interrogation are clearly grammatical, we have no grammatical framework to deal with this kind of implication that is carried by the intonation. The reason is obvious—it is a feature of the spoken language only.

There are differences of a minor but striking kind between the grammar of the spoken and written language. For instance, it would be agreed that there are three common ways of forming the plural of nouns:

(i) add -*s*	e.g. *cat*/*cats*
(ii) no change	e.g. *sheep*/*sheep*
(iii) change vowel	e.g. *foot*/*feet*

Most nouns in English fall into the same class in speech and writing but some do not. *Postman*/*postmen* is clearly an example of (iii) in written language but in speech it belongs to (ii) since there is but one form—/poustmən/. If we say "The /poustmən/ came up the street" we do not know if there was one or more than one postman, just as we cannot tell how many sheep there are in *The sheep ran across the field*. Furthermore *house*/*houses* is a regular member of (i) in written language—we merely add an -*s*. But in speech it is totally irregular since the plural is /hauziz/ with the sibilant of *phases*, not */hausiz/ with the sibilant of *faces*. Then again there are some verbs with irregular -*s* forms e.g. *has* not **haves*. But while *does* is quite regular in the written form—just like *goes*, in speech it is quite irregular since it is /dʌz/ not */duːz/. Most of the verbs with irregular -*s* forms are auxiliary verbs. Indeed they all are except one. I make it a regular practice to ask my first year students to identify that single one, and always without success, so unaware are native speakers of the facts of the language they speak every day. It is, of course, *says* which is /sez/, not /seiz/, though oddly enough the orthographic form *sez* is often used to indicate sub-standard speech.

Thirdly, grammar books take over quite uncritically categories that are not appropriate to English, almost all of them from Latin. It has often been claimed that a knowledge of Latin helps with the understanding of English grammar. This is, or has been, true in a paradoxical way—true because the English grammar that the pupil learnt was really Latin grammar applied to English, and as long as he knew only English much of it seemed pointless and obscure; when, however, he learnt Latin it all became clear! It is some time since the grammar imposed the six cases of Latin on English—

9

table, O table, table, of a table, to or for a table, from or by a table, though we still hear talk of the English genitive and the dative. There is a great deal left over still from Latin in the traditional books. English has no gender, except perhaps in the *he/she/it* distinction which is a matter of sex rather than grammatical gender, and sex is not the same as gender as you can see from the German word for "wife", which is neuter. More serious than this is the survival of a three tense system in English, of past, present and future, though this trio appears nowhere in the formal patterns of the language, but is merely an example of thinking in the Latin mould. Why after all should we expect our three-fold division of time to be expressed in the verb? There is no natural or universal reason that it should be. Professor J. R. Firth used to deal with those who with their traditional and largely Latin training confused tense, a GRAMMATICAL category, with time by suggesting that tense was equally a feature of the English noun with *ex-wife* as past, *fiancée* as future and *grandfather* as pluperfect!

Fourthly, the traditional grammars are too concerned with PRESCRIPTION rather than DESCRIPTION, with normative rules telling us what English ought to be like rather that what it is. But what authority do they have for such rules? Most of them were invented at some time, largely on the model of Latin, in the eighteenth century or thereabouts. But there seems to be little point in insisting on these rules for our own children, and it is a greater mistake to insist on them for students overseas, for at least our own children will recognize them for what they are and ignore them once they are out of the classroom. Admittedly bad rules are on their way out, but some are still with us—witness the correspondence columns of the newspapers and the Radio Times where complaints against newsreaders and politicians who cannot speak "correct" English abound. Many of the rules are pure Latin. This is true of the insistence on *It is I* and *He is bigger than I* where all of us, I trust, would usually use *me*. But the corresponding Latin forms would require *ego* in the nominative, not *me* in the accusative. But why look to Latin? Why not to French where the form *je* would be proscribed in both examples. French has the form *moi*; what then is wrong with English *me*? Of course, the proponents of such rules do not admit they are derived straight from Latin, but give specious explanations. For *He is bigger than I* it is said that *than* is a conjunction and not a preposition, and that the sentence is short for *He is bigger than I am.* But one could argue on precisely the same lines for *He came after I*, which could be short for *He came after I did.* The simple fact is, of course, that *than* and *after* are both prepositions and conjunctions and that *He is bigger than I* is as unnatural as *He came after I* but recommended only because of the Latin model. There are many other rules of this kind. A notorious one, that we should not end a sentence with a preposition, was first propagated by Dryden. But it has no use or validity. There is nothing odd or undesirable about *I wasn't spoken to* or *the man I spoke to.* You may recall in this context Churchill's alleged reference to something "up with which I will not put" and the little girl who said "Mummy what did you bring that book I didn't want to be read to out of up for?"

AREAS OF INTEREST FOR LINGUIST AND TEACHER

I should like now to look, in some detail, at some of the areas of the English language in which a student of traditional grammar would be unfamiliar but which I feel should be included in any teaching programme. I would divide them roughly into three, the first concerned largely with English as a spoken language, the second with the grammar of English and the third with the varieties and use of English. I shall, however, say nothing more about the third of these as they are amply dealt with by Professor Bernstein and Professor Quirk.

First, then, let us consider the characteristics of the spoken language. Few speakers of English have any idea at all even of the phonological system, the system of sounds—how many vowels and consonants there are. Most of them are aware of the apparent vagaries of English spelling in regard to such oddities as the *ough* words but do not realize that we have, for instance, two "th" sounds [ð] and [θ] as in *this* and *thin*, or that we have a vowel system that cannot, except with very suspect manipulations be reduced to five. How many vowels there are in the spoken language depends on the way in which we analyse the dipthongs and the so-called long vowels. But it seems to be an unescapable fact, that if we consider just the short vowels, which are better referred to as the non-final vowels, since they do not occur at the end of a word, we shall end up with six. The full set is found between /r/ and /k/ and /p/ and /t/ as in

rick	*pit*
wreck	*pet*
rack	*pat*
rock	*pot*
ruck	*putt*
rook	*put*

It is interesting to notice the devices the written language uses to allow for the extra vowel—*rook* has a double *o*, while *putt* has a double *t*.

More knowledge of the phonemic system—the system of distinct sounds can, however, be in itself a dangerous thing. It has sadly misled spelling reformers and educators who have concentrated too much upon the inventory of distinct sounds, the phonetic alphabet, so to speak, of the English language, without paying attention to the function of the sounds. A very good and obvious example is in the -*s* ending of the plurals. For although in writing we merely add -*s* to *cat*, *dog* and *horse* to produce *cats*, *dogs* and *horses* in speech we add /s/ for /kæts/ /z/ for /dɔgz/ and /iz/ for /hɔːsiz/. But what is often overlooked is that although /s/ and /z/ are distinctive sounds in *Sue* and *zoo* they are not distinctive IN THE PLURAL FORMATION, since we could never have in English* /kætz/ with /z/ or */dɔgs/ with /s/. There is nothing to be gained, therefore, by making a distinction here just because a distinction has to be made elsewhere in the language, and, not surprisingly, native speakers of English are unaware that they have any distinction here—because, in fact, they do not! Notice, incidentally, that though I have spoken about the -*s* plural, the same remarks apply to the -'*s* possessive, the abbreviated form of *is* and *has* and even to the third person singular form of the verb. This -*s* formation with its phonetic alternations, entirely determined by the phonological shape of the word, is a very common feature of English and nothing at all is gained by associating it, or rather confusing it, with the phonemic contrast of /s/ and /z/. The conclusion is obviously that the orthography is not always as foolish as it seems. A more striking example of this is to be found in the words of the pattern *photograph*, *photography*, *photographic*. If we write in a phonemic orthography, we have /ˈfoutəgraːf/ /fəˈtɔgrəfi/ /foutəˈgræfik/. The second of these has no vowel in common with the first or the third, while the vowel of the third syllable is different in all three. Yet no native speaker of

English has any difficulty with the recognition of the orthographic form. Moreover, he is so familiar with the patterning involved that if we invent a new set of words, he would have no difficulty in producing the whole series if given the first of them. He would know, for instance, that if a "lomograph" were invented, its use will be "lomography" and its results "lomographic" (/ˈloumǝgraːf/, /lǝˈmɔgrǝfi/, /loumǝˈgræfik/). Once again the orthography which keeps the same shape for all the forms is totally adequate because the variations of sound are totally predictable.

Any study of the spoken language would have to include a study of intonation and stress. Here, however, we have a very real problem in establishing precisely what the facts are, partly because of the great complexity of our system of intonation and partly (perhaps even largely) because of the lack of a simple correlation between intonation and either grammar or semantics. It is not true, for instance, that we always make statements with a falling intonation and ask questions with a rising intonation and, indeed, there are very few statements of the kind that can ever be made about intonation. Nevertheless, it is perfectly possible to teach the recognition of the more obvious features of intonation. The earlier and less sophisticated works on the subject distinguish a small number of intonation tunes—the fall, the rise, the fall-rise with perhaps also a distinction between the low rise that is often associated with statements and the high rise that belongs more with questions. It is not difficult, too, to give an understanding of the way English makes use of sentence stress or tonicity—the placing of the main stress on different words in the sentence. One can do this with considerable effect (with a rising intonation) on the question: *Is Mary going to wear that hat?* There are seven words and seven possibilities in terms of sentence stress placement (with seven different interpretations).

In grammar the field is almost limitless, but I would particularly draw attention to the verbal system—not merely because I have written a book on the subject, but because it is basically interesting and quite unlike the picture given by traditional grammar books. In brief we have to recognize that the verbal system of English is operated largely by the use of the auxiliary verbs BE, HAVE, DO, WILL, SHALL, CAN, MAY, MUST and OUGHT (with several other marginally auxiliary verbs). These are important for three quite distinct reasons. First that they are different from verbs like

KEEP, WANT, BEGIN is shown by the fact that they cannot be freely combined. We can say *He keeps wanting to begin talking, He begins to want to keep talking, He wants to begin to keep talking* etc. But we can only say *He must have been talking* not **He has must be talking* or **He must be having talked* and in the case of all but the first of these auxiliaries we cannot combine them at all. There is no **will must* or **can may*. Secondly, BE and HAVE alone provide the progressive (*is eating*), the perfect (*has eaten*) and the passive (*is eaten*) as well as combinations as in *has been eaten*. These together with tense, past and present, which alone in English is formed by inflection—by actual change in the verb itself, go to make up the central system of the verb, while the others—WILL, SHALL, CAN, MAY, MUST and OUGHT add to this the modal system. Then, thirdly, with these verbs alone can we form negation and question in English by the devices of the *-n't* ending and the inversion of the subject and the auxiliary verb—*He wasn't going, He hasn't gone, He can't go, Is he going? Has he gone?, Can he go?,* but not **He wantsn't to go* or **Wants he to go?* Where there is no auxiliary verb we use DO. *He doesn't want to go. Does he want to go?* DO is the empty auxiliary verb—it has no function except to be an auxiliary verb in such places in the grammar as negation and question where an auxiliary verb is obligatory.

But even these important and fascinating facts about the English language are essentially on the "surface" of the grammar. A little "deeper" there are other problems. Why do we make the distinction between *He can't have been there yesterday* and *He couldn't be there yesterday*? i.e. what are the grammatical structures that make both forms possible and account for their difference in meaning? In both cases we appear to be denying past possibility and even if we can isolate the difference of meaning between these two sentences, how can we make any kind of systematic grammatical statement about them? It turns out to depend on several factors, first that there are two quite distinct uses of *could*—one to refer to the subject's ability, the other to refer to general possibility, and secondly on precisely what it is that is being placed into past time. Paraphrase shows what is meant—*It is not possible that he was there yesterday* and *He was not able to be there*. But this is not enough. We can generalize much more first by showing that this kind of distinction is possible with all the modals to some degree—cf. *He wouldn't be there* and *He won't have been there*—and secondly by evolving a different syntax for the two structures.

I could go on to talk for hours about negation—that *I don't think he'll come* is formed from *I think he won't come*, that *He mustn't come* is not the true negative of *He must come*—for the negative is *He needn't come*, and *He mustn't come* is rather *He must not-come*. Then there is a familiar problem of *some* and *any*. *Some* seems to be used with positive verbs and *any* with negative ones—*He has some money, He hasn't any money*. Why then can we distinguish between *Didn't you earn any money last week?* and *Didn't you earn some money last week?* Frankly I do not know the best way of handling this distinction, but once again the paraphrase may point the way—*Is it true that you didn't earn any money?* and *Isn't it true that you earned some money?* But if I leave this as yet an unsolved problem it is only to show that there is still much to be done.

TEACHING ENGLISH AS A SECOND OR FOREIGN LANGUAGE

I must now, very briefly, make some remarks on the teaching of English as a second or foreign language. The problems are different, and, I think, much more difficult.

There have been major misconceptions in the field—representing two major and conflicting approaches. The first is that we should, as in native language teaching, teach a great deal *about* the language—in fact that this is largely what teaching a language is. This is a major facet of the much despised traditional "Grammar-translation" approach. It seems to me, and others, fairly clear that there is not much point in teaching grammar, i.e. teaching about the grammar of English, to children in Africa, Asia, or Europe for that matter. They want to learn to speak and to write the language, not to be able to provide a linguistic description of it. However, it is possible to be too dogmatic. I know that if I wish to learn a new language, the simplest way to approach it is to spend some hours with a grammar book. It helps a great deal if, when I try to practise the new language, I already understand the major grammatical and phonological characteristics. I am not, of course, in the same position as the child at school and what is useful to me is not necessarily, not even probably, appropriate to him. But I do not think we know as yet how much formal teaching, if any, would be useful for the more intelligent child, particularly the child who has to learn more than one language. Are we sure, for instance, that there is no truth in the old belief that learning Latin grammar was a good training for the acquisition of other languages—simply because it gave an insight into the way languages "behave"?

The second misconception is that a foreign language can be learnt in the same way as one's own native language. This is found in the approach that a few years ago was supposed to replace the out-dated grammar-translation method—the "direct method" in its various forms. Here children were merely presented with a situation in which the language was simply provided and they were required to respond—in a situation very like that of the child learning to speak his own tongue. But this was wholly mistaken for two reasons. First there is not enough time. The child learning his own language does so at every hour of the day, while the child learning a new language probably has no more than a few hours a week. If we are to have any success with these few hours obviously some short cuts involving some kind of concentrated directed teaching are needed. Secondly, the child already knows one language—cannot we in all seriousness make use of that knowledge? It is easy enough to make fun of a method that so deliberately refuses to make use of any previous knowledge. One story I like is of the teacher in Africa trying to put over by the direct method an English Christmas. The children were obviously puzzled about the turkey, when he heard a whisper (in their language)—"It's an ostrich". And there is another of the teacher who illustrated trains by making puffing noises and going under his desk to suggest a tunnel. Naturally every time the word occurred the children pretended they did not know the meaning!

What has the linguist to provide in this field? Three things I think. First, he can and must provide an accurate description of English. This will probably, almost certainly, not be made available to the pupils, but the teacher should be fully cognisant of it and it must to some degree determine the material that is taught and tested. Grading of teaching material is obviously a linguistic exercise in the sense that it can be stated only in linguistic terms. But it does NOT necessarily follow that the grading of the material can be determined wholly or even largely by linguistic factors. This is an important point. The specification of what is to be taught can only be done in linguistic terms but decisions about that specification are not necessarily linguistic. There are many other factors of educational, social, psychological kinds. So there is, or should be, no clash between the linguist and the educationalist—any more than in teaching mathematics there can be any clash between the professors of mathematics and those who are solely concerned with teaching the subject at school. This is why I dislike the term "applied linguistics". I do not really know what it is. I know only that linguistics is a valuable tool in language teaching, but the two are quite different.

Secondly, the linguist can provide relevant information about the learner's own language. I am now thinking of what are usually called contrastive studies. Unfortunately this is one of the weakest areas of language study related to language teaching. There are a few contrastive studies of this kind, comparing the phonological and grammatical systems of two languages, but they are of very limited use. They do, of course, account for the fact that a French child fails to pronounce his *th*'s or that an African child cannot distinguish between *cat, cut, cart, caught* and *cot*. But contrast at this level (very much on the "surface") is of little value simply because for both languages a number of equally valid descriptions are possible. For instance, if we wish to compare the vowel system of English with that of another language, which analysis of the system are we to take? We can think in terms of a six-vowel system (and even a five-vowel system) or of an eleven-vowel system or of almost any number up to twenty-five or so, depending on the way we wish to analyse. Clearly we cannot rightly contrast unless we have some non-arbitrary systems to contrast. *And* phonology is simple compared with grammar! But there is a straight-forward descriptive problem—that of describing what actually happens when a class of, say, French children learns English. Such a description would be tedious and unrewarding for any one who looks for simple solutions but is, surely, a very valid and important exercise. Linguists, unfortunately, are today less and less inclined to get down to the job of minute and careful investigation of real languages—be they the languages of native speakers or of language learners.

Thirdly, the linguist ought to be able to state in more general terms what happens when a child learns a language and in particular when he learns a second language. There is, of course, much speculation along the lines of the distinction between competence and performance and into the nature of linguistic universals, but I do not believe that this is what we need. Research is required to find out whether certain kinds of linguistic "knowledge" in one language

9*

facilitate the acquisition of similar knowledge in another. For instance, how relevant is it that a language has a passive or how relevant that the passive involves features similar to that of English, when the pupil tries to learn the English passive? It could be possible to investigate such problems—though as with all linguistic investigations, a vast amount of tedious painstaking work is required.

Again and again in the paper I have spoken of the need for careful linguistic investigation and description, for this in my belief is the essence of linguistics. I do not in any way doubt the need for a sound theoretical basis for our subject, but much of linguistic theory is pure speculation and often speculation with the false basic assumption that the answers are easy, that the basic systems are simple. Meanwhile the need for detailed research is overlooked.

NOTES

1 Bloomfield, L.: "Twenty one years of the Linguistic Society", *Language* 22 (1946), p. 3.
2 Pike, K. L.: *Phonemics* (Ann Arbor: The University of Michigan, 1947).
3 Flesch, Rudolf: *Why Johnny can't read—and what you can do about it* (New York: Harper, 1955).
4 Hockett, C. F.: *A course in modern linguistics* (New York: Macmillan, 1958), p. 4.
5 Nesfield, J. C.: *Manual of English grammar and composition* (London and New York: Macmillan, 1898).

FURTHER READING

CRYSTAL, D.: *What is Linguistics?* (London, 1968).
GLEASON, H. A.: *Linguistics and English grammar* (New York, 1965).
HALLIDAY, M. A. K., McINTOSH, A. and STREVENS, P.: *The linguistic sciences and language teaching* (London, 1964).
HORNBY, A. S.: *A guide to patterns and usage in English* (London, 1954).
PALMER, F. R.: *A linguistic study of the English verb* (London, 1965).

PALMER, H. E. and BLANDFORD, F. G.: *A grammar of spoken English*, third edition, revised and rewritten by R. Kingdon (Cambridge, 1969).

QUIRK, R.: *The use of English* (London, 1968).

13

Language and extra-linguistic communication

COLIN CHERRY

Imperial College, London

"IDEAS AND IMAGES"

THE RUDE SHOCK THAT AWOKE THOMAS HOBBES

One afternoon in the year 1629 Thomas Hobbes was browsing in a gentleman's library, somewhere near Paris, when he chanced upon a copy of Euclid's "Elements", an event which was to have a profound effect upon his life. It is to be remembered that he was then 41 years old and that he had been educated at Oxford in the traditions of scholarly logic—of which he confessed he could make no sense whatever. In later life he also confessed that he had read very little, saying that those who read most seemed to know least, (a view to which I shall be offering a certain subscription in this lecture).

However, Hobbes did not read this book of Euclid in the way in which it is customary to do so—from page 1 onwards—but he read it *backwards*, "from proposition to its demonstration, then to the preceding proposition with its demonstration", and so on. In the words of his biographer John Aubrey,[1] he is said to have exclaimed: "By g———— this is impossible!..." (for, we are told, "he would now and then *sweare* by way of emphasis"). By this unusual means "he was demonstratively convinced of that trueth". "This made him in love with geometry".[2] It was from this moment that his philosophical work began.

CHARLES SANDERS PEIRCE (1839-1914)
THE FOUNDER OF "PRAGMATISM"

I start with this story because it crystallizes several themes of my talk tonight. Now, I am neither artist nor mathematician, but a student of "human communication", a subject which is not centred on any traditional academic field, but has forced me over the past 35 years to enter several of them (technology, psychology, social sciences and epistemology in particular) and to try to reconcile these varied points of view. To do this and to guide experimentation, some consistent system of thinking has had to be adopted, some philosophy. I confess that I myself am a confirmed "Pragmatist", a follower of Charles Sanders Peirce, who invented the philosophy of Pragmatism, that curious, eccentric American, a one-time teacher of William James (in whose stables, I believe, he once took up residence).

Sanders Peirce[3] was essentially a logician, probably the leading one of his day, but his theories were not coldly detached from human life. To him it was human beings who have knowledge; it was living creatures who communicate. Nor did he divide the world into its traditional dualism (the world of "reality", outside ourselves, and the internal world of "private" thought and experience) but he united them by starting with the concept of *signs*. To him, this word *sign* referred not just to spoken and written words, but included all forms of gesture, drawing, numbers, tokens (like money), painting . . . all forms, from simple reflexes like blushes and frowns, to the heights of sonnets and symphonies.[3] Any thought or concept must be *signified*, both to the thinker himself and to other people. In Peirce's terms: "all thought *is* in signs".

On this base Peirce built up his theory of knowledge in such a way that not only behavioural aspects of communication could be discussed, but also such words as *meaning, truth, knowledge*, and other value terms. I believe it is true to say, also, that Peirce's views are wholly consistent with the sociological theory of Emile Durkheim (1858–1917)[5].

THE CHOICE OF SIGNS FOR EXPRESSION CAN REVEAL OR CONCEAL TRUTH

But to start. When I was taught Euclid's geometry at school, one theorem stood out a mile as having something fishy about it. It was Pythagoras's Theorem—illustrated by Fig. 1a. To me, the proof of this theorem seemed far too complicated, to produce such an elementary *idea*, an idea expressed more simply in the symbols of algebra as:

$$A^2 = B^2 + C^2$$

So simple! This idea is "beautiful", in a sense, but its conventional proof seemed unaesthetic, to me.

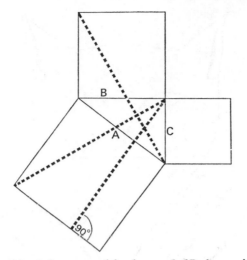

Fig. 1a. The traditional diagram used for the proof of Pythagoras's Theorem—a complicated image for a simple idea.

I was older than Thomas Hobbes before I was "demonstratively persuaded of the trueth". This truth is that this conventional form of expressing this Theorem *conceals* a far greater truth. Let me illustrate.

I had been taught to recite this Theorem in the form of an incantation: "The Square on the hypotenuse equals the sum of the squares on the other two sides", as endless generations of schoolboys must have been too. But we can divide both sides of this equation by 2 and see that what is also true is that: "the triangle on the hypotenuse is the sum of the triangles on the other two sides".

So we could go on, hacking off corresponding pieces from these triangles . . . and so produce *any similar* shapes. In private discussion recently, Professor Hyman Levy gave me the most "demonstratively persuasive trueth" by saying that Pythagoras's Theorem might just as well be "the cat on the hypotenuse equals the sum of the cats on the other two sides!" (See Fig. 2). The Theorem, in fact, has no specific relevance to square or any other *shapes* at all; it is about *areas*, not shapes. (A^2 is an area, not a square shape).

Now, you can search the Book of Euclid from beginning to end,

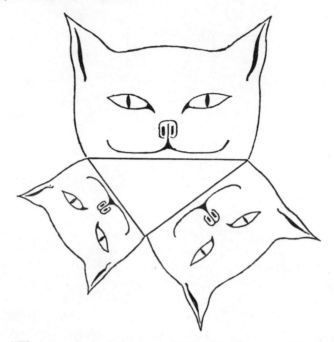

Fig. 2. "The cat on the hypotenuse equals the sum of the cats on the other two sides." (With full acknowledgement to Professor Hyman Levy.)

and find no reference to cats anywhere. Nor to cows nor trees. Why not? The answer to this fascinating question is not to be sought in mathematics, but rather in social institutions. The answer is that these Ancient Greeks were not concerned with logical thought of cats, cows or trees (though they have been of religious significance to them as to other cultures). They were interested only in straight lines, squares, circles, triangles, etc. probably by virtue of their practical needs for navigation by the fixed stars.

It was also a *static* geometry. They did not accept "movement" as one of the concepts in their logic. Briefly, as in all systems of human thought, certain restrictive bounds or "disciplines" were dominant—these are the "rules of the game".

If movement is accepted as a geometric concept, Pythagoras's Theorem requires no proof at all—it is obvious. Let me demonstrate with the diagram in Fig. 1b. The four black right-angled triangles are now set around the four sides of the white square, of

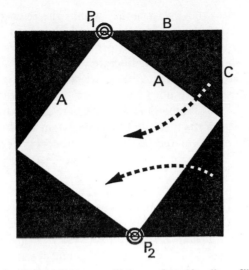

Fig. 1b. An alternative diagram which renders the "proof" obvious, if movement be accepted. See *Fig. 1c*.

side Λ. If we swing two of these triangles into new positions the white area becomes two squares, of sides B and C, (See Fig. 1c). The Theorem is obvious.

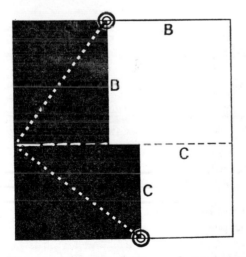

Fig. 1c. The white area A² in *Fig. 1b* has now become converted into two squares of areas B² and C².

Any system of thought, whether within the sciences or the arts, aims to produce expressible *forms*, and the distinction between form and formlessness can be expressed by the one word: *rules*. Sometimes these rules are deliberately set up and known; sometimes we merely conform to them without knowing them in any articulate sense (as we obey the laws of the land without knowing much about them). Sometimes the rules are dictated by Nature (as an artist or sculptor is restricted to some extent by the properties of paint or stone). Form requires rules, perhaps better described as "constraints", rules which are mostly man-made (self- or socially-imposed).

This concept of "form" is one of the strongest bridges between the Sciences and the Arts. No concept can exist without a conceiver, and its revelation requires some concrete, expressible, *sign*. There can be no substance without form. Even in thinking in privacy, we are conversing—"I" with "myself"—and we are deceiving ourselves if we feel, sometimes, that we have ideas that we cannot express.

Another simple example from "moving geometry" can be illustrated by another model, illustrated by Fig. 3—probably well-

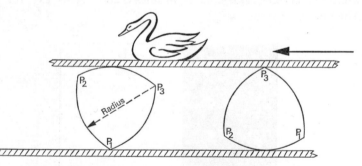

Fig. 3. Parallel motion without round rollers or wheels. Our thinking can be inhibited by our technological expectations. (During the lecture the curvilinear triangular "rollers" were concealed by a cardboard wall.)

known to many of you, but I have found that it deceives many non-scientific people. Here I have shown a long platform which you can see I can push backwards and forwards behind this wall. The little folded-paper model of a swan, on the platform, seems to glide smoothly along, parallel always to the table. What can the platform be rolling upon? Wheels? Rollers? No; these are the shapes that naturally spring to minds of people raised in industrial societies. There are, in fact, an infinity of other possibilities, for any odd-sided curvilinear polygon would do. Our new "50 new pence coin" would serve for example.

That certain forms dominate our thinking is evidenced by the fact that we have words for them. Thus, in our European culture, we speak of shapes as *straight*, *square*, *round*, etc. or by referring to common objects or conventional icons like heart-shaped, four-legged, etc. But we do not have words for *all* shapes! Knowledge requires categorization, peculiar to the culture. In Christian culture we speak of *the Cross* with much significance, whilst the words "the Crescent" are mainly confined to naming suburban roads, without any Islamic associations.

Enough of geometry. I have deliberately taken examples from elementary geometry tonight, because they are easy to talk about. But the main points that I am trying to make are relevant to all fields of human thought—and therefore to human nature. Knowledge, in Sanders Peirce's view, is all socially derived.

THE INSTITUTIONAL ORIGINS OF OUR IDEAS AND IMAGES OF THE WORLD

When I was born I formed a part of my own mother, with no knowledge of any separate existence. I was taught to be myself, and to see the world as I do, not through direct observation, but first through verbal and other play, initially by my mother and family, then by friends, acquaintances, school—throughout life. I have been taught to see my reality, that is, through the language and all other signs and symbols of the many institutions of my culture. As Durkheim argued, the individual and his society are inseparable, being two sides of the same coin. Our views of the world then continually change as our varied experiences build up in us, not so much by our objective view of some idealistic, ultimate, metaphysical reality "out there" but created by our ever-changing social contacts. Since the detailed experiences of each one of us differ we each see the world in different ways. Nevertheless, there is a general "consensus of opinion" about many aspects of the world, especially of the "outward aspects", within any culture, or within its various institutions, deriving from the very fact of sharing that

Fig. 4. A fine example of international symbolism, confined in interpretation to the institution we call "sports". Bodily features are almost absent.

culture—the language, signs and symbols taught us by society through its institutions. As the great physicist Schrödinger has put it: "only a minute fragment of what any one of us may call our picture of the world is drawn from our own sense-experience—the greater part coming from other people's experience (of which the lion's share is preserved in writing and print)".[4]

That is to say, we are *taught* to see and imagine that we know about places we have never visited, about people we have never met, and about ideas and institutions we have never lived with. We can but imagine we know and we shall deceive ourselves; we can do no more than view other peoples, with their funny ways, only through the spectacle of our own institutions.

We can understand past history, too, only in this way, and for this reason alone I would quarrel with those Marxists who say that we can comprehend the social conditions and exploitations of early times, *as they were felt at that time*, through study of, for example, paintings or of Egyptian inscriptions. We can but speculate.[6]

We can understand foreign peoples today only to the extent that we may share common institutions with them, say those of the division of labour, or of money, or of science, or of sports or, fast-increasing today, of law.[7] Fig. 4 shows one of the finest examples of international symbolism yet designed (in my opinion)—confined in interpretation to the institution of "sport"; notice the almost total absence of the human body.

"TRUTH" IS A PLURALITY. ARTS AND SCIENCES DISTINGUISHED

"Reality" is then something drawn out of ourselves, as our institutions largely decide, by the circumstances of the moment, and truth, like beauty, is relative to the person and his beliefs, it is not heaven-decided. In the words of the Pragmatist William James, one answer to Pontius Pilate's question, "What is truth?" is simply "Truth is what you firmly and soundly believe".[8] Because it is upon these beliefs that you will act.[9]

These personal variations in our views of the world are, of course, far greater in the Arts than in the Sciences, and purposefully so, a distinction which has increased with the rapid spread of printed journals. If Art be considered as the creation of new symbols to express new hypotheses, it presents challenges to us each as individuals; then Science is concerned rather with challenging society, by exposing its hypotheses to the public test.

These views may seem trivial to those of you who believe that Science consists of the *discovery* of the "Laws of Nature" or as the dictates of Mother Nature. To the Pragmatist, however, this use of the word "law" is interesting, for it is suggestive of a written body of edicts which Nature must obey or be punished, a suggestion of Holy Writ. This misconception has never been more clearly put than by William James when he thundered to his pupils:

"When the first mathematical, logical, and natural uniformities, the first *laws* were discovered, men were so carried away by the clearness, beauty and simplification that resulted, that they believed themselves to have deciphered authentically the eternal thoughts of the Almighty. *He* also thought in conic sections, squares and roots and ratios, and geometrized like Euclid. *He* made Kepler's laws for the planets to follow . . . *He* established the classes, orders, families and genera of plants and animals . . . *He* thought the archetypes of all things, and devised their variations; and when we rediscover any one of these His wondrous institutions, we seize His mind in its very literal intention".[10]

PROGRESS IS THE RESULT OF COURAGE. THE COMFORTS OF TRADITION

Such biting sarcasm is perhaps unnecessary today, though I feel we cannot be harmed if we remind ourselves occasionally that rather it is we men and women who "obey" the laws of Nature; inanimate Nature cannot *obey*. It is *we* who obey the laws of Newton, or Kepler, or Maxwell when we talk with one another in scientific discourse. The "laws of Nature" are really the rules of the Community of Scientists and, like all man-made laws, they may be broken—by the ignorant, the stupid or, far more important, by those persons of great insight and courage who seek to reform them. I say "courage" because, though science has at its very centre the ideal of anti-dogma, its laws become named after famous men. There is an authoritarianism about it. It took a Galileo to say that Copernicus was wrong and an Einstein to tell Newton that his Laws needed reforming. But all truth is sought this way, by people who have the courage to challenge established beliefs, the *status quo*. This thought is not mine, of course, but Samuel Johnson's:

"All great truth begins as heresy". It is more important to creative change, and so to the possibility of progress, to be able to say "No!" than to say "Yes", for you will be defying established belief and laying yourself open to challenge and demand for an explanation.

In Durkheim's view, for any action to be moral it must be both desired by the actor and accepted by his society. All really new ideas, *revealed* by new symbols, must therefore to some extent or other be seen by the majority as momentary acts of immorality (of various degrees). They may be desired by the creator, but not immediately by the rest of society. Only later, when others of the society have been "demonstrably persuaded of the trueth", does the act become moral and built into the new conservatism. The original thinker, to whom the new idea has been first revealed, has not created it for the "good of the masses" of his present day. He is communicating with himself, the person he is about to become, and so with people of the future. A creative thought *must* be ahead of its time and, momentarily, immoral, to some extent, greater, or lesser, or trivial. Any reformer will be seen by some sections of the population to be bloody-minded. Otherwise there could be nothing to reform. Quite simply: the country is going to the dogs.

Perhaps we shouldn't let this worry us unduly, for it always has been. It is an inevitable feeling deriving from social change itself. In a changing society, whether progressive or not, there must be some sections, large or small, who feel and express some sense of outrage. Progress contains an element of pessimism and offence. Heaven on Earth is a contradiction in terms, for nobody would notice their bliss. Perhaps we are here close to the Buddhist view that in a world of ceaseless change, man is born to sorrow, for that which he loves today will be changed by tomorrow. A "progressive" society must always, to some extent, be a dissatisfied society, with its established beliefs constantly under criticism or challenge. All creative thought, in both Science and Art is then, like crime, a form of deviant behaviour. Today, we don't often burn such critics to death, or crucify them—we shove them into special institutions, under the care of enlightened authority—into prisons, or mental homes, or universities—where their dangerous potential can be watched by the public. There they are categorized and labelled, so that the public comes to *expect* certain things of them, in the traditions of such institutions.

The quest for truth, as it seems to oneself, cannot be divorced from moral searchings. This thought is not miue either; you will find it in the Third Book of Genesis. In simplest terms, those old clichés: "Art for Art's Sake" and, worse: "Science for Science's sake" are either semantic nonsense or they are immoral statements. The criterion of "sake" involves living people. Both Artists and Scientists are morally responsible for their productions. It is not moral that any system of thought be judged wholly by its own criteria. This is obvious today in the field of Science. In the Arts it is most clearly seen perhaps in political cartoons, in advertisements of certain kinds, and in all creation of knowingly false images.

COMMUNICATION WITH OTHER WORLDS AND ALL THAT

But to return. I have offered the Pragmatists' view of knowledge that it is all socially derived, even knowledge that we exist and of who "we" are. Rather than speak, as I did earlier, of "understanding" foreign peoples or peoples of earlier history, it may perhaps be the most clear way of expressing this view to consider that present-day obsession—communicating with "intelligent beings" in outer space.

In common discussion, confusion sometimes arises through casual usage of words like "intelligent" and "language". Communication requires *signs*, as does thought; for a concept to be distinguished from any other concept, it must be signified. We may then ask, as did Charles Sanders Peirce, "What *is* a sign?" Concepts in other people's heads, whether Earthmen's or Martian's, are not observable; only their consequences are. Peirce argued that, for any stimulus to act *as* a sign, it must be interpretable by some response sign. How would we know that any signals received from Mars, however regular, represent Martian signs, symbols or language? The real difficulty lies not in the (assumed) recognition of regular signs, as such, but in *interpreting* them and in assessing their significance to Martians.

Bees and termites, for example, have highly developed systems of communicating which were first elucidated by Karl von Frisch.[11]

Briefly here, when a scout bee finds food, at any distance up to 6, 7 or even 8 miles, she returns to the hive where, in total darkness she "dances" on the vertical comb in a figure-of-eight, with its axis inclined to the vertical by an angle equal to the angle of the food's direction to that of the sun. To indicate distance, she waggles her posterior at a number of waggles per second more or less inversely proportional to the distance to the food. The other bees touch her, mimic her, and "get the itch", until all eventually are excited into a kind of ritualistic pop-session which drives them forth from the hive with the Message in their eagerness to serve the State. They communicate in other ways too, for other community-preserving purposes—but let this suffice. Here we have primitive counting and measuring systems. They have also achieved division of labour and the most rigid system of Trade Unions ever known. Heaven help any blackleg. They are stung to death.[12]

Are bees "intelligent" therefore? They go on using the same signs through countless generations—an undevelopable language. Discussion with them is somewhat difficult! More important, they can learn little about *us*. Thus the mere possession of a sign-system is not enough for intercultural communication; there must be other shared institutions before signs can expose their significance to both parties. For the word "communication" means *sharing*.

So, too, with the Martians. When I was a boy we used to see pictures of scratches on Mars and were told that these were "canals" (I imagined little coloured barges moving along them). Recently a film has appeared at the Classic Cinema, Piccadilly, ("Easy Rider") which depicts the opposite; Martians in flying saucers, hovering over an American freeway, observing the curious ways of Earthmen—those highly-coloured and shiny beetle-like creatures who creep along their canals, in long lines, every now and again stopping to shake out a few parasites . . .

Why do people want to communicate with Mars anyway? To invite more trouble than we have already? We can't even communicate with China yet! It is usually mathematics which is cited as the most likely medium often, we are told, because it is "fundamental". What does fundamental mean? Is mathematics more fundamental than death? Is it more universally shared?

The real question is exposed only when the specific type of *symbolism* is considered, for symbols are derived out of experience and history,[13]—i.e. out of institutions.

I shall never forget the opening scene of the pre-war revue on the London stage, based upon the book by Sellars and Yeatman, called "1066 and All That" in which a Roman centurion marched on to the stage, leading a line of 10 soldiers dressed in full armour, with shields and swords. "Squad . . . *shun!*" shouted the officer, "Squad . . . *number!*" Smartly the soldiers obeyed:

"I II III IV V VI VII VIII IX!"

It is an old joke told against the Romans that, whilst they could use their numerals for denoting and counting, they must have found great difficulty in square-rooting. Am I right in saying that the concept of square-rooting is actually unthinkable in Roman numerals alone? I believe it is true that the Romans could not keep accounts readily and were forced to transport large quantities of coinage about in bulk.

Symbols (the icons, names, diagrams, numerals, token, words . . . all sign *forms*) are theoretically infinite in their possible forms, but the forms actually used by a society arise out of their social needs, their environment, their inheritance, and their varied institutions. To reduce the problem to its most absurd limits, let us indulge again in Science Fiction. Centuries ago the Martians were scanning the skies with their telescopes, searching for "intelligent life" in space. To make these telescopes they of course possessed an

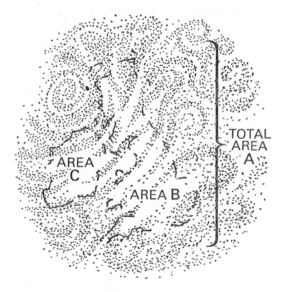

Fig. 5a. The bizarre sign from Earth, once espied by Martians. What could these symbols mean? (The surrounding fuzz was known to be enveloping gas—mainly water vapour.)

advanced technology, an industry, a social structure, educational services and a host of other institutions of their own peculiar kinds. They also possessed a morality, an imaginative life, even Art, a mysticism . . . of which more in a moment.

For years they watched the planet Earth, a cold place enveloped in a cloud of gas, (perhaps water vapour?). Was there life there?

One day a fantastic success was achieved for, through a rare opening in the enveloping gas they espied a bizarre signal from Earth, which they photographed and pondered over. Here is my Personal Press Release, shown in Fig. 5a. What strange language was that?

What were the Earthmen trying to signal? Mathematics, of course! Ah, but how should this remarkable signal be interpreted? It was not long before they deciphered the message, being "intelligent". They knew that a sign standing alone can have no meaning; there must be relationships. How to get these? Looking closely at their treasured photograph, the Martians quickly realized the significance of there being *two* enclosed areas. Now, Martian society was dominated by a ruling clique of landowners, whose status depended upon the area of land that each owned; their mathematics had evolved out of the need to measure and share land. Obviously, therefore, Earthmen were using the symbols natural to landlordism—the curious *shapes* meant nothing; only the areas did. To interpret this they naturally wrote in mathematical symbols: (translated here into Earth Language)

$$\text{Area A} = \text{Area B} + \text{Area C.}$$

This equation alone told them little. Now comes the *mystical* element of their belief and symbolism—the belief element of truth,

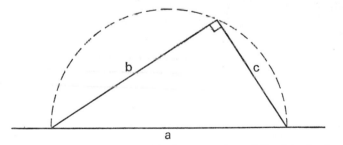

Fig. 5b. The Martians' only possible interpretation of Earthman's signal— Pythagoras's Theorem.

as they themselves could possibly see it and ought to see it. Martian
cultural and spiritual life was obsessed with a certain symbol—the
Square. Square shapes were as important to the religious life of the
Martians as the Crescent is to Islam, or the Red Star to the
Marxists or for that matter, as the Circle is to Industrial Society
today. So the Martians naturally first packed these areas into
squares of side *a b* and *c* giving

$$a^2 = b^2 + c^2$$

The Earthmen knew Pythagoras's Theorem!

They next went down the slippery slope of sound reasoning
further, much further. Surely, they asked themselves, this could be
generalized? Earthmen could not possibly know about Martian
spiritual life, nor about the great significance of the Square. But, of
course, they didn't need to know this—any other shape would do
instead—triangles, semi-circles—even cats' faces, as we mentioned
earlier—any shapes whatever, so long as they are "similar". Earthmen, therefore, being in a dilemma as to what symbolic shapes to
choose for symbolizing Pythagoras's Theorem, had wisely sent out
purely arbitrary, random, shapes like those of Fig. 5a. Only the
areas mattered to people dominated by land-covetousness.

In Charles Peirce's terms, any sign to act *as* a sign must be
interpreted. We can only interpret other people's beliefs and intentions through our own beliefs. It is not the signs and symbols
themselves that do the trick; it is the community's institutions,
within which the signs are interpreted. Meaning is always social.

Suppose that these distant Earthmen *did* know that Pythagoras's
Theorem applies to any shape whatever, the Martians might have
asked themselves. Then random shapes like those of Fig. 5a would
be the very thing they would choose! If by any chance the opening
in the clouds had revealed another land area about equal to B + C
(say part of Scandinavia) the belief that Earthmen knew trigono-
metry might have become eradically stamped upon the Martians'
minds!

Often the sun is referred to as being an object which we share
with "the Martians", with the implication that the circle is a
possible common symbol. This is not at all obvious—many of us do
indeed see the sun as a circular disc on many occasions, but there
are endless other ways of seeing it and its significance—if this is

doubted, the reader should take a walk around many a gallery of impressionist paintings.

So we could go on with this nonsense . . . mere observation of other people's signs may communicate anything. It is *discourse* that brings comprehension.

If this sounds fantasy, look back on Earth itself. Islamic mathematics developed co-ordinate geometry, perhaps an eventual result of their great concern with sundials and the shadows cast by gnomons, before Descartes in Europe (who was inhibited by the Greek geometrical tradition). Yet the algebra of Islam remained for long comparatively unknown in medieval Europe. Why? For reasons of symbolism—no Latin translation appears to have been made.[14]

Hieroglyphic and ancient icon symbols of all kinds offer endless examples of the traps into which we can fall if we assume too rashly the nature and significance of the social institutions within which these signs were used.

The same thing could be said of our own times. Is it too absurd, for example, to suggest that the "magic" of binary counting, which is so prominent today, is associated, amongst other things, with another modern binary obsession—sex? There is nothing special

Fig. 6. Binary symbols, suited to (a) illiterates, (b) the erudite.

about the number 2—it is merely the first plural number.[15] Long before computers were invented, binary icon signs were in widespread use, and appeared in many parts of the world, on certain important doorways, looking something like those shown in Fig. 6. Symbols like 1 or 0 mean little to illiterate peasants—or Martians.

What institutional interpretation should we make? Are these in Fig. 6 not the "simplest" binary symbols—more "simple" than 1 or 0? They are nearer to Nature! I am speaking not of concepts, remember, but of their symbolic expressions.

People who are genuinely concerned with mathematical communication with Mars, or what-not, must make assumptions, or hypotheses, about their symbolisms, and so their concepts, through other social institutions than mathematics. Thus, if one night I saw some strange signal which I could interpret (by some hypothesis) as representing the prime numbers, I have no *logical* reason to be surprised, any more than if I saw any other *pre-stated* set of numbers. Similarly, if a Barbary Ape types out Hamlet, we have no cause for surprise at all—for this sequence of letters is just as probable as any other *pre-stated* sequence.[16] Hamlet lies in ourselves, not in the Ape. In order to test the knowledge and scholarship of Martians or Apes, it is utterly useless merely to *observe* their signals. We must respond to them, i.e. interpret, and observe the consequences.[17] That is, we must question or challenge; following Sanders Peirce, meaning is only revealed within discourse. This is utterly distinct from assessment of the "intelligence" of animals merely by watching their behaviour in groups. Communication within their own kind is one thing; communication with *us* is another.

HUMAN LANGUAGE AND SIGNS; THE VEHICLES OF PERSONAL BELIEFS

Human language differs from animal sign-systems by a gulf, which Suzanne Langer[18] refers to as "one whole day of creation". It is essentially, *developable*. Whereas the beasts can do nothing with their indicator signs except indicate, in rigid, unchanging ways, generation after generation, we humans can always modify our sayings;[19] we can express, argue, plead, threaten, greet, comfort and utter the profoundest thoughts, all with a vocabulary of 2 or 3 thousand words. Whatever you say, I can always *choose* to say something different. I can distinguish myself from each of you by language in more ways than by any other means. Through language I have been taught to think of myself as an individual, separate from you, starting with my earliest baby babblings and my mother's responses, and then through my interactions within all the social institutions which have given me identity and make up "me".[20]

THE AUTHORITARIAN BASIS OF KNOWLEDGE— THE EXISTENTIALIST'S "THEY"

This faculty of language, and use of endless sign-systems combined with Art and all our other means of expression, then gives us the illusion that we are separate, individual creatures, with wills of our own, unhampered by others. At least in the so-called developed countries this has become increasingly so, with the rapid growth of science and spread of rationalism. In other areas of the world, no independent action by any individual is conceivably possible, so harsh is Mother Nature. We live in the industrial countries under the illusion that we have "thought things out for ourselves". The word *proof* is flung about too readily what is "proof" but a very strong faith? How many people here could *prove*, here and now, that the earth is not flat? Or that Shakespeare wrote Macbeth? Or that water consists of hydrogen and oxygen? Or that King Charles I was beheaded in 1649? No; the truth is that we live, day by day, taking virtually all our decisions and actions, by *faith* or trust—instilled in us by various Authorities forming our institutions, our schools, Governments, text-books, famous names, . . . our own father and mother; perhaps more, too, than we often realize, by that awful Jehovah called *They*, ("They say it's going to rain"; "They say that Frenchmen eat frogs" . . .) to which the existentialist thinker Heidegger has drawn attention. It is all these and other authorities who have taught us our essential beliefs. Faith, in the sense of trusting belief, is the starting-point of human awareness and action, and it is socially derived.

The consequences of this can sometimes be surprising. For example, when Marconi proposed to attempt radio transmission across the North Atlantic in 1901, between the U.S.A. and Britain, he received a scathing letter (now held in the Munich Museum) from one of the greatest scientists of his day—Heinrich Hertz. Hertz pointed out that the earth is *round* (as everybody knows) and that radio waves travel in straight lines (as everybody ought to know); therefore, Marconi's transmissions would not go round the earth, but would pass straight out into space, unless reflected back to earth by (quote) "a mirror the size of a continent" (which, as nobody then knew, actually does exist in the form of ionized particles. It was discovered later, and called "the Heaviside Layer"). Marconi pressed on with his trials and succeeded. What was the result? Not surprisingly, the experiment gave massive evidence to the Society of Flat Earthists[21] and *they were absolutely justified*, being supported by the two most highly prominent scientists of the day!

IMPORTANCE OF THE HISTORICAL PERSISTENCE OF SYMBOL FORMS

Finally, I should like to comment upon the amazing historical *persistence* of symbols and signs.

As history passes and social conditions change, ideas change, slowly, sometimes reluctantly, sometimes in a revolutionary way. It is the outward and visible symbols which persist so obstinately; it is their forms which remain whilst they take over new content and meanings in their new environments. If these outward and visible signs were to change each time our ideas became modified, then our worlds would crumble. We would never know who we were or where we stood. When a modern office block or shoe-box of a factory suddenly appears in an 18th century town or near a cathedral, its incongruity is the result of the mere appearance —not of the use to which it is going to be put.

Decoration, motifs, icons, rituals and symbols of all kinds are continually adapted to new significances, but it is those forms themselves which compose so much of our emotional worlds. Their changing meanings, with their unchanging forms, gives us part of our sense of change itself, of continually moving away from the past. When we speak of some symbolic form as "old-fashioned" or some rituals and customs as "out-of-date", we mean that they have become symbolic merely of the past itself and not of any particular element of the past to which we can now relate ourselves, at the present day. They have failed to adapt to any modern needs.

This is not to deny, of course, that many symbols are in widespread use today whose origins have been totally forgotten by most people. Many of the pagan symbols used for Xmas,[22] for example, or the ritual burning of Guy Fawkes. We still speak of Monday,

Tuesday, Wednesday, Thursday, Friday without giving a thought to Nordic times. We see the Greek Acanthus plant widely used for decoration; Pallas Athene has become Britannia.

Although we speak of some symbolic forms as "old-fashioned" or as "out-dated", I personally hold that, as actual forms, they never became lost to us entirely, any more than a language can be said ever to be totally destroyed. Fashions change and become revived. Often their very old-fashionedness makes them rare articles of greater value. We "treasure" what we believe to be the past, in spite of revolutions. Further, we can only invent for ourselves what were the real significances of early symbols as used by our distant ancestors. I can never *be* an ancient Greek, or a Viking— any more, for that matter, than I can be a modern Chinaman.

Similar comments could be made of the signs and symbols used by mathematics and science. Throughout their long history, certain symbols have retained their forms, with renewed content, giving us the illusion that we understand the past In a formal sense we may. Thus, when I read Euclid, I may feel that I have some common understanding with the ancient Greeks—but this can only be in a limited sense. On the contrary, I can have no true *feeling* as to the aesthetic, or religious, or nationalistic values and significance of Greek mathematics and sciences, to them, at their time, any more than I can have the slightest certainty of what meaning say, the cave-drawings of the Dordogne had to those stone-age artists.

Undoubtedly, one can read in history books, and accept intellectually, that the origins of Greek geometry lay partly in coastal navigation and that the mathematics of Islam arose first from their needs to make sundials.[14] But I can no more experience the feeling that, for example, Venus could at one and the same time be a goddess, a star in the sky and a legendary person on earth symbolized in fables, any more than a New Guinea head-hunter can grasp the concept of the Holy Trinity.

NOTES

1 John Aubrey, *Brief Lives*, Vol. 1, 1680.
2 "Geometry (which is the only science that it hath pleased God hitherto to bestow on mankind)", Leviathan, Part 1, Chapter 4.
3 Peirce, C. S.: "The Collected Papers of Charles Sanders

Peirce", 6 Vols., C. Hartshorne and P. Weiss. (Eds.), Harvard University Press, Mass. 1931–1935. Peirce's original writings are extremely difficult to understand, because so much of them are expressed in his own invented jargon. The reader is first referred to some excellent modern interpretations, e.g. see Gallie, W. B.: *Peirce and Pragmatism*, Harmondsworth, 1952.

4 Among the physical scientists Erwin Schrödinger has accepted this sign basis of knowledge and "reality" most strongly. See his book, *My View of the World*, Cambridge University Press, England, 1964.

5 Bierstedt, R.: *Emile Durkheim*, London, 1966.

6 Fischer, E.: *The Necessity of Art (a Marxist Approach)*, Harmondsworth, 1963.

7 Not because we are better people, but through the explosive growth of international organizations (i.e. shared institutions) which increasingly *define* the laws. E.g. see Mangone, G. H.: *A Short History of International Organisations*, McGraw-Hill Inc, New York, 1954.

8 Cf. Peter Strawson's discussion of truth, Lecture 5, pp. 99–101 (Ed.)

9 On another occasion James said "Truth is what we ought to believe" (a moral definition, linking it with goodness). Lecture in Boston 1906 on "What Pragmatism Means". On yet another occasion he said "True ideas are those which we can assimilate, validate, corroborate, and verify. False ideas are those we cannot".

10 James, William: Lecture II "Pragmatism, A New Name for an Old Way of Thinking", New York, 1907.

11 Von Frisch, Karl: *Bees, Their Vision, Chemical Senses and Language*, Cornell University Press, Ithaca, 1950.

12 This summary of bee-behaviour is a gross simplification of the whole business. (See also Claire and W. M. S. Russell, Lecture 8, pp. 168–73 (Ed.))

13 The same point is made by Claire and W. M. S. Russell in relation to monkey communities. Lecture 8, p. 181 (Ed.)

14 Winter, H. J. J.: "Some Features of the Mathematical Sciences in Islam", *Endeavour* XXVIII, September 1969.

15 The Ogam "script", carved some 1,500 years ago on stone pillars in Ireland and Wales, is mighty close to discovery of binary symbols. It was an invented code, based upon Latin letters.

16 This is a simple result of Probability Theory—all conceivable finite sequences of signs, coming from a *random* source, are equally probable.

17 See M. M. Lewis on the interaction between mother and baby leading to the development of language in the child, Lecture 9, pp. 197–8 (Ed.)

18 Langer, S.: *Philosophy in a New Key*, Harvard University and Oxford University Presses, 2nd Edition, London, 1951.

19 For a fuller discussion of the difference see Claire and W. M. S. Russell, Lecture 8, pp. 163–7 (Ed.)

20 See Basil Bernstein's discussion of socialization, Lecture 11, pp. 230 ff. (Ed.)

21 Stathan, Commander E. P. (R.N.): The Navy and Army Illustrated, August 26, 1899.

22 Even the X in Xmas has been retained, not through laziness of spelling, but because it is really the Greek letter χ.

FURTHER READING

BIERSTEDT, R.: *Emile Durkheim* (London, 1966).

CHERRY, E. C.: *On Human Communication* (New York, 1957, reprinted 1966).

GALLIE, W. B.: *Peirce and Pragmatism* (Harmondsworth, 1952).

JAMES, William: Various lectures and essays, which may appear in various editions. E.g. see, in particular: "The Dilemma of Determinism" (1884); "The Varieties of Religious Experience" (1902); "The Tiger of India" (*Psychological Review*, Vol. II, 1895), p. 105; "What Pragmatism Means" (Lecture, Columbia University, 1907). In the present writer's opinion, James should be read *after* Charles Peirce. Peirce created the logical and consistent philosophy of Pragmatism, but he needs an interpreter (e.g. Ref. 3) whilst James tried to persuade us of its value for thinking about many daily problems and dilemmas, with much literary force and rhetoric.

MEAD, G. H.: *Mind, Self and Society* (Chicago and London, 1934).

SCHRÖDINGER, E.: *My View of the World* (Cambridge, 1964).

14

Linguistics, usage, and the user

RANDOLPH QUIRK

University College London

The lectures in this series have tried to answer three prime questions: first, what is the nature of human language; second, how is the study of linguistics organized, the scientific study of human language; and thirdly, what bearing do language and linguistics have upon our understanding of other areas of inquiry. My task in bringing the series to a close is to ask what bearing linguistics has on language—on our language and on us as users of English.

Linguistics has provided us with our dictionaries and grammars of English. But this rather bald and deceptively self-evident statement requires careful scrutiny. It does not mean, for example, that the dictionaries and grammars of English in common use have been designed by linguists: it means that the compilers of dictionaries and grammars have been informed by some linguistic theory or other, because they could not otherwise have even made a start on such work. But so venerable is the tradition of lexicography and grammar writing that very few of those carrying out such work have felt the need to engage in the issues that have been especially exciting linguists of the past twenty years. It is necessary to insist on this because it is sometimes alleged that, because dictionaries by Onions, Barnhart, Gove, or grammars by Curme, Long, Zandvoort seem to reflect so little of what is currently dominant in linguistics, they reflect no linguistics at all. They do, of course. The work of such men rests confidently, if not exactly securely, on the accumulated wisdom of linguistic scholarship stretching back over centuries, on the whole retaining what has been found permanent and true, skimming off what has been suspected to be merely fashionable and false. This is why English grammars and dictionaries of 1870 do not strike us as wildly different in approach, format or content from grammars and dictionaries of 1970, whereas if we take Chomsky's *Aspects* of 1965 and W. D. Whitney's *Language and the Study of Language* of 1867, we appear to have two separate disciplines with widely differing frames of reference.

EVALUATING DICTIONARIES AND GRAMMARS

But my statement that linguistics has given us dictionaries and grammars requires further scrutiny. It implies—correctly and very importantly—that linguistics supplies us with standards by which we can speak of one dictionary or grammar as being better in some respect than another. We need to be careful, however, about the use of "better" here. For reasons that are by no means fully understood, there is a widespread deep-seated and apparently well-nigh ineradicable belief that good usage comes to us from dictionaries and grammars; and that it is the task of these works not merely to identify the rules of good lexical or grammatical use but to determine them—perhaps even, in some sense, create them. On this basis, a grammar or dictionary may be adjudged less good than another according as the author has described the rules for a usage of which the critic disapproves, much as one Anglican bishop might be adjudged less good than another if he had added a tenet from Buddhism to the thirty-nine articles.

Let me illustrate the two ways in which "not good" could be applied to a single rule. If a grammarian said that all English verbs were made negative by the introduction of the auxiliary *do* followed by *not* and the infinitive, as in *He drank—He did not drink*, a linguist might criticize the rule because it would permit the ungrammatical *He did not be cold* as the negative of *He was cold*. No such objection would cross a lay critic's mind, but he might on the other hand object that the grammarian's rule would permit *He used to go* to be negated as *He didn't use to go*, and this, he may say, is "bad grammar".

Similarly, a linguist may criticize a dictionary entry because a word is poorly defined or given an incorrect etymology. A lay critic may object to a definition because a meaning is given of which he disapproves (*terrific* with the sense "splendid", for example); and he will object to the appearance of some entries altogether: many Americans protested at Gove's including *ain't* in the 1961 *Webster*, and there are plenty of four-letter words which the British too would want to exclude, even in our present permissive phase.

It is easy to see the two senses of "good" and to confer a superior smile on the layman's use of it. This is not to say, however, that the lay use can be dismissed as involving an attitude that is irrelevant, or a sociolinguistic problem for which we already have the solution.

The attitude is so far from being irrelevant as to underlie a large part of the layman's purpose in interesting himself—even to the small extent that he does—in dictionaries and grammars at all. And the lexicographer's and grammarian's problem lies to no small extent in trying to satisfy the perfectly legitimate needs and interests of the lay user. He must ask himself which or how many of the varieties of English he is going to take into account in his grammar or dictionary; how he is going to categorize them and their interrelations; how— even more fundamentally—he is going to acquire the data on these varieties. Though the native grammarian or lexicographer has in one sense complete knowledge of the language he is describing and this can be used as an invaluable gauge to check data and test rules, he knows that variation among individuals can be very considerable and that he must make sure that it is the community's language he is describing and not his own idiolect. Moreover, it is no easy task to pour out all the knowledge even of one's own language, let alone do so in a systematic, well-ordered, and of course objective manner. Both on theoretical and on practical grounds, therefore, grammarians and lexicographers have had to devise ways of observing other people's usage, paying careful attention to objectivity and to principles of selection.

CORPUS AND ELICITATION

The Survey of English Usage is concerned with grammar rather than with lexicology, but the categorization of sources in Fig. 1 is

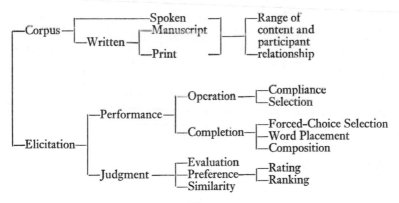

Fig. 1

applicable to both fields. Broadly speaking, all present-day dictionaries of English place ultimate reliance solely on a *printed corpus*. This is of course a great advance over the days when items were included on a haphazard basis and when definitions were promoted primarily by the lexicographer's own opinion of the correct meaning. Modern practice still leaves a good deal to be desired, however. For example, it has been possible now for a quarter of a century to collect a corpus of spoken English fairly easily and inexpensively through the advent of the tape recorder. Every lexicographer knows that most new words and most new meanings of existing words are current in speech before they appear in print—and that it is a matter of chance not merely *when* but *whether* they get into print. One respects the lexicographer's reasons for clinging to printed sources (notably, their public verifiability) but it is high time that methods were evolved to admit this primary type of source material. Secondly, little or nothing has been done in lexicography to develop scientific techniques for supplementing corpus (in which the occurrence of "self-defining" quotations is necessarily fortuitous) by elicitation techniques in order to attain a fuller record of the words we know and the meanings we assign them. One obvious reason for this is that a corpus can give us only positive information: that a word exists and exists in a certain sense; it cannot give us the negative information that a word or meaning has ceased to exist. As a result, it is extremely difficult for dictionaries to be other than out of date, since in revising an earlier edition the lexicographer has not the means of proving that his predecessors' work is invalid in any respect except incompleteness. For example, the latest *Concise Oxford* (1964), in most respects an excellent revision, gives as its entire and sole definition of *terrific*, "Causing terror, terrible".

Another reason for needing elicitation techniques is that definition solely by scrutiny of corpus-derived quotation, while admirable in inhibiting the lexicographer's imagination and personal prejudice, is almost inevitably prevented from achieving the full semantic subtlety that characterizes verbal usage. For example, for all its 2000 handsome pages, the new *Random House Dictionary* (1966) is not alone in equating the adverb *utterly* with *completely*. But we have found that, in articial supplementation of corpus by completion tests (where subjects were asked to complete sentences where a beginning was supplied like "The man utterly ————"),[1] the adverb was freely used to intensify verbs like *hate, disagree, detest, despise* but we were not offered verbs like *love*, *mend*, *restore*. The point is clinched by an elicitation technique that we call "forced-choice selection" testing. Given

> I –––– detest her
> I –––– agree with you
> (completely, utterly)

where we require the two blanks to be filled from the alternatives (each of which can be used once only), subjects predominantly put *utterly* into the blank before *detest*, where of course if it really was equivalent to *completely* there would be a random distribution of the two adverbs.

Again, we will not easily find a dictionary that explains the reason for our unhesitating choice between *munch* and *chew* in this pair of sentences:

> He –––– the bacon
> He –––– the bacon reluctantly
> (chewed, munched)

and indeed we will be lucky if our dictionary attempts to make any distinction at all between the two verbs. The *Concise Oxford* defines *scuttle* solely in terms of hurrying from danger; it even uses the verb "fly" as a gloss in this connexion. If this were the whole truth recognized by even the least sensitive native user of English, *scuttle* would fit either of the following blanks with equal satisfaction for him:

> The mouse –––– towards the door
> The mouse –––– silently towards the door
> (darted, scuttled)

But it is very unlikely that many of us would agree to a random use of the two verbs here.

In short, and without going into other aspects of contemporary dictionaries that could be improved in the light of recent linguistic research, we may look for a great deal of change in lexicographical method during the next generation, which will result in dictionaries reacting to usage much more sensitively than they do at present, and without sacrificing the admirable standards of objectivity they have developed.

GRAMMATICAL DESCRIPTION

The problems in compiling a grammar are much greater than in compiling a dictionary, since the objects to be described (sentences, clauses, phrases, modal usages etc.) are much more abstract and less discrete. There are, it is true, some respects in which the grammarian's task seems easier: his field of study seems to be more limited and more stable than that of the lexicographer. No one knows all the words even in the *Concise Oxford* and not even the most widely read lexicographer can have a week go by without coming upon a new word in his daily paper. By contrast, we rarely have the impression that we are reading or hearing a new grammatical structure.

Even so, the grammarian's problem in assembling the data for his description is not dissimilar from the lexicographer's, and we may refer back to Fig. 1. Again, we have the need for a corpus of other people's usage as our basis: the risk of bias, idiosyncracy or sheer uncertainty is even greater with a grammarian's introspection than with a lexicographer's. How do we decide when to say "I gave the girl a book" and when to say "I gave a book to the girl"? How do we decide whether we normally say "I didn't dare to answer", "I didn't dare answer" or "I dared not answer"?

As for extending the corpus beyond the traditional type of printed material, the Survey of English Usage considers that for grammatical research it is essential to have adequate samples of unprepared speech and free conversation and also to collect written material in manuscript form as well as in print. There is no reason to doubt that our organization of sentences is very different as between speaking and even the most casual letter, irrespective of whatever difference there may or may not be in our use of vocabulary. We know that a perhaps even greater change comes over our sentence structure when we are preparing a more formal piece of writing—even some announcement for a notice board. Finally, anyone who has had a piece of work published knows that house style makes numerous changes necessary before a manuscript goes into print.

But essential as a carefully planned and representative corpus is, we are still left with the obvious deficiencies that are inherent in any corpus: it is inevitably an incomplete inventory of the possible grammatical patterns in a language, and quotations are in any case too often inadequate to enable us to specify the precise rules governing their structure. We therefore pay close attention to the need for acquiring information by means of elicitation techniques. Most of our work in this area has been with *compliance* tests, in which subjects hear (not see) a sentence and are told to carry out some small change and then to write down the sentence otherwise unaltered. For example, they might be given the sentence "He probably will buy a car" and be told to replace *He* by *She*. The interest to us would be of course the number of subjects who—despite the instructions— would write down *She will probably buy a car*, having moved the adverb from in front of the auxiliary verb, thus giving us unsolicited a clear indication of their preference in the matter. But since I used forced-choice selection tests to illustrate elicitation for lexical information, let me use this type[2] also to show how grammatical information can be elicited.

If we were asked what difference there was between *I heard the door slam* and *I heard the door slamming*, we would be quite likely to say that there is very little. This certainly has been the view of most authors of English grammars. But if we were given the following and asked to fill the blanks with *slam* or *slamming*

> I heard the door ———— all night
> I heard the door ———— at midnight

we would probably associate *slamming* with the former and *slam* with the latter, thus indicating that we recognize an aspectual difference. Similarly, although we have all known that the verb *to wet* had two alternative forms of past tense ("He wet it", "He wetted it"), it has not been generally known, until the Survey's tests demonstrated it, that there is a semantic distinction between them in that they will not be randomly distributed by a forced choice in the two sentences:

> The artist ———— the paper carefully
> The baby ———— the bed last night

ATTITUDES TO USAGE

Yet another reason for needing elicitation technique is that we need to know not merely the facts of usage but also the attitudes to particular usages. It is still not sufficiently realized that, between the universally acknowledged well-formed structures and the opposite

pole of structures whose ill-formedness is acknowledged equally
universally, there is a large mass of usage where opinion is divided.
Fig. 2[3] represents the gradations for fifty sentences on which reactions were sought some time ago at University College. We should

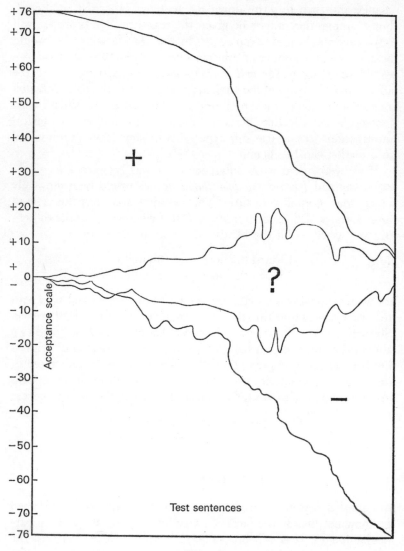

Fig. 2

take particular note that, for a few examples, neither acceptance nor rejection was in a majority, but actual uncertainty.

But it is still less clearly realized that both our usage and our attitudes to usage are conditioned by several sharply different factors and that the relation between acceptability and usage is complex and indirect. Fig. 3 attempts to display some of the chief variables.[4]

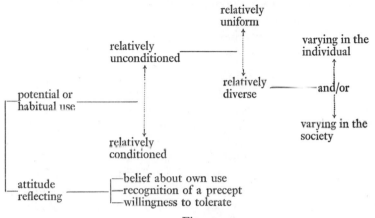

Fig. 3

It will be noticed that, within the material derived from elicitation techniques, we need a distinction between "habitual" and "potential" usage. In particular, it is often useful to distinguish those features of an elicited sentence which an informant can be presumed to have commonly experienced: the past of *learn* or the placing of *hardly* between auxiliary and main verb, for example. These could be regarded as "habitual". By contrast, elicitation might seek the use of an item that the informant may never have experienced but which is nevertheless in some sense "available" to him. For example, he might have to supply a past for a strange new verb like /flaiv/ or show where he would place the adverb *introductorily* in a sentence. Not all instances of "potential" use are as clear as these, but when it is considered how invariant or "idiomatic" usage can be at the opposite pole (for example "Far be it from me" which does not allow us to form *"Near be this to her") one realizes the significance of rules that are to be derived from "potential" rather than relatively "habitual" use.

The diagram goes on to state that use may be conditioned or

unconditioned. Such conditioning may be situational (as when a formal occasion prompts a formal usage) or it may be linguistic. For example, although one can generally permute the prepositional phrases in the structure *talk to N_1 about N_2* there is a linguistic condition forbidding this when N_1 and N_2 are co-referential. Thus

>   I talked to Harry about the play
>   I talked about the play to Harry
>   I talked to Harry about himself
> but not *I talked about himself to Harry
> or   *I talked about Harry to himself

Where an item is towards the relatively unconditioned end of the graded scale, use may be relatively uniform or relatively diverse. The latter pole is sometimes referred to as "free variation", a term which my colleagues and I tend to avoid since we doubt the validity of its implications. Finally, this type of diversity may be a property of the individual (as when Mr X vacillates between /saiˈkɔlədʒi/ and /psaiˈkɔlədʒi/ (*psychology*) without this reflecting any such variation in society) or it may be a property of society itself (as for instance the variation between /iðə/ and /aiðə/ (*either*) which need not affect a Mr Y who says only /aiðə/).

The lower limb of Fig. 3 concerns attitude—a reminder that someone's attitude to usage may have a by no means simple relation to his actual usage, either natural or elicited, habitual or potential. Attitudes to usage seem to us to reflect three potentially independent but often intimately interacting factors. A person may have strong beliefs about what forms he habitually uses; and he may also have strong views on the forms that ought to be used. These may be in harmony or he may confess that he believes them to be in conflict. But we must all realize that our beliefs about our own usage by no means necessarily correspond to the actual facts of our usage—as our wives or children or other unkindly frank observers are liable to remind us from time to time. Moreover, we may tolerate usage in others that corresponds neither to what we think we say ourselves nor to what we think is most commendable.

LINGUISTICS AND THE USE OF ENGLISH

At which point it may be expected that I should tackle the vexed question of the relation between actual usage and opinion about the most commendable usage. What can linguistics do, one may ask, to maintain or improve the quality of everyday usage? Most linguists this century have tended to use linguistic insights to show that the whole notion of maintaining or improving the quality of a language is misconceived. Very properly. Language fulfils its rôle to no small extent by the very fact that its users are able to change it. Linguists have therefore rightly poured scorn on those who have stood Canute-like against waves of change on principle. In December 1969 a member of the House of Lords wrote what is a typical protest to *The Times*:

> It seems that the American "this" has become established when the word "that" should properly be used.
> Now one finds that in almost every other sentence . . . the word "viable" occurs. I have always understood that the word referred to the capability of a living creature to maintain life. Is its new use another Americanism? Surely, to refer to a business, an industry, a film . . . being "viable" is nonsense?

If we can set aside the suspicion that the main basis for irritation here is the influence of America (or perhaps a more laudable dislike of cliché and "OK" jargon), the protest seems to stem from the fact that etymologically *viable* is related (through French *vie*) to Latin *vita*. But of course this gets us nowhere. We do not attempt to be governed by etymological meanings with words like *pen*, *pert* or *pending*, and presumably the noble critic allows himself to call a play *lively*, to say that there is no *life* in British industry, and to insist that it is *vital* to use English correctly—though no danger to life and limb is conceivable.

It is right that linguistics should not be invoked in the interests of so dubiously motivated a conservationism: right indeed that it should actually be used to give some reassurance to people who might be inhibited in the natural use of English by eminent protesters of this kind. But this does not mean that linguistics is committed in principle to any rigorous insistence on *laissez-faire* in matters of language use. Just as linguistic scholarship helps us to understand why change is inevitable, so the insights of linguistics can make us more alert in what we are saying or writing, so that we can avoid ambiguity or obscurity, anticipate irrelevant or unwanted overtones and *doubles entendres* (as in the questionnaire which asked "How many people do you employ, broken down by sex?"), and achieve our objective more efficiently by well-formed and efficient phraseology, elegant and precise choice of words, sensitive and effective control of metaphor. We should not, for example, have to wrestle with clumsiness, involving trivial ambiguity, like the following sentence on "the pill":

> All the present preparations contain a mixture of two synthetic hormones, which appear to suppress the secretion by the pituitary gland in the brain of a substance which plays a crucial part in the process of ovulation. (*Sunday Times*, 26 July 1964)

Or we may consider a more serious infelicity where—without obscurity of expression—there was genuine ambiguity. In connexion with the decision whether or not to sell a house to a coloured immigrant, a builder's statement was reported as follows:

> We would not jeopardise our business by selling a house to you. (*The Times*, 18 June 1969)

Especially on so grave an issue, a user of English ought to be aware of the two structural possibilities here, the one involving conditional *would*, the other volitional:

> We would not jeopardize our business if we sold a house to you.
> We would not be willing to sell a house to you and so jeopardize our business.

Let me illustrate also the point I made about control of metaphor. A metaphor involves simultaneously a *paradigmatic* relation between the literal element it replaces and the figurative one it introduces, and a *syntagmatic* relation between the literal and metaphorical elements in the linguistic environment.[5] Thus "the seeds of discord" must be understood as "the initial signs, a growing murmur, the first spark of discord": but the effectiveness of this relation depends on the syntagmatic relations and we must not go on to speak of the seeds of discord rumbling in the background or bursting into flame. Obviously. But unfortunately, the mixed or wasted metaphor is not always so easy to avoid, and there is a real difficulty in that we can forget or not even know what degree of "life" a metaphor possesses for other members of our speech community. Even Hamlet could speak of taking arms against a sea of troubles.

In September 1969, when it was clear that Herr Brandt was about to become Chancellor, the *Daily Express* commented on

> the tense and almost certainly squalid political horse-trading which will inflict Bonn over the next few days. (30 September 1969)

If *inflict* (which requires a human subject) is an error for *infect* or *afflict* (with their implication of disease or disaster) the syntagmatic relation with *horse-trading* is unsatisfactory—and it is little better if we are meant to understand "which [events] will inflict [on] Bonn", or if *inflict* is an error for the semantically more vacuous *affect*.

A more interesting example of rhetorical misfire because of metaphor appeared in the opening of a leading article on the Pinkville massacre. The point at issue was whether one was being disloyal to the United States in showing horror at the alleged atrocities in Vietnam. The article began thus:

> There is a treason worse than criticism of governments. It is the treason that betrays the values for which one's country stands. (*Sunday Times*, 30 November 1969)

The intended metaphorical climax of the second sentence is linguistically well-formed. The *moral lapse* which departs from the traditionally upheld values is paradigmatically replaced by "treason" which is given a congruent syntagmatic relation with "betrays", and so the offence is made more vivid and serious. Or it should be. Unfortunately the climactic metaphor has been preceded by a sentence which, although presumably intended to affirm literal treason, unhappily undermines the succeeding metaphor by using it in a diluted and figurative sense. The first sentence thus says "*treason* is here defined as mere anti-government criticism", and we need not be surprised that in place of a climactic metaphor in the second sentence, we get bathos and no metaphor at all.

This laborious exposition is tedious and bathetic itself, but my point has been merely to claim that a linguistic analysis of "poor" English can point to ways in which we can use our language more effectively and more enjoyably. The message of linguistics on the native language was useful enough when it was largely confined to condemning the pedantries of prescriptive grammar. It can be made constructive in the normal educational process.

Even more obviously, it has a constructive contribution to make in therapy for the linguistically abnormal. The miracle of a Helen Keller or a Christy Brown brings home to us the potential of the deprived individual when once the mechanism of language can be brought into operation. But when we see the thousands of children who remain deprived of language powers or the adults who have been so deprived by accident or illness, we are humiliated by the realization of how little we yet understand the means by which language is learnt, the way in which semantic and syntactic rules operate in the human brain, how little we understand the very nature of language itself. In the past fifty years enormous strides have been made in the diagnosis of articulatory defects and in the construction of therapeutic drills precisely directed at the specific malarticulation detected. Where the breakthrough is needed is in the understanding of the deeper strata of linguistic organization, and here we look for fruitful co-operation between linguistics and psychological medicine.

CONCLUSION

It is commonly regarded as a triumph to have the last word, but there are grave disadvantages when this means trying to find something new to add when thirteen distinguished people have already had their say. They have harvested and led away the corn, as Chaucer puts it,

> And I come after, glenynge here and there,
> And am ful glad if I may fynde an ere
> Of any goodly word that they han left.

Rather this, at any rate, than attempt a resounding peroration. All the same, we might for a moment reflect where we have arrived in our study of linguistics and where we might further direct our thoughts after these lectures.

One of the fruits of the course must surely be a wiser, sadder awareness of language's complexity and of our abiding ignorance. This is not to belittle the profound thought that generations of linguists have applied to human language, or their solid achievements, but rather to adopt a posture of proper humility in the face of all that still challenges us. If the degree of deeper understanding these lectures have conveyed leads only to a keener sensibility, a greater tolerance of language variety, and less rigid preconceptions about the uniqueness or inviolability of a national standard language, they will have served a valuable enough purpose. A realization of the almost spiritual relation between a person and the language he speaks is essential if languages and dialects are not to mutate grotesquely from badges of pride to barriers of hate and fear. The potential for harm can be seen in Belgium's language riots and the terrible immolations in Madras: but it can be seen nearer home in the recent demonstrations for Welsh and—more insidiously—in the continued promotion of vaudeville "comedy" where the humour lies in pecularities of immigrants' English which can be made to seem as uproariously funny as hunchbacks, bearded ladies or the mentally ill were to our great-grandfathers.

We need only a little linguistics to give us enough ability to observe other people's language with intelligent interest rather than the scornful rejection that is born of ignorance and fear. And I do not think "fear" is too strong a word. There is no form of xenophobia more irrational than its application to what we significantly call our *own* language, our *mother tongue*. Impassioned but impracticable plans for repatriation of linguistic immigrants have been repeatedly made since the sixteenth century, and post-imperial insecurities have not reduced such urges. A society which could accept the need by some to wear linguistic badges such as the accents associated with Oxford or Harvard is disturbed that others want to express a comparable identity through "Soul talk".

Add to this not merely the emergence of American English; the reluctant admission that this implies the existence of *British English*; distant strains of "Strine" from down under; talk in Dublin about the standards of Hiberno-English; and it is not surprising that the dissolution of empire has been accompanied by fears about the balkanization of English. Add to that again complaints that block language like "probe", "bid" and "cut" is proceeding beyond the headlines to everyday speech, and we have the basis for fears that English is being reduced to a sort of pidgin. "No word not in current kindergarten use," writes Miss Nancy Mitford (*Listener*, 16 May 1968), "may be introduced into the dialogue of a film. When working on a script I once wrote 'ineluctable'; I was told to take it out at once as nobody would know what it meant."

Again, we need only a little linguistics to sharpen our observation sufficiently to know whether these fears are justified or not. Beside the fissiparous tendencies that are natural to language (they produced Spanish, French and Rumanian out of Latin, for example), English is responding to powerful counteractive tendencies of a centripetal kind that result from the special conditions of the modern world: the political affiliation of the English-speaking countries, the ease and speed of modern communications, the democratization of education, and the trend to uniformity in material culture, to mention some of the obvious factors. In many ways, we are linguistically much less insular in Britain than we were even as little as twenty years ago, having learnt to respond with great immediacy not merely to American English but to the English of Australia, the West Indies, Africa and the Indian subcontinent—not to speak of the English of Merseyside. Inevitably, this has meant our adopting many words from these varieties of English—especially American English of course—but the spread of language habits has not been a one-way process. Through broadcasting, books and the British news-agencies, we have continued to increase the world's familiarity with British English; and even the all-powerful American English has yielded to our influence in certain fields—not least, the language of pop. In short, although a century ago it seemed that English might indeed break up into different languages as the Romance group did, more recent tendencies have been in the reverse direction. A word no sooner becomes fashionable in San Francisco than it is equally so in Bradford and Brisbane. Rather than talk of English being balkanized or pidginized, it might be more accurate to think of its being *homogenized*. And if this particular image helps us to realize that British English is no longer the cream of English, that we have instead the concept of a language measured out in labelled cartons all of which are guaranteed equally creamy, we may end these lectures with an analogy which has implications for our sociolinguistic health. At any rate, we may hope that there is no analogue to Strontium 90.

NOTES

1   Greenbaum, S.: *Verb Intensifier Collocations in English* (The Hague, 1970), pp. 73 ff.

2   Kempson, R. M. and Quirk, R.: "Controlled Activation of Latent Contrast", *Language* 47 (1971).
3   Quirk, R. and Svartvik, J.: *Investigating Linguistic Acceptability* (The Hague, 1966), p. 52.
4   Greenbaum, S. and Quirk, R.: *Elicitation Experiments in English: Studies in Use and Attitude* (London, 1970), pp. 1 ff.
5   Leech, G. N.: *A Linguistic Guide to English Poetry* (London, 1969), pp. 150 ff.

FURTHER READING

BOLINGER, D. L.: *Aspects of Language* (New York, 1968).
CRYSTAL, D. and DAVY, D.: *Investigating English Style* (London, 1969).
GREENBAUM, S. and QUIRK, R.: *Elicitation Experiments in English: Studies in Use and Attitude* (London, 1970).
LEECH, G. N.: *English in Advertising* (London, 1966).
LYONS, J.: *Introduction to Theoretical Linguistics* (Cambridge, 1968).
QUIRK, R.: *The Use of English*, 2nd edition (London, 1968).
STRANG, B. M. H.: *Modern English Structure*, 2nd edition (London, 1968).
SVARTVIK, J.: *On Voice in the English Verb* (The Hague, 1966).
TURNER, G. W.: *The English Language in Australia and New Zealand* (London, 1966).

Notes on Contributors

Basil B. Bernstein. Born London 1924. BSc Economics from London School of Economics and Political Science. Assistant Teacher, City Day College 1954–60. Honorary Research Assistant, University College London 1960–62. Reader in Sociology of Education and Head of Sociological Research Unit, University of London Institute of Education 1962. Professor of the Sociology of Education 1967.

Colin Cherry. Born St Albans 1914. Educated at St Albans School. Took first degree as evening student at Northampton Polytechnic whilst laboratory assistant with General Electric Company, Research Laboratory, Wembley. Joined University of Manchester 1947, and Imperial College 1949. First as Lecturer then as Reader. Appointed to Chair in Telecommunication in 1958. Early research concerned with Theory of Electric Circuits. Later interest moved towards the human being in communication, especially experimental psychology of speech and hearing. In recent years has been particularly interested in philosophical and sociological aspects of human communication and its technological extensions. Has travelled widely in many countries on lecture tours.
  Publications: *On Human Communication* (M I T Press).

Eugénie J. A. Henderson. Graduated University College, London, 1935. Lectureship in Phonetics Department, University College and work at BBC until 1939. Work during war in Ministry of Economic Warfare and, later, on intensive Japanese courses for the Services. Lecturer in Phonetics, SOAS, 1943–52, Reader in Phonetics 1952–65, Professor of Phonetics since 1965. Visiting Professor, University of Rangoon, 1954. Head of Department of S.E. Asia and the Islands, SOAS, 1960–65; Head of Department of General Linguistics and Phonetics, 1965–70. Special academic interests include the phonetics and phonology of the languages of South East Asia. Field work in tribal languages of Burma. Married, with four sons.
  Publications: *Tiddim Chin* (OUP). *The Indispensable Foundation: a selection from the writings of Henry Sweet* (OUP). (Forthcoming)

Firthian Linguistics (Holt, Rinehart and Co.). Co-editor (with G. B. Milner) of *Indo-Pacific Linguistic Studies, Vols I and II* (North Holland Publishing Co.).

Edmund Leach. Born 1910. Read Mathematics and Mechanical Sciences at Cambridge, obtained BA 1932. After several years of civilian life in China returned to England to study Social Anthropology under Malinowski and Raymond Firth. An abortive field trip to Kurdistan in 1938, frustrated by the Munich crisis was followed by a prolonged trip to Burma in 1939, frustrated by the war. From autumn 1939 to the summer of 1945 saw much of Northern Burma as an officer in the Burma Army. In 1947–48 took his PhD, carried out a survey in Sarawak and accepted a first teaching appointment at LSE. Relinquished a Readership at this school in 1953 to return to Cambridge as Lecturer 1953–58, then Reader in Anthropology. In 1966 succeeded Lord Annan as Provost of King's College, Cambridge. The 1967 Reith Lectures brought him to the attention of the general public but he continues his research work as one of this country's leading social anthropologists.

M. M. Lewis. Born 1898. Scholar and Morley Medallist in English Literature at University College, London. BA English; MA Education, and PhD. Taught English at Newport Grammar School and William Ellis School 1918–24. Lecturer and Senior Lecturer at University College, Nottingham 1924–40. Vice-Principal Goldsmith's College, London 1940–7. Director of the Institute of Education, Nottingham 1947–63. Professor of Education 1956, Professor Emeritus 1963.

Professor Lewis has long studied the development of language in children, and he has explored the subject in several books. His recent research has been into the development of deaf children, and he was chairman of the DES committee whose report "The Education of Deaf Children" appeared in 1968.

His wife is Hilda Lewis, the novelist, and they have one son.

Publications: *Infant Speech* (London 1936). *Language in School* (London 1947). *The Importance of Illiteracy* (London 1953). *How Children Learn to Speak* (London 1957). *Language, Thought, and Personality* (London 1967). *Language and Personality of Deaf Children* (NFER). *Language and the Child* (NFER 1969).

John Lyons. Born Manchester 1932. Educated St Bede's College, Manchester 1943–50 and Christ's College, Cambridge 1950–54. BA in Classics 1953 and Diploma in Education 1954. Military service in the Navy 1954–56. Lecturer in Comparative Linguistics at the School of Oriental and African Studies University of London 1957–61. PhD (Cambridge) for research on the vocabulary of Plato 1961. Lecturer in Linguistics at the University of Cambridge 1961–64. Has held visiting appointments at the Universities of Indiana, California, Texas and Illinois. Married with two daughters.

Publications: *Structural Semantics* (Blackwell, Oxford). *Introduction to Theoretical Linguistics* (Cambridge University Press, London and New York). *Chomsky* (Fontana, London and Viking, New York). Editor of *New Horizons in Linguistics* (Penguin Books), *Journal of Linguistics. Psycholinguistics Papers* (Edinburgh, with R. J. Wales).

Noel Minnis. Born 1926. Principal Lecturer in English, Wall Hall College of Education. Served in Royal Navy 1945–47. Read German and Russian at Trinity College, Oxford 1944–45, then English Language and Literature, 1948–50—MA Oxon. 1951. Taught English and studied French History in Dijon, France 1950–1951. Taught English, History and French at the Royal Grammar School, Colchester, and at King Alfred's School, Wantage 1951–1959. Joined the staff of Wall Hall College 1959. Modern English Language Course at University College, London, 1968–69. MA London 1969. Married with four children.

Frank Palmer. Educated: Bristol Grammar School 1932–40. New College Oxford 1941–42, 1945–48. Merton College Oxford 1948–49. MA (Oxon). Lecturer in Linguistics, School of Oriental and African Studies 1950–60. Professor of Linguistics, University College of North Wales 1960–65. Professor of Linguistic Science, University of Reading since 1965. Professor Palmer has travelled widely on behalf of the British Council, the Ford Foundation and the Inter-University Council. Editor of the *Journal of Linguistics* since 1969.

Publications: *The Morphology of the Tigre Noun* (OUP). *A Linguistic Study of the English Verb* (Longmans). (Ed) *Selected Papers of J. R. Firth* (Longmans and Indiana). Also various articles on Linguistic Theory, English and Ethiopian languages.

Randolph Quirk, MA, PhD, DLit, Hon. FIL Fellow of University College London and Quain Professor of English Language and Literature. Sometime Professor of English Language in the University of Durham. Educated London, Yale, Michigan. Has lectured on problems of English grammar in USA, Europe, USSR, Africa, India, Australia and New Zealand. Director of the Survey of English Usage. Chairman, Committee of Inquiry into the Speech Therapy Services.

Publications: *The Concessive Relation in Old English Poetry* (Yale UP). *An Old English Grammar* (with C. L. Wrenn; Methuen). *The Teaching of English* (with A. H. Smith; OUP). *Investigating Linguistic Acceptability* (with J. Svartvik; Mouton). *Systems of Prosodic and Paralinguistic Features* (with D. Crystal; Mouton). *The Use of English* (Longman). *Essays on the English Language* (Longman). *Elicitation Experiments in English: Studies in Use and Attitude* (with S. Greenbaum; Longman). General Editor, English Language Series, Longman.

R. H. Robins. MA Oxford University 1948. DLit University of London 1968. Lecturer in Linguistics, School of Oriental and African Studies 1948–54. Reader in General Linguistics, University of London 1954–64. Professor of General Linguistics, University of London since 1965. Honorary Secretary Philological Society since 1961. Visiting Research Fellow, University of California, 1951: field work on Yurok (American Indian Language). Visiting Professor, University of Washington, Seattle 1963. Visiting Professor, University of Hawaii, 1968.

Publications: *General Linguistics* (Longmans). *A Short History of Linguistics* (Longmans). *The Yurok Language* (University of California Press).

Claire Russell and *Dr W. M. S. Russell*. At an International Conference in 1955, the Russells introduced the study of Human Ethology, which is now beginning to arouse wide public interest. In 1957, they published the first scientific paper on the subject, and in 1961 the first book, *Human Behaviour: A New Approach* (André Deutsch). Other publications on human and animal behaviour and the relations between them include the recent *Violence, Monkeys and Man* (Macmillan), plus two other books, some 60 scientific articles, and numerous broadcasts. Claire Russell devotes most of her time to research and writing. W. M. S. Russell is Lecturer in Social Biology at the Department of Sociology, at the University of Reading.

George Steiner. Born Paris 1929. Bachélier des Lettres et Philosophie Paris 1947. BA University of Chicago 1948. MA (Bell Prize Am Lit) Harvard 1950. DPhil (Rhodes Scholar 1950–52) Oxford 1955. Member Institute Advanced Study, Princeton 1956–58. Fellow Churchill College Cambridge 1961. Schweitzer Professor New York University 1966–67. Recipient O. Henry Short Story Prize 1959. Fellow Royal Society of Literature. School of Letters Kenyon College and Indiana University. Gave the 1970 T. S. Eliot Memorial Lectures. Married with two children.

Publications: *Tolstoy or Dostoevsky* (Faber). *The Death of Tragedy* (Faber). *Anno Domini* (Faber). *Language and Silence* (Faber). Editor *The Penguin Book of Modern Verse Translation. Homer* (Prentice-Hall, with R. Fogles). Member Editorial Staff London *Economist* 1952–56.

P. F. Strawson. Born 1919. Educated Christ's College Finchley, St John's College Oxford (Scholar). Served World War II, RA, REME, Captain. Assistant lecturer in Philosophy, University College North Wales 1946, John Locke Scholar, University of Oxford 1946. Lecturer in Philosophy 1947, Fellow and Praelector 1948 University College Oxford. Fellow of University College Oxford 1948–68, subsequently Fellow of Magdalen College. Waynflete Professor of Metaphysical Philosophy in the University of Oxford since August 1968. FBA 1960. Visiting Professor Duke University 1955–56. Fellow Humanities Council and Visiting Associate Professor Princeton University 1960–61. Married with four children.

Publications: *Introduction to Logical Theory* (Methuen). *Individuals* (Methuen). *The Bounds of Sense* (Methuen). Editor: *Philosophical Logic* (OUP). *Studies in the Philosophy of Thought and Action* (OUP).

Stephen Ullmann. Born Budapest 1914. PhD Budapest 1936. DLit Glasgow 1949. MA Oxford 1968. War work with BBC Monitoring Service 1940–46. Lecturer, Senior Lecturer Romance Philology and General Linguistics, University of Glasgow 1946–53. Professor

11

Romance Philology, University of Leeds 1953–64. Professor French Language and Romance Philology and Chairman Department of French Language and Literature, University of Leeds 1964–68. Professor Romance Languages, University of Oxford and Fellow of Trinity College Oxford since 1968. Visiting Professor University of Toronto 1964 and 1966, University of Michigan 1965, University of Poona 1966. Invited to Visiting Professorship in the University of Western Australia 1970. Married with one son and two daughters.

Publications: *Words and Their Use* (Blackwell). *The Principles of Semantics* (Blackwell). *Précis de sémantique française* (Francke, Berne, Switzerland). *Style in the French Novel* (Blackwell). *The Image in the Modern French Novel* (Blackwell). *Semantics. An Introduction to the Science of Meaning* (Blackwell).

Editor: *Language and Style* (Oxford, Blackwell). Joint editor *Archivum Linguisticum* 1949–64. Member Editorial Board *Archivum Linguisticum, French Studies, Romance Philology, Style*.

Oliver Zangwill. Born 1913. BA King's College Cambridge 1935. MA King's College Cambridge 1939. Research Student Cambridge Psychological Laboratory 1935–40. Psychologist Brain Injuries Unit, Edinburgh 1940–45. Assistant Director Institute of Experimental Psychology, Oxford 1945–52. Senior Lecturer in General Psychology, University of Oxford 1948–52. Visiting Psychologist National Hospital for Nervous Diseases London since 1947. Professor Experimental Psychology University of Cambridge since 1962. Professorial Fellow King's College Cambridge since 1955.

Publications: *An introduction to Modern Psychology* (Methuen). *Cerebral Dominance and its Relation to Psychological Function* (Oliver and Boyd). *Current Problems in Animal Behaviour* (Cambridge University Press, with W. H. Thorpe). *Amnesia* (Butterworths, with C. W. M. Whitty). Editor: *Quarterly Journal of Experimental Psychology* 1958–66. President Experimental Psychology Society. Member Biological Research Board, Medical Research Council 1962–66.

Index